THE TECHNOSYSTEM OF FREE SPEECH

In this book, Christoph Graber explains how the fundamental right of freedom of expression is gradually being enriched to cover its technological prerequisites. It challenges the predominant legal view that technology is merely an instrument, arguing that this overlooks the complex interplay between technological materiality and communicative sociality. It builds on a core argument of science and technology studies, that there is interpretative flexibility in both the design and social reception of a technology, which lays the groundwork for a critical stance towards smart technologies and the corporations that control them. This approach can then be transposed into the legal sphere via Luhmann's systems theory. This book shows how normative expectations about digital technologies are formed and develop into legal norms and fundamental rights. It argues that, in order to achieve the implementation of fundamental rights, it is important to recognise their dimension as objective value judgments of a constitution, which the state has a duty to protect.

Christoph B. Graber is Professor of Law, Chair for Legal Sociology with special focus on Media Law at the University of Zurich. He has been a visiting professor/scholar at leading universities in the USA, Australia and Italy and has published widely in monographs and high-impact journals.

LAW IN CONTEXT

Since 1970, the Law in Context series has been at the forefront of a movement to broaden the study of law. The series is a vehicle for the publication of innovative monographs and texts that treat law and legal phenomena critically in their cultural, social, political, technological, environmental and economic contexts. A contextual approach involves treating legal subjects broadly, using materials from other humanities and social sciences, and from any other discipline that helps to explain the operation in practice of the particular legal field or legal phenomena under investigation. It is intended that this orientation is at once more stimulating and more revealing than the bare exposition of legal rules. The series includes original research monographs, coursebooks and textbooks that foreground contextual approaches and methods. The series includes and welcomes books on the study of law in all its contexts, including domestic legal systems, European and international law, transnational and global legal processes, and comparative law.

Books in the Series

Acosta: *The National versus the Foreigner in South America: 200 Years of Migration and Citizenship Law*
Alaattinoğlu: *Grievance Formation, Rights and Remedies*
Ali: *Modern Challenges to Islamic Law*
Alyagon Darr: *Plausible Crime Stories: The Legal History of Sexual Offences in Mandate Palestine*
Anderson, Schum & Twining: *Analysis of Evidence, 2nd Edition*

Ashworth: *Sentencing and Criminal Justice, 6th Edition*
Barton & Douglas: *Law and Parenthood*
Baxi, McCrudden & Paliwala: *Law's Ethical, Global and Theoretical Contexts: Essays in Honour of William Twining*
Beecher-Monas: *Evaluating Scientific Evidence: An Interdisciplinary Framework for Intellectual Due Process*
Bell: *French Legal Cultures*
Bercusson: *European Labour Law, 2nd Edition*
Birkinshaw: *European Public Law*
Birkinshaw: *Freedom of Information: The Law, the Practice and the Ideal, 4th Edition*
Blick: *Electrified Democracy: The Internet and the United Kingdom Parliament in History*
Broderick & Ferri: *International and European Disability Law and Policy: Text, Cases and Materials*
Brownsword & Goodwin: *Law and the Technologies of the Twenty-First Century: Text and Materials*
Cakal: *Law and Torture: Widening the Apertures, from the Doctrinal to the Critical*
Cane & Goudkamp: *Atiyah's Accidents, Compensation and the Law, 9th Edition*
Clarke: *Principles of Property Law*
Clarke & Kohler: *Property Law: Commentary and Materials*
Collins: *The Law of Contract, 4th Edition*
Collins, Ewing & McColgan: *Labour Law, 3rd Edition*
Corrias, *Law and Inhumanity: Dehumanization, Silent Claims and Atrocity Crimes*
Cowan: *Housing Law and Policy*
Cranston: *Making Commercial Law Through Practice 1830–1970*
Cranston: *Legal Foundations of the Welfare State*
Darian-Smith: *Laws and Societies in Global Contexts: Contemporary Approaches*
Dauvergne: *Making People Illegal: What Globalisation Means for Immigration and Law*
David: *Kinship, Law and Politics: An Anatomy of Belonging*
Davies: *Perspectives on Labour Law, 2nd Edition*
Dembour: *Who Believes in Human Rights?: Reflections on the European Convention*
de Sousa Santos: *Toward a New Legal Common Sense: Law, Globalization, and Emancipation*
Diduck: *Law's Families*
Douglas-Scott: *Brexit, Union, and Disunion: The Evolution of British Constitutional Unsettlement*
Dowdle: *Transnational Law: A Framework for Analysis*
Dupret: *Positive Law from the Muslim World: Jurisprudence, History, Practices*
Dutta: *A Jurisprudence of Conversations: Law, Life and Feminism in Post-colonial India*
Emon: *Jurisdictional Exceptionalisms: Islamic Law, International Law, and Parental Child Abduction*
Estella: *Legal Foundations of EU Economic Governance*
Fortin: *Children's Rights and the Developing Law, 3rd Edition*
Garnsey: *The Justice of Visual Art: Creative State-Building in Times of Political Transition*
Garton, Probert & Bean: *Moffat's Trusts Law: Text and Materials, 7th Edition*
Ghai & Woodman: *Practising Self-Government: A Comparative Study of Autonomous Regions*
Glover-Thomas: *Reconstructing Mental Health Law and Policy*

Gobert & Punch: *Rethinking Corporate Crime*
Goldman: *Globalisation and the Western Legal Tradition: Recurring Patterns of Law and Authority*
Goodrich, Kimmel & Meyler: *Performing Law: Actors, Affects, Spaces*
Graber: *The Technosystem of Free Speech: Enriching Fundamental Rights in a Digital Society*
Haack: *Evidence Matters: Science, Proof, and Truth in the Law*
Harlow & Rawlings: *Law and Administration, 4th Edition*
Harris: *An Introduction to Law, 8th Edition*
Harris, Campbell & Halson: *Remedies in Contract and Tort, 2nd Edition*
Harvey: *Seeking Asylum in the UK: Problems and Prospects*
Herring: *Law and the Relational Self*
Hervey & McHale: *European Union Health Law: Themes and Implications*
Hervey & McHale: *Health Law and the European Union*
Holder & Lee: *Environmental Protection, Law and Policy: Text and Materials, 2nd Edition*
Hommes: *The Convention and the Kingdom: How the Netherlands Received the European Convention on Human Rights*
Jackson & Summers: *The Internationalisation of Criminal Evidence: Beyond the Common Law and Civil Law Traditions*
Jeutner: *The Reasonable Person: A Legal Biography*
Kennedy: *Inducing Intimacy: Deception, Consent and the Law*
Kostakopoulou: *The Future Governance of Citizenship*
Kreiczer-Levy: *Destabilized Property: Property Law in the Sharing Economy*
Kubal: *Immigration and Refugee Law in Russia: Socio-Legal Perspectives*
Lewis: *Choice and the Legal Order: Rising above Politics*
Likosky: *Law, Infrastructure and Human Rights*
Likosky: *Transnational Legal Processes: Globalisation and Power Disparities*
Lixinski: *Legalized Identities: Cultural Heritage Law and the Shaping of Transitional Justice*
Loughnan: *Self, Others and the State: Relations of Criminal Responsibility*
Lunney: *A History of Australian Tort Law 1901-1945: England's Obedient Servant?*
Maughan & Webb: *Lawyering Skills and the Legal Process, 2nd Edition*
McGaughey: *Principles of Enterprise Law*
McGlynn: *Families and the European Union: Law, Politics and Pluralism*
Mertens: *A Philosophical Introduction to Human Rights*
Miller: *An Introduction to German Law and Legal Culture: Text and Materials*
Moffat: *Trusts Law: Text and Materials*
Monti: *EC Competition Law*
Morgan: *Contract Law Minimalism: A Formalist Restatement of Commercial Contract Law*
Morgan & Yeung: *An Introduction to Law and Regulation: Text and Materials*
Nash: *British Islam and English Law: A Classical Pluralist Perspective*
Ng: *Political Censorship in British Hong Kong: Freedom of Expression and the Law (1842–1997)*
Nicola & Davies: *EU Law Stories: Contextual and Critical Histories of European Jurisprudence*
Norrie: *Crime, Reason and History: A Critical Introduction to Criminal Law, 3rd Edition*
Norrie: *Rethinking Criminal Justice: Punishment, Abolition And Moral Psychology*

O'Dair: *Legal Ethics: Text and Materials*
Oliver: *Common Values and the Public–Private Divide*
Oliver & Drewry: *The Law and Parliament*
Palmer & Roberts: *Dispute Processes: ADR and the Primary Forms of Decision-Making, 1st Edition*
Palmer & Roberts: *Dispute Processes: ADR and the Primary Forms of Decision-Making, 3rd Edition*
Petersen: *Practices of Restitution: Law and Aesthetics in Modern Germany*
Picciotto: *International Business Taxation*
Pieraccini: *Regulating the Sea: A Socio-Legal Analysis of English Marine Protected Areas*
Probert: *The Changing Legal Regulation of Cohabitation, 1600–2010: From Fornicators to Family, 1600–2010*
Qiao: *The Authoritarian Commons: Neighborhood Democratization in Urban China*
Radi: *Rules and Practices of International Investment Law and Arbitration*
Reed: *Internet Law: Text and Materials*
Richardson: *Law, Process and Custody*
Roberts & Palmer: *Dispute Processes: ADR and the Primary Forms of Decision-Making, 2nd Edition*
Rowbottom: *Democracy Distorted: Wealth, Influence and Democratic Politics*
Sauter: *Public Services in EU Law*
Scott & Black: *Cranston's Consumers and the Law*
Seneviratne: *Ombudsmen: Public Services and Administrative Justice*
Seppänen: *Ideological Conflict and the Rule of Law in Contemporary China: Useful Paradoxes*
Siems: *Comparative Law, 3rd Edition*
Stapleton: *Product Liability*
Stewart: *Gender, Law and Justice in a Global Market*
Tamanaha: *Law as a Means to an End: Threat to the Rule of Law*
Taylor: *Fortin's Children's Rights and the Developing Law, 4th Edition*
Trundle: *Injurious Law: Nuclear Exposure and the Harms of Redress*
Tuori: *Properties of Law: Modern Law and After*
Turpin & Tomkins: *British Government and the Constitution: Text and Materials, 7th Edition*
Twining: *General Jurisprudence: Understanding Law from a Global Perspective*
Twining: *Globalisation and Legal Theory*
Twining: *Human Rights, Southern Voices: Francis Deng, Abdullahi An-Na'im, Yash Ghai and Upendra Baxi*
Twining: *Jurist in Context: A Memoir*
Twining: *Karl Llewellyn and the Realist Movement, 2nd Edition*
Twining: *Rethinking Evidence: Exploratory Essays, 2nd Edition*
Twining & Miers: How to Do Things with Rules, 5th Edition
Varney: *Disability, Human Rights and Contract Law*
Wan: *Film and Constitutional Controversy: Visualizing Hong Kong Identity in the Age of 'One Country, Two Systems'*
Ward: *A Critical Introduction to European Law, 3rd Edition*
Ward: *Law, Text, Terror*
Ward: *Shakespeare and Legal Imagination*

Watt: *The Making Sense of Politics, Media, and Law: Rhetorical Performance as Invention, Creation, Production*
Wells & Quick: *Lacey, Wells and Quick: Reconstructing Criminal Law: Text and Materials, 4th Edition*
Woodhead: *Caring for Cultural Heritage: An Integrated Approach to Legal and Ethical Initiatives in the United Kingdom*
Yeungs & Ranchordá: *An Introduction to Law and Regulation: Text and Materials, 2nd edition*
Young: *Turpin and Tomkins' British Government and the Constitution: Text and Materials , 8th Edition*
Zander: *Cases and Materials on the English Legal System, 10th Edition*
Zander: *The Law-Making Process, 6th Edition*

International Journal of Law in Context: A Global Forum for Interdisciplinary Legal Studies

The *International Journal of Law in Context* is the companion journal to the Law in Context book series and provides a forum for interdisciplinary legal studies and offers intellectual space for ground-breaking critical research. It publishes contextual work about law and its relationship with other disciplines including but not limited to science, literature, humanities, philosophy, sociology, psychology, ethics, history and geography. More information about the journal and how to submit an article can be found at http://journals.cambridge.org/ijc

THE TECHNOSYSTEM OF FREE SPEECH

Enriching Fundamental Rights in a Digital Society

Christoph B. Graber

University of Zurich

CAMBRIDGE
UNIVERSITY PRESS

CAMBRIDGE
UNIVERSITY PRESS

Shaftesbury Road, Cambridge CB2 8EA, United Kingdom

One Liberty Plaza, 20th Floor, New York, NY 10006, USA

477 Williamstown Road, Port Melbourne, VIC 3207, Australia

314–321, 3rd Floor, Plot 3, Splendor Forum, Jasola District Centre, New Delhi – 110025, India

103 Penang Road, #05–06/07, Visioncrest Commercial, Singapore 238467

Cambridge University Press is part of Cambridge University Press & Assessment, a department of the University of Cambridge.

We share the University's mission to contribute to society through the pursuit of education, learning and research at the highest international levels of excellence.

www.cambridge.org
Information on this title: www.cambridge.org/9781009688307

DOI: 10.1017/9781009688314

When citing this work, please include a reference to the DOI 10.1017/9781009688314

First published 2026

Cover image: War Flower Afrin Rose Yellow 2017, Stefan Gritsch

A catalogue record for this publication is available from the British Library

A Cataloging-in-Publication data record for this book is available from the Library of Congress

ISBN 978-1-009-68830-7 Hardback

To Monika

Contents

Acknowledgements

Over the last decade, I have been teaching my annual course 'Regulation without Law? Law and the Technologies of the 21st Century', as well as seminars on law and technology at the University of Zurich (UZH), Faculty of Law. This experience has shown me that many students and young scholars from law and other disciplines (including sociology, philosophy, economics and political science) are overwhelmed by the rapid pace of technological development and its societal impact. Many of them have expressed the need for a theoretical framework that would enable them to understand what the law can do to help shape today's digital ecosphere. Inspired by this experience, I have written this book for current and future law students and young scholars from a variety of backgrounds and jurisdictions who are interested in digital technologies and their effect on the normative order and free communication.

The theme of the book was inspired by the observation that, with regard to freedom of expression, legal practice is 'technology-blind', failing to engage with digital technologies in a way that goes beyond a trivial instrumental assessment. For example, in its case law on the freedom of expression and information (Article 10 of the European Convention on Human Rights), the European Court of Human Rights only superficially acknowledges differences between the various distribution media, treating technology as a 'black box' rather than undertaking an in-depth analysis of the interactions between the technological medium and the process of receiving and transmitting information. While this approach may have been unproblematic in the age of the press and broadcasting, it requires revision now that the internet is the leading distribution medium. In order to achive this, I had to delve deep into social theory and examine the relationship between technology, society and the law on a profound level.

I wrote the bulk of the book during a research sabbatical that I spent in 2023 as a Fernand Braudel Senior Fellow at the European University Institute (EUI) in Florence. Villa Salviati was the perfect place to work. The vast park and massive walls of the eternal Renaissance castle made for a pleasant contrast with the ephemeral digital world in which my book was developing. I am grateful to Peter Drahos and Nicolas Petit for the many lunch discussions, which gave me new energy each time. I am particularly indebted to Peter Drahos for generously sharing his extensive knowledge with me and for his critical feedback on some of my ideas. My thanks are also due to the EUI for this fellowship and to the UZH for its generous support of focused research.

Many people helped me along with the writing of this book by discussing theoretical issues with me or by reading drafts of chapters and making critical comments. I would like to thank José Luis Alonso, Tilmann Altwicker, Ulrike Babusiaux, Giovanni Biaggini, Sandra Braman, Emilios Christodoulidis, Oliver Diggelmann, Monika Dommann, Camilla Dul, Elena Esposito, Michael Fässler, Thomas Gächter, Urs Gasser, Andreas Glaser, Angelo Golia, Florian Grisel, Moritz Hany, Helmut Heiss, Mireille Hildebrandt, Jonas Kaiser, Vagias Karavas, Regina Kiener, Raffaela Kunz, Karl-Heinz Ladeur, Lorenz Langer, Johannes Liebrecht, Matthias Mahlmann, Alice Margaria, Loredana Martignetti, Jörg Paul Müller, John Palfrey, Johannes Reich, Alexander Rom, Sarah Summers, Brigitte Tag, Gunther Teubner, Andreas Thier, Marc Thommen, Florent Thouvenin, Chris Thornhill, Kieran Tranter, Felix Uhlmann, Thomas Vesting, Giulia Walter, Dan Wielsch and Peter Yu. Many thanks to Emilios Christodoulidis for a dear friendship that dates back to 1989, when we were both PhD students at the EUI. My discussion of constitutional history and the implementation of fundamental rights with Giovanni Biaggini, Regina Kiener and Andreas Kley was especially illuminating. It was Giovanni Biaggini who encouraged me to use the Swiss system of constitutional adjudication as a concrete example to discuss issues related to the enrichment of fundamental rights. I also learned from him that, in 1874, the Swiss Bundesverfassung became the first constitution in the world to explicitly allow citizens to appeal against violations of their constitutional rights to a supreme court.

Stefan Gritsch kindly gave me the permission to use his artwork, 'War Flower Afrin Rose Yellow 2017', for the book's cover. I am extremely grateful for this!

I would like to thank Chad Jorgenson for his skilful editing of the manuscript. Without him, the language would not have reached the desired level of clarity. Many thanks are also due to Camilla Dul and Mona Gubler, who helped me in the final stages of footnote formatting and indexing.

Finally, I would like to thank Maks del Mar for vigorously supporting my project and including the book in the Cambridge University Press 'Law in Context' series, as well as to express my profound gratitude to the three anonymous reviewers who meticulously evaluated the book proposal and provided invaluable suggestions for improvement. At Cambridge University Press, I am grateful to Matt Gallaway and Toby Ginsberg for their interest in my book and to Jadyn Fauconier-Herry, Gemma Smith and Laura Blake for their help.

CHAPTER 1

Introduction

On two recent occasions, Swiss MPs have called for the incorporation of new fundamental rights into the Federal Constitution, in order to strengthen the protection of freedom of expression in the face of threats posed by digital technologies on the internet. The first parliamentary initiative, launched in 2018, called for a constitutional amendment that would introduce a new fundamental right to net neutrality.[1] The MP who sponsored it, Mathias Reynard, justified the initiative by pointing out that there was no mention of net neutrality in the Swiss Telecommunications Act (FMG), even though it arguably has the status of an 'unwritten law'. The initiative was subsequently withdrawn, after Parliament amended the FMG to include the open internet principle (and the associated concept of net neutrality) in the new Article 12e FMG. The second parliamentary initiative, submitted in 2022 by another MP, Samuel Bendahan, called for the right to digital integrity to be enshrined in the Constitution.[2] Specifically, the initiative sought to give citizens the right to know what data is being collected about them on the internet and by whom. However, the National Council (the lower house of Parliament) decided not to follow suit, arguing that existing gaps and difficulties in protecting citizens' digital

[1] Mathias Reynard, parliamentary initiative of 1 March 2018 (18.407 'Netzneutralität in der Verfassung verankern [Anchoring Net Neutrality in the Constitution]'), www.parlament.ch/de/ratsbetrieb/suche-curia-vista/geschaeft?AffairId=20180407.

[2] Samuel Bendahan, parliamentary initiative of 29 September 2022 (22.479 'Das Recht auf digitale Unversehrtheit in die Verfassung aufnehmen [Include the Right to Digital Integrity into the Constitution]'), www.parlament.ch/de/ratsbetrieb/suche-curia-vista/geschaeft?AffairId=20220479.

integrity, which is already covered by Article 10 of the Constitution, should be addressed through statutory legislation.

The two initiatives are linked by the desire to guarantee freedom of communication under the conditions created by the technical and economic development of the internet. Moreover, they are both grounded in a conception of fundamental rights that, in two respects, is at odds with the prevailing understanding of the Constitution in legal doctrine and jurisprudence: first, because they invoke fundamental rights in cases where it is *not* a matter of defending freedom against *state* interferences and, second, because they see the technological infrastructure of the internet itself as representing an issue of fundamental rights. From a sociological perspective, the two initiatives reflect an understanding of constitutional law which acknowledges that the dynamics of producing constitutional norms can also involve issues of fundamental rights that fall outside the formal boundaries of the written constitutional text. They evince an understanding of the constitution that embraces bottom-up social change and is thus cognitively open to developments in the production of constitutional norms in society. Under the prevailing conditions in the digital ecosphere, these dynamics of social norm production respond to the effects of technological change and economic globalisation.

The present book seeks to present a critical perspective on freedom of expression, by focusing on the technological preconditions of this fundamental right. The term 'technosystem' was originally introduced by Andrew Feenberg.[3] In his groundbreaking work *Technosystem: The Life of Social Reason*, Feenberg combines philosophy with science and technology studies (STS) in an attempt to make a critical account of the development of technology conceivable. In this spirit, the present book intends to adopt a critical perspective on the complex relationships between normative ordering and internet technologies. A second reason for using the term 'technosystem' is that this book aims to bring together STS and sociological systems theory. These sociological perspectives are

[3] Andrew Feenberg, *Technosystem: The Social Life of Reason*, Cambridge, MA: Harvard University Press, 2017.

then set in relation to legal practice, enabling the following three methodological approaches to be distinguished:

1) STS, which represents the most advanced sociology of technology
2) Sociological systems theory, which provides an accurate description of the complexity of present-day society and, arguably, makes it possible to conceptualise the relationship between law, technology and society
3) Legal sociology, which combines a sociological perspective on law with legal practice

Needless to say, this is a methodologically challenging undertaking, which requires us to make a clear distinction between a normative-prescriptive perspective and an empirical-descriptive one. The former is typical of legal practice (including legal doctrine), which deals with the form of law. It focuses on the systematic relationship between abstract principles, whose application in concrete cases leads to logically justified decisions. Legal sociology, in contrast, examines the social context of the law from an empirical-descriptive perspective, asking questions such as: Why is there a norm? What effect does it have? Is it socially accepted and respected? When it comes to the problem of freedom of expression and technology, the sociological perspective allows us to identify issues relating to the production of fundamental rights norms outside the legal (and political) system, in areas of society where legal doctrine would not typically expect to find them. However, sociology does not see *more* than the law, but merely something different. Every approach has its blind spot, because every observation uses a distinction to observe its object. The blind spot is precisely the initial distinction that guides the observation.[4] While an observer cannot see her own blind spot, she can see that of another observer. It is in order to overcome this predicament that the dual perspective of sociology and law is adopted throughout this book.

Chapter 2 begins the enquiry into free speech under the conditions of a globally networked digital environment by clarifying the meaning of

[4] Niklas Luhmann, *Theory of Society*, translated by Rhodes Barret, vol. 1, Stanford: Stanford University Press, 2012 (1997), at 35.

the term 'constitution'. Under the banner of 'transnational constitutionalism', intense discussions have taken place in recent years about constitutional thinking that seeks to break free from statehood and formalism. The question of the constitutional subject is of great importance here. In the twenty-first century, nation-states remain the primary constitutional actors, as they have been since the revolutions of the eighteenth and nineteenth centuries. However, the modern era has also witnessed the emergence of transnational corporations, which have developed into powerful players within a globalised economy. As telecom service providers, equipment manufacturers and platform operators, they have a particularly strong influence over the conditions governing freedom of expression. This raises a number of questions: What does it mean, on the theoretical and practical level, to conceive of transnational corporations as constitutional subjects? How do concrete developments on the internet relate to processes of producing constitutional norms? How should the relationship between state-centred and societal constitutional legitimacy be conceptualised?

Chapter 3 then addresses the thesis that law has undergone a process of transnationalisation through the development of internet regulation in the wake of the invention of the World Wide Web in the 1990s. This chapter addresses questions such as: Is it true that a transnational law is developing that is largely free of state influence? What does a close analysis reveal about the relationship between non-state governance and state regulation in addressing pressing social problems related to the 'network of networks'? How do approaches to the regulation of content and technology differ between the United States and the European Union? Net neutrality is taken as a case study for an in-depth examination of the transnationalisation thesis in the context of the technological preconditions of free speech. In addition to the debates on net neutrality in the United States and the EU, this chapter also examines the debate in India, where the example of Meta Free Basics illustrates how the actions of large technology companies can lead to restrictions on freedom of expression. The question is then whether the history of net neutrality in these three jurisdictions, where regulatory solutions have been found along national territorial lines, reflects the spectre of the 'splinternet' and undermines the thesis of the transnationalisation of the law.

Chapter 4 critically examines how the European Court of Human Rights (ECtHR) has conceptualised the technological requirements of freedom of expression in its case law on Article 10 of the European Convention on Human Rights (ECHR). Differences between the technical media used to express opinions (print media, broadcasting and the internet) are only superficially taken into account in the ECtHR's practice. The Court treats technology as a 'black box' rather than conducting an in-depth analysis of the interaction between the technical medium and the process of receiving and transmitting information. Such an instrumental understanding of technology may have been unproblematic in the age of print media and broadcasting, but now that the internet has become a leading medium, it needs to be revised. In order to do so, it is necessary to shift our point of observation from legal doctrine to the social sciences. This chapter correspondingly reviews two leading perspectives on the relationship between technology, society and law, namely media theory of law and STS. Media theory of law is remarkable for the general account it has developed to explain how the historically dominant means of information dissemination influence the law. However, it has two main drawbacks: 1) its uncritical perspective on the technology involved and 2) the fact that it underestimates the importance of normative social structures in the digital environment. In contrast, the strength of STS lies in its use of detailed case studies involving complex interactions between society and materiality/technology. The key concept of co-production helps us understand the interdependencies between technology developers and social responses. However, STS reaches its limits when it deals with the law, since its practitioners generally lack a solid legal background.

Chapter 5 proposes to address these weaknesses of STS with regard to the law by incorporating a perspective from legal sociology that is informed by Niklas Luhmann's theory of *autopoietic systems.* The claim made here is that such an approach can provide a theoretical framework that serves as a bridge between STS and law. On the theoretical level, this is a very ambitious undertaking, since although sociological systems theory is strong when it comes to understanding the role of law in society, critics have argued that it is blind to technology and therefore poorly suited to the digital age. Luhmann did indeed write very little about technology, but this does not mean that systems theory is unable to conceptualise the interface between the materiality of a distribution medium (e.g., the internet) and the sociality of communicative systems (e.g., law). It should not be overlooked that Luhmann distinguishes not only living systems, conscious systems and communicative systems but also machine systems.[5] All four types of systems are operatively closed, with structural coupling explaining how such operatively closed systems can relate to each other. 'Structural coupling' is the name given to the mechanism that allows a system to orient its own operations towards structures constructed as facts in its environment or towards the structures of other systems.[6] How can the coupling of different types of systems be explained in the case of computer-aided interactions? In opposition to the theoretically unsatisfactory conception of the internet as a social-material hybrid found in media theory, systems theory demands that a clear distinction be made between the sphere of technological materiality (the technosystem) and the sphere of communicative sociality (the social system and its sub-systems). This is the prerequisite for adopting a critical or normative position vis-à-vis technological media. The distinction between the material and the social makes it possible, at the next stage, to study with precision the diverse factual interrelations between the two spheres that exist in online communication. In order to do so, it is essential to understand technologies as artefacts possessing *affordances*, in the sense of possibilities and constraints. A key question is then that of how affordances enter into digital technologies. The final piece in this theoretical mosaic relates to the concept of normativity in the digital ecosphere and, in particular, the question of whether normative expectations about digital technologies can emerge. Since normative expectations constitute the structures of the legal system, the answer to this question will provide a micro-level explanation of how the structural coupling between law and technology works.

5 Niklas Luhmann, *Social Systems*, translated by John Bednarz with Dirk Baecker, Stanford: Stanford University Press, 1995 (1984), at 40–41.

6 Dirk Baecker, 'Digitalisierung als Kalkül', in Dirk Baecker, et al. (eds.), *Post-digitales Management*, Wiesbaden: Springer VS, 2023, pp. 23–37, at 26 (translation by the author).

While the previous chapters focused on the sociological question of how a normative order adapts to technology-induced social change, Chapter 6 reconstructs the technology-specific normative-prescriptive contours of freedom of expression as a fundamental right in the internet age. The aim here is to gather evidence of the growing importance of the technological environment for freedom of expression at the national and global levels, with a specific focus on legal practice and regulation. Recognising that the trustworthiness of data-processing technology is a prerequisite for freedom of expression, privacy law is taken as the starting point for this enquiry. An important distinction ought to be made here between the integrity of the data and the integrity of the network. I also revisit the discussion of net neutrality and the open internet from Chapter 3. From a free-speech perspective, it is crucial that online data be distributed in a non-discriminatory way. The chapter therefore reconstructs the main steps in the development of net neutrality and open internet norms in the United States and the EU. While the United States originally set the tone, the EU has now taken the lead, with the European Court of Justice (ECJ) clearly defining the contours of the relevant provisions of the Open Internet Regulation (OIR). This chapter also examines the evidence found in the case law of the ECtHR on Article 10 ECHR of a tendency to recognise an independent right of transmission. Moreover, the activities of the Internet Corporation for Assigned Names and Numbers (ICANN) can be seen as producing technology-related standards that are relevant to freedom of expression. One of ICANN's tasks is to manage the internet's Domain Name System (DNS). Domain names play a central role when we surf the internet or send emails, but in order for the data packets exchanged between computers to reach their destination, the alphabetical domain names must be translated into numerical IP addresses. This translation work is carried out by a hierarchically organised system of so-called root servers, which is administered by ICANN within a multistakeholder legal structure. ICANN thus controls the 'master key' to the entire global internet and can influence the conditions under which freedom of communication is possible. Finally, the technical standards for the internet, which are developed by the Internet Architecture Board (IAB) and the Internet Engineering Task Force (IETF), are also important for freedom of expression. The technical documents produced by these bodies have a significant impact on how people use the internet to communicate. The IAB and IETF are organised on a global basis, and their operations are wholly or largely independent of the government.

Having thus identified the technological dynamics that are most likely to determine the direction in which the doctrine of freedom of expression will evolve, Chapter 7 addresses the broader issues of changes of fundamental rights within the framework of the tension between social evolution and constitutional stability. Telecom companies, equipment manufacturers and platform operators are new private actors who provide the hardware and software that can, in various ways, co-determine the conditions of freedom of expression on the internet. The emergence of such non-state actors poses a challenge to the doctrine of fundamental rights, which must be addressed. This leads us to ask: How is constitutional thinking responding to this challenge? What further developments are needed to take account of the increasing relevance of technological conditions for freedom of expression? These questions lie at the heart of the sociological view of fundamental rights as social institutions that have become differentiated in the course of modernisation. From this perspective, the focus is on how fundamental rights function, as well as the emergence, growth and impact of these norms. This view contrasts with the largely defensive, state-centred understanding of fundamental rights that prevails in legal practice. However, drawing on sociological insights within the framework of legal practice represents a methodological challenge. In order to avoid the famous is-ought problem, the sociological and legal perspectives must be clearly distinguished. From a legal perspective, questions concerning the enrichment of fundamental rights are discussed, taking the Swiss system of constitutional adjudication as a case study. The Swiss legal system is particularly interesting in this regard, because of its long, uninterrupted development of constitutional adjudication and its pioneering role at the international level.[7] In 1874, the Swiss Federal Constitution

[7] Giovanni Biaggini, 'Constitutional Adjudication in Switzerland', in Armin von Bogdandy, et al. (eds.), *The Max Planck Handbooks in European Public Law*, Oxford: Oxford University Press, 2020, pp. 779–840, at 781–782.

(Bundesverfassung der Schweizerischen Eidgenossenschaft, BV) became the first constitution in the world to *explicitly* allow citizens to appeal to a supreme court in the event of the violation of their constitutional rights.[8] A special feature is that, since that time, the BV has provided for a *special legal remedy* to protect constitutional rights (constitutional complaint), which is also easily accessible and effective. The Federal Supreme Court is not limited to merely finding that a violation of constitutional rights has occurred, but can also annul the administrative or legislative act in question. At the end of the 1950s, the Federal Supreme Court began expanding the catalogue of constitutional rights guaranteed by the BV, recognising various unwritten fundamental rights in a manner unknown in other constitutional systems.[9] These fundamental rights include essential guarantees, such as the right to own property, freedom of expression, personal freedom, freedom of assembly, the freedom to use any language and the right to assistance and care.[10] During the complete revision of the BV in 1999, these rights were all formally incorporated into the revised constitutional document. The power of the Federal Supreme Court to recognise unwritten fundamental rights, where necessary, remains under the new constitution.[11] As highlighted throughout this book, the power of the courts to effectively protect freedom of expression is limited in the context of global digital networks and powerful private technology companies. It is therefore even more important to understand fundamental rights as positive obligations to protect objective constitutional value judgments which, under certain technical and social conditions, can only be implemented through legislation. This brings us full circle to the parliamentary initiatives to enrich freedom of expression mentioned at the beginning of this introduction and how the Swiss legislator intends to deal with them.

[8] Ibid., at 786. [9] Ibid., at 789.

[10] Christoph B. Graber, 'Bottom-Up Constitutionalism: The Case of Net Neutrality' (2016) *Transnational Legal Theory*, 7 (4), pp. 524–552, at 532.

[11] Regina Kiener, et al., *Grundrechte*, 4th edn, Bern: Stämpfli, 2024, at 21; Giovanni Biaggini, 'Grundrechtsinnovation im Bundesstaat – ein Streifzug durch 175 Jahre Verfassungsgeschichte', in Frédéric Bernard, et al. (eds.), *Le droit au service de l'humanité: Mélanges en l'honneur de Michel Hottelier*, Zurich: Schulthess, 2023, pp. 33–50, at 44.

Writing this book was a long process. I benefited greatly from the conversations I have had over the past ten years with law students at the University of Zurich in my annual course 'Regulation without Law? Law and the Technologies of the Twenty-First Century', as well as in seminars on law and technology. Inspired by this experience, I have written this book for current and future law students and young academics from a variety of backgrounds who are interested in new technologies and their impact on free communication. They are called upon to make critical use of their knowledge of digital technologies and relate it to the fundamental question: How is normative order possible under the conditions of a digital society?

CHAPTER 2

Free Speech and the 'Digital Constitution'

Examining the potential development of the fundamental right to freedom of expression in relation to its technological preconditions is closely linked to the concept of a 'digital constitution', a topic about which much has been written in recent years.[1] The concept of a digital constitution is discussed in the broader context of transnational constitutionalism, which is defined in the literature as constitutional thinking that seeks to move away from statehood and formalism. Given that the world's digital infrastructure is controlled by private, transnational corporations, a conceptual opening-up of this kind seems to be a matter of some urgency. However, since such an approach conflicts with commonly held views in public law and political philosophy, it is necessary to begin by clarifying the meaning of the concept 'constitution' as it applies in the digital environment.

[1] A selection of only the most recent contributions includes Edoardo Celeste, *Digital Constitutionalism: The Role of Internet Bills of Rights*, London: Routledge, 2022; Edoardo Celeste, 'Internet Bills of Rights: Generalisation and Re-specification towards a Digital Constitution' (2023) *Indiana Journal of Global Legal Studies*, 30 (2), pp. 25–54; Dan Wielsch, 'Political Autonomy in the Digital World: From Data Ownership to Digital Constitutionalism' (2023) *Indiana Journal of Global Legal Studies*, 30 (2), pp. 115–130; Giovanni de Gregorio, 'Digital Constitutionalism Across the Atlantic' (2022) *Global Constitutionalism*, 11 (2), pp. 297–324; Angelo Jr Golia, 'Critique of Digital Constitutionalism: Deconstruction and Reconstruction from a Societal Perspective' (2023) *Global Constitutionalism*, 13 (3), pp. 1–31; Christoph B. Graber, 'Net Neutrality: A Fundamental Right in the Digital Constitution?' (2023) *Indiana Journal of Global Legal Studies*, 30 (2), pp. 197–226.

2.1 THE CONCEPT OF A CONSTITUTION IN THE DIGITAL ENVIRONMENT

Talk of a 'digital constitution' must sound strange to legal practitioners and political philosophers. In these circles, as in everyday language, the word 'constitution' is usually associated with a codified document that lays out the political system of a nation-state and contains a set of norms that represent the hierarchical apex of that state's legal order.[2] This formal concept of a constitution is linked to statehood and the nation-state's need to define boundaries between the private and the public, as well as the internal and the external.

The term 'constitution' was coined at the end of the eighteenth century in the context of the revolutions in the United States and France and since then refers to a written text.[3] The constitutional documents drawn up in the United States and France symbolised the distance of the revolutionary project from the old regime, constituted the state's power as a monopoly and legally regulated the exercise of power.[4] As an expression of the social differentiation of law and politics in modern society, 'constitution' acquired a double meaning, political and legal. Jurists subsequently associated the term with a written document containing the highest normative order that prevails over all other legal norms.[5] Of course, generalised processes of legal formalisation already existed in Europe's high medieval society. However, as Chris Thornhill has pointed out, this 'involved little more than the establishment of formally drafted summaries of existing common laws or customs'.[6]

The current debate on transnational constitutionalism proposes to understand the notion of a constitution in a way that departs from

[2] See, e.g., Rainer Wahl, 'In Defence of "Constitution"', in Petra Dobner and Martin Loughlin (eds.), *The Twilight of Constitutionalism?*, Oxford: Oxford University Press, 2010, pp. 220–242.

[3] Chris Thornhill, *A Sociology of Constitutions: Constitutions and State Legitimacy in Historical-Sociological Perspective*, Cambridge: Cambridge University Press, 2011, at 74.

[4] Dieter Grimm, 'Constitution Beyond the Nation State?' (2011) *Zeitschrift für Rechtssoziologie*, 32 (2), pp. 181–188; Harold J. Berman, *Law and Revolution*, Cambridge, MA: Harvard University Press, 1983, at 396.

[5] Dieter Grimm, 'The Achievement of Constitutionalism and Its Prospects in a Changed World', in Petra Dobner and Martin Loughlin (eds.), *The Twilight of Constitutionalism?*, Oxford: Oxford University Press, 2010, pp. 3–22.

[6] Thornhill, *A Sociology of Constitutions*, at 57–58.

formalism and attachment to statehood. This development is a reaction to the changes in the nation-state and globalisation that have occurred since the end of the Second World War. It is of critical importance for the topic under discussion here, because the practices of private intermediaries, such as large telecom companies (which can block or slow down the distribution of specific content), equipment manufacturers and platform operators (who can interfere with user privacy), have a significant impact on freedom of expression and raise new constitutional questions. A conceptual opening-up is therefore a prerequisite for reflecting on a possible constitutionalisation of the technological preconditions of free speech online. In this chapter, an assessment will be conducted to determine which expansions of the concept of a constitution can be empirically verified from the perspective of law and sociology. I will then present some reflections on the results from a normative perspective.

2.2 THE EXTENSION OF THE CONCEPT IN LAW AND SOCIOLOGY

A desire to move away from the state-centred understanding of constitutions is visible in the literature on international law, which addresses the thesis that public international law since the end of the Second World War has become a stratified structure composed of different, mutually supportive legal orders, with the Charter of the United Nations serving as a constitution at the summit.[7] Similarly, constitutional language has been used in interpreting human rights instruments as an 'international bill of rights',[8] as well as in processes related to the

[7] Bardo Fassbender, *The United Nations Charter as the Constitution of the International Community*, Leiden: Nijhoff, 2009; Bardo Fassbender, '"We the Peoples of the United Nations": Constituent Power and Constitutional Form in International Law', in Neil Walker and Martin Loughlin (eds.), *The Paradox of Constitutionalism: Constituent Power and Constitutional Form*, Oxford: Oxford University Press, 2007, pp. 269–290; Erika de Wet, 'The International Constitutional Order' (2006) *International and Comparative Law Quarterly*, 55 (1), pp. 51–76.

[8] Francesco Francioni, 'An International Bill of Rights: Why It Matters, How Can It Be Used' (1997) *Texas International Law Journal*, 32 (3), pp. 471–482; B.G. Ramcharan, 'The Legal Status of the International Bill of Human Rights' (1986) *Nordic Journal of International Law*, 55 (4), pp. 366–383; John P. Humphrey, 'The International Bill of

creation of an international trade regime under the World Trade Organisation.[9] At the regional level, the establishment of the European Convention on Human Rights (ECHR),[10] as well as the primary law of the European Union, including the Charter of Fundamental Rights,[11] have been associated with developments in constitutionalisation.

These approaches are of great interest in the context of this book, because the technological infrastructure that makes communication on the internet possible in the first place is controlled by *transnational* actors. This is evident in the field of telecommunications, for example, where transnational telecom corporations dominate the market. Debates about open internet access/net neutrality have as their underlying aim to arrive at an understanding of the concept of a constitution that is detached from the territorial boundaries of statehood.[12] Since telecommunications cross national borders, such a perspectival broadening seems necessary if we are to examine concrete developments in net neutrality. At the same time, we must ask whether this is sufficient. Most decisions that are of significance for the future of open internet access are made not by states, but by telecommunication companies that operate transnationally. Moreover, the issues of free expression, technology and privacy

Rights: Scope and Implementation' (1976) *William and Mary Law Review*, 17 (3), pp. 527–542.

9 Joel P. Trachtman, 'The Constitutions of the WTO' (2006) *European Journal of International Law*, 17 (3), pp. 623–646; Deborah Z. Cass, *The Constitutionalization of the World Trade Organization*, Oxford and New York: Oxford University Press, 2005; Ernst-Ulrich Petersmann, 'The WTO Constitution and Human Rights' (2000) *Journal of International Economic Law*, 3 (1), pp. 19–25.

10 Richard Bellamy, 'The Democratic Legitimacy of International Human Rights Conventions: Political Constitutionalism and the European Convention on Human Rights' (2014) *European Journal of International Law*, 25 (4), pp. 1019–1042; Christian Walter, 'Die EMRK als Konstitutionalisierungsprozess' (1999) *Zeitschrift für ausländisches öffentliches Recht und Völkerrecht*, 59, pp. 961–983.

11 Ingolf Pernice, 'The Treaty of Lisbon: Multilevel Constitutionalism in Action' (2009) *Columbia Journal of European Law*, 15 (3), pp. 349–407; Ingolf Pernice, 'Multilevel Constitutionalism and the Treaty of Amsterdam: European Constitution-Making Revisited' (1999) *Common Market Law Review*, 36 (4), pp. 703–750; Joseph Weiler, *The Constitution of Europe: "Do the New Clothes have an Emperor?" and Other Essays on European Integration*, Cambridge: Cambridge University Press, 1999.

12 For a critique, see Wahl, 'In Defence of "Constitution"', at 232–237.

should be seen as interrelated.[13] The risk of an invasion of one's privacy on the internet does not arise solely from government activities, as private-sector device manufacturers and platform companies with opaque operations also pose a threat. Finally, although the above-mentioned developments in international law involve decentring the nation-state, they remain rooted in a formalistic understanding of what a constitution is, one that does not reflect what is actually happening in relation to global connectivity and free speech.

One promising alternative to such a formalistic approach is a *sociological* analysis of tendencies towards constitutionalisation in the context of the technological conditions that frame the exercise of free speech online. If we adopt a sociological perspective, it is the *functions* of a constitution that come to the fore.[14] The sociologist Niklas Luhmann, in particular, is a pioneer when it comes to analysing *constitutional functions* from a system-theoretic perspective.[15] He argues that modern state constitutions are characterised by the close structural coupling of the legal system and the political system, leading him to emphasise the cooperation between these two systems.[16] Since law and politics are operationally closed systems that exclude any input/output relationship, the constitution is a crucial mechanism that enables them to be structurally coupled. Notably, the constitution of a nation-state is understood differently in each system: 'For the legal system it is a supreme statute, a basic law. For the political system it is an instrument of politics.'[17]

Drawing on Luhmann's work, Thornhill has reassessed the development of political constitutionalism from a historical-sociological

[13] Timothy Garton Ash, *Free Speech: Ten Principles for a Connected World*, New Haven and London: Yale University Press, 2016, at 285.

[14] For a critique of functional constitutional perspectives in the social sciences, see Jon Elster, 'Don't Burn Your Bridge Before You Come to It: Some Ambiguities and Complexities of Precommitment' (2003) *Texas Law Review*, 81 (7), pp. 1751–1788, at 1783–1784.

[15] See Chapter 5 for an introduction to a system-theoretic approach to law.

[16] Niklas Luhmann, *Die Politik der Gesellschaft*, edited by André Kieserling, Frankfurt: Suhrkamp, 2000, at 391–392; Niklas Luhmann, 'Verfassung als evolutionäre Errungenschaft' (1990) *Rechtshistorisches Journal*, 9, pp. 176–220, at 193.

[17] Niklas Luhmann, *Law as a Social System*, translated by Klaus Alex Ziegert, Oxford and New York: Oxford University Press, 2004 (1993), at 410.

perspective and, at a high level of abstraction, identified *constitutive* and *limitative* functions of political constitutions.[18] He argues that these functions evolved over the course of a lengthy historical process, first becoming visible at the end of the Middle Ages with the development of a certain degree of political or legal autonomy. In the process of societal differentiation, Thornhill writes, 'political actors (later, in some instances, to become states) evolved by separating themselves from the highly diffuse and personalized loci of pre-modern or feudal power and from the power vested in ecclesiastical institutions'.[19] He explains the establishment of politics as a separate societal realm by appealing to modern society's need for power 'that could be detached from specific social sectors, roles, and status indicators and applied generally and reproducibly to a variety of objects and contents'.[20] Like Luhmann, Thornhill understands the relationship between politics and law in the constitutionalisation of the nation-state as involving a co-evolution, insofar as the law enabled the formation and general application of political power, thus making possible the constitution of political autonomy in the first place. At the same time as political autonomy came to be constituted in the form of the nation-state, law, religion, science and art emerged as distinct social spheres.[21] As these spheres sought to become autonomous through the development of their specific media of communication, politics was forced to reduce the scope of its interference in the particular affairs of these systems. Once again, the law played a crucial role in institutionalising the necessary political self-restraint in the form of constitutional limitations. Constitutional rights (and the rule of law more broadly) were codified as a way of separating the political from its social environment, which was a prerequisite for the further functional differentiation of society and the emergence of autonomous communication media other than power.[22]

The codified constitutions of modern nation-states provide broad empirical evidence for Thornhill's hypothesis. For example, the constitutive

[18] Thornhill, *A Sociology of Constitutions.*

[19] Chris Thornhill, 'Towards a Historical Sociology of Constitutional Legitimacy' (2008) *Theory and Society*, 37 (2), pp. 161–197, at 170.

[20] Ibid., at 172. [21] Ibid., at 174. [22] Ibid., at 175.

function of the Swiss Federal Constitution is anchored in those provisions that establish the legislative, executive and judicial powers. Generally speaking, the limitative function can be recognised in the catalogues of fundamental rights found in the constitutions of nation-states, as well as in the checks and balances that regulate the relationship between the three branches of government. In federal states, such as Switzerland, the constitutional norms dividing the responsibilities between the federal and the sub-federal levels of government represent an additional element of self-limitation with regard to power.[23]

The fact that the scope of this conceptualisation of constitutions is limited to national territories potentially contradicts Luhmann's thesis that we live in a 'world society'. Rather than defining society in terms of national borders, the concept of a world society is characterised by the general elision of territorial differentiation in favour of expanding processes of functional differentiation at the global level.[24] According to Luhmann, the structural principle of functional differentiation applies to most social sub-systems, especially the economy, science, art, mass media and education. While all these systems unfold their functionality at the global level, this is only partially the case for law and not at all for the political system. Luhmann argues that the political system remains centred on the nation-state; indeed, it is at the level of the nation-state that political decisions are taken. With regard to the law, territorial differentiation continues to structure communication to a large extent, mainly because the court system (a sub-system of law) is generally organised at the national level.[25] Beyond the national realm, the legal system has extended its reach to incorporate international, transnational and global legal dynamics.[26] For Luhmann, '[t]he result

[23] Christoph B. Graber, 'Bottom-Up Constitutionalism: The Case of Net Neutrality' (2016) *Transnational Legal Theory*, 7 (4), pp. 524–552, at 528.

[24] Niklas Luhmann, 'The World Society as a Social System' (1982) *International Journal of General Systems*, 8 (3), pp. 131–138.

[25] Niklas Luhmann, *Theory of Society*, translated by Rhodes Barret, vol. 1, Stanford: Stanford University Press, 2012 (1997), at 96.

[26] Thornhill argues that international law is increasingly penetrating into national laws. Chris Thornhill, 'The Mutation of International Law in Contemporary Constitutions: Thinking Sociologically About Political Constitutionalism' (2016) *The Modern Law Review*, 79 (2), pp. 207–247, at 224–225.

is that the structural coupling of the political system and the legal system through constitutions does not have an equivalent at the level of global society'.[27] Consequently, there is an asymmetry between politics and law at the global level, which seems to be indicative of a decline in constitutionalism.

Nevertheless, a new strand in sociological thinking about constitutions has emerged, known as societal constitutionalism (SC), which opposes the thesis of a decline of constitutionalism in the age of globalisation. The focus here is on the emergence of constitutions outside of international politics in the 'private' sectors of global society.[28] While this approach is also functionalist, it differs from Thornhill's version of constitutionalism in that it examines constitutional developments not only in the spheres of politics and law but also in all social subsystems. The radical novelty of SC is that it adopts a very broad concept of constitutions, leaving behind the boundaries of the nation-state and the legal-political sphere as the focal point of constitutional reflection. While the current debate on SC has been deeply marked by the writings Gunther Teubner has published over the last two decades, the roots of SC can be traced back much further, primarily to the American sociologist David Sciulli, who laid the foundations of this theory in the 1980s.[29]

Sciulli asks what strategies are available to modern society to escape the rationalisation dilemma diagnosed by Max Weber and counter the resulting danger of a drift towards authoritarian structures.[30] The

[27] Niklas Luhmann, *Law as a Social System*, at 487–488; Gunther Teubner, '"Global Bukowina": Legal Pluralism in the World Society', in Gunther Teubner (ed.), *Global Law Without a State*, Aldershot: Dartmouth, 1997, pp. 3–28, at 6.

[28] Gunther Teubner, 'The Project of Constitutional Sociology: Irritating Nation State Constitutionalism' (2013) *Transnational Legal Theory*, 4 (1), pp. 44–58, at 45.

[29] David Sciulli, 'Voluntaristic Action as a Distinct Concept: Theoretical Foundations of Societal Constitutionalism' (1986) *American Sociological Review*, 51 (6), pp. 743–743; David Sciulli, 'Foundations of Societal Constitutionalism: Principles from the Concepts of Communicative Action and Procedural Legality' (1988) *British Journal of Sociology*, 39 (3), pp. 377–407; David Sciulli, *Theory of Societal Constitutionalism: Foundations of a Non-Marxist Critical Theory*, Cambridge: Cambridge University Press, 1992.

[30] David Sciulli, *Theory of Societal Constitutionalism*, at 56; see Gunther Teubner, 'Societal Constitutionalism: Alternatives to State-Centred Constitutional Theory?', in Christian Joerges, et al. (eds.), *Transnational Governance and Constitutionalism*, Oxford and Portland: Hart, 2004, pp. 3–28, at 10.

dilemma identified by Weber consists in the fact that, on the one hand, the pressure to rationalise the organisation of labour, the use of capital and the legal system is a prerequisite for modernisation, while, on the other, this systemic pressure leads to the increasing bureaucratisation of productive enterprises in the economy as well as of the state administration, stifling informal coordination and fuelling authoritarian social tendencies.[31] Reformulating a thesis first put forward by Talcott Parsons in the 1930s, Sciulli argues that the only way for actors to resist systemic pressures towards collapse and drift is through 'the maintaining of the integrity of institutions of voluntaristic action'.[32] By combining Lon Fuller's account of collegial formations with a procedural approach, Sciulli is able to move from simple voluntarism to a more sophisticated theory of societal constitutionalism.

Extending societal constitutionalism to the whole of society, Sciulli elaborates a generalised account of the functions of a constitution beyond the nation-state. On this account, the critical potential of practices rooted in societal constitutionalism can check the drift towards authoritarianism, provided that restrictions on the social diffusion of power are institutionalised in the form of collegial organisations, 'the vehicles by which civil society can be constituted'.[33] According to Sciulli, the collegial form of organisation can be found wherever professionals develop and follow a professional ethics, for example in public or private research institutes, artistic and intellectual networks, universities, professional associations, rule-making bodies, non-profit organisations and so on.[34] The collegial formation provides an arena within civil society that is relatively insulated from instrumental rationality and the more unmediated competition between interests in politics or the economy.[35]

Sciulli emphasises the development of internal and external procedural restraints, in the hope that these will counteract the shift towards authoritarianism. In emphasising that these restraints are *procedural*, he

[31] Sciulli, *Theory of Societal Constitutionalism*, at 42–46.

[32] Sciulli, 'Voluntaristic Action as a Distinct Concept', at 748.

[33] David M. Frankford, 'The Critical Potential of the Common Law Tradition: Theory of Societal Constitutionalism: Foundations of a Non-Marxist Critical Theory' (1994) *Columbia Law Review*, 94 (3), pp. 1076–1124, at 1077.

[34] Sciulli, *Theory of Societal Constitutionalism*, at 80.

[35] Ibid., at 169.

invokes a debate in law-and-society circles about the advantages of a procedural form of rationality over a substantive one.[36] While a substantive approach focuses on specific outcomes, procedural methods stress the form of institutional structures (especially generality and abstractness, the clarity and publicity of legal rules and a prohibition on retroactive application), as well as how participation in a legal proceeding is organised. Firmly convinced that substantive approaches are ineffective, Sciulli postulates a procedural rationality practised within collegial formations as a possible source for the voluntary emergence of external procedural restraints as norms.[37] While internal procedural restraints are essential, since they guarantee a normative minimum standard for the interpretation of the law, external procedural controls are needed to prevent private corporations from deliberately engaging in the arbitrary exercise of collective power.[38] Because the law of modern nation-states does not protect the integrity of the dynamics of civil society, external procedural constraints must also be used to monitor the institutionalisation of collegial formations in civil society.[39]

Teubner's interpretation of societal constitutionalism builds on Sciulli's work, stressing that the constitution must no longer be state-centred.[40] Instead, the constitution's functions should be generalised 'to all social spheres', thus imposing limitations on the expansive tendencies 'of the dominant instrumental (economic) rationality'.[41] For twenty years, Teubner has reconstructed the constitution's central functions in various transnational contexts.[42] While Sciulli did not specifically examine the real effects of globalised communication, Teubner developed a particular interest in the digitally networked environment and the

[36] For an influential account, see Gunther Teubner, 'Substantive and Reflexive Elements in Modern Law' (1983) *Law and Society Review*, 17 (2), pp. 239–285.

[37] Sciulli, *Theory of Societal Constitutionalism*, at 189.

[38] Ibid., at 190–191.

[39] Ibid., at 183.

[40] Teubner, 'The Project of Constitutional Sociology' (2013), pp. 44–58.

[41] Angelo Jr Golia and Gunther Teubner, 'Societal Constitutionalism: Background, Theory, Debates' (2021) *ICL Journal*, 15 (4), pp. 357–411, at 373.

[42] A comprehensive account of the theory can be found in Gunther Teubner, *Constitutional Fragments: Societal Constitutionalism and Globalization*, translated by Gareth Norbury, Oxford: Oxford University Press, 2012.

globalised economic sphere.[43] The inclusion of the organisational structures of collective actors in his theory is a second point where Teubner goes beyond Sciulli.[44]

2.3 THE SELF-CONSTITUTIONALISATION OF TRANSNATIONAL CORPORATIONS

One of the key topics in Teubner's theory is the role and constitutional status of transnational corporations (TNCs). TNCs are generally defined as multinational firms that distance themselves from the nation-state in which they originated[45] and that are characterised by a disjunction between their economic strategy and legal liability.[46] While their economic strategy is developed at the global level, only the subsidiary, and not the parent company, is legally liable under the law of the state where it is incorporated. For international law, transnational corporations are 'invisible', since their legal personality is conceived through their affiliation to a nation-state.[47] As a result, the parent companies of TNCs operate in a legal vacuum, while the subsidiary chooses the legal system that suits it best.

Transnational corporations play a significant role in the context of the internet, especially since certain globally active tech giants have acquired power and wealth that exceeds that of the average nation-state. Meta/Facebook, for example, is so powerful that language associated with statehood is used in the literature to describe the influence of

[43] Teubner, 'Societal Constitutionalism', pp. 3–28; Gunther Teubner, 'Transnational Economic Constitutionalism in the Varieties of Capitalism' (2015) *The Italian Law Journal*, 1 (2), pp. 219–248.

[44] Golia and Teubner, 'Societal Constitutionalism', at 374.

[45] See Alessandro Bonanno and Robert J. Antonio, 'Multinational Corporations', in George Ritzer (ed.), *The Wiley-Blackwell Encyclopedia of Globalization*, Chichester: Wiley-Blackwell, 2012, pp. 1–9, at 1–2, 7.

[46] John G. Ruggie, 'Multinationals as Global Institution: Power, Authority and Relative Autonomy' (2018) *Regulation & Governance*, 12 (3), pp. 317–333, at 320.

[47] This also applies in principle to human beings. See Fleur Johns, 'The Invisibility of the Transnational Corporation: An Analysis of International Law and Legal Theory' (1994) *Melbourne University Law Review*, 19 (4), pp. 893–923, at 894.

this global platform.[48] Already in his earliest writings on social constitutionalism, Teubner wrote that mighty internet actors, such as Yahoo, should be seen as new constitutional subjects, alongside states and international organisations, the only legal subjects formally recognised by public international law.[49] Google, he later argued, challenges constitutional theory, because the worldwide dominance of its search engine, 'its questionable handling of users' private data and its massive expansionist tendencies into other sectors of the internet raise not only political but also constitutional questions in the strict sense'.[50] Tech giants and other TNCs have made themselves into new players in the global economy, with the goal of freeing their corporate strategies from the legal and political constraints imposed by nation-states.[51] As organisations, TNCs are sub-systems of the economic system, operating within that system's organised professional sphere, as distinguished from its spontaneous sphere:[52] while the former brings together highly specialised skills, the latter is mainly a gathering of forces from civil society, which channel 'external impulses and pressures into the system'.[53] By bringing together opponents in a deliberative process within a social system, these two spheres facilitate the formation of diverse opinions, as well as creating learning opportunities and chances to overcome disagreement through compromise.[54]

From a micro perspective, Teubner argues that TNCs are organisations within the economic system that create their own constitutions, distinguishing *internally* between constitutive and limitative functions. The development of *constitutive constitutional functions* by TNCs reflects the effort all social systems make to secure the autonomy of their

[48] Examples include terms like 'Facebookistan', 'Zuckerberg Law' and 'Facebook's Supreme Court'. See Anupam Chander, 'Facebookistan' (2012) *North Carolina Law Review*, 90 (5), pp. 1808–1844.

[49] Teubner, 'Societal Constitutionalism', at 3–6.

[50] Teubner, 'The Project of Constitutional Sociology', at 44.

[51] Bonanno and Antonio, 'Multinational Corporations', at 2 and 7.

[52] Teubner, *Constitutional Fragments*, at 88–102.

[53] Golia and Teubner, 'Societal Constitutionalism', at 380.

[54] I will return to these mechanisms, which are important for Teubner's theory, in more detail in Chapter 7.

communication media.[55] Teubner suggests that TNCs constitute themselves with the double aim of escaping 'from nation-state regulation' and providing 'legal security for their transactions'.[56] He thus generalises the distinction between constitutive and limitative constitutional functions originally made in relation to the constitutions of nation-states and applies it to constitutional phenomena in the sphere of the economy and corporations. Seen in this way, a social system striving to constitute its autonomy seeks to expand the scope of its specific communication medium as much as possible. Teubner describes the effect of this mechanism in terms of a compulsion to grow, leading the system to collide with and affect other social sub-systems.[57] He argues that TNCs, as a corrective to such growth compulsions, create *limitative constitutional functions* 'to overcome the primacy of shareholder value in favor of a stakeholder-orientation as well as to realize self-restraint in the areas of labor, product quality, environment, and human rights'.[58]

States, for their part, are interested in attracting large companies as taxpayers and employers. Since governments are aware that TNCs like to establish themselves in states offering the most favourable legal, economic or cultural conditions for developing their business strategies, this creates competition between states for the favour of powerful transnational corporations, usually to the detriment of the common good. The result is often a race to the bottom when it comes to human rights, labour standards, taxation and environmental protection. If the political circumstances in a country change, there are no cultural ties or sense of responsibility to the public interest that can be counted on to prevent a TNC from moving its headquarters to another country where it can expect better conditions that enable it to optimise the pursuit of its economic goals.[59] In the digital sphere, this rationality is illustrated by

[55] Teubner, *Constitutional Fragments*, at 75.

[56] Gunther Teubner, 'Self-Constitutionalizing TNCs?: On the Linkage of "Private" and "Public"' Corporate Codes of Conduct' (2011) *Indiana Journal of Global Legal Studies*, 18 (2), pp. 17–38, at 22.

[57] Teubner, *Constitutional Fragments*, at 81.

[58] Teubner, 'Self-Constitutionalizing TNCs?', at 23.

[59] The shifting of profits out of tax collectors' grasp by TNCs is a major problem. See 'What Could a New System for Taxing Multinationals Look Like?', *The Economist*, 13 May 2021.

Meta/Facebook's decision to choose Ireland as its European headquarters: public-interest advocates maintain that this was done to avoid tax,[60] while data protectionists point to the notoriously light touch of the Irish data-protection authorities.[61]

Nevertheless, while there is ample evidence that TNCs are developing constitutive functions in their constitutions, there is little to suggest that TNCs are institutionalising any limiting functions. Teubner argues that the necessary pressure on TNCs to submit to limitations cannot be expected to come from states. While he does not deny that states have improved their cooperation when it comes to regulating TNCs – indeed, many soft-law instruments have recently been endorsed by the United Nations (Guiding Principles on Business and Human Rights), the Organisation for Economic Co-operation and Development (Guidelines for Multinational Enterprises), the International Labour Organisation (Tripartite Declaration of Principles Concerning Multinational Enterprises and Social Policy) and other recognised international frameworks – few tangible steps have been taken to institutionalise binding constraints on TNCs, with the exception of the EU and rich countries, such as Switzerland, where these ideas have triggered a national legislative process to strengthen corporate social responsibility reporting.[62] This failure is due to the mechanisms described above, according to which TNCs can quickly instrumentalise their attractiveness

[60] Christian Fuchs, *The Online Advertising Tax as the Foundation of a Public Service Internet*, London: University of Westminster Press, 2018, at 26–27.

[61] See William McGeveran, 'Friending the Privacy Regulators' (2016) *Arizona Law Review*, 58 (4), pp. 959–1026, at 961.

[62] For the EU, see in the first instance Directive 2014/95/EU of the European Parliament and of the Council of 22 October 2014 amending Directive 2013/34/EU with regard to the disclosure of non-financial and diversity information by certain large undertakings and groups, OJ L 330, 22 October 2014. The directive refrains from imposing direct liability for the foreign activities of large companies based in the EU. Instead, its scope is limited to reporting obligations on topics such as the environment, human rights and corruption. In addition, there are specific due diligence and reporting obligations on child labour and sensitive minerals for companies above a certain size. The solution adopted in Switzerland broadly follows EU Directive 2014/95; see Swiss Code of Obligations (indirect counterproposal on the Swiss Responsible Business Initiative), amendment of 19 June 2020, entry into force on 1 January 2022, AS 2021 846.

as taxpayers and employers at the level of national politics to argue against binding regulation.

Given the limited prospects for effective government action, Teubner asks what means other than coercive state action can push or nudge TNCs to voluntarily develop restrictive functions in their constitutions.[63] His answer is that the necessary pressures can only come from the spontaneous sphere within the economic system – that is, from civil society circles, such as consumer organisations, trade unions, social movements and activists. In the following, Teubner's claim will be empirically tested using the social network Facebook as an illustration.

2.4 FACEBOOK AS A CASE STUDY

One conspicuous example of the pressure exerted by civil society on a transnational tech company is the so-called Facebook leaks, a series of revelations culminating in the disclosure by former Facebook employee Frances Haugen of secret company documents to *The Wall Street Journal* in 2021. Haugen's whistleblowing led to a hearing before a US Senate sub-committee, which shed light on Facebook's strategy of downplaying its 'harmful impact, including fanning teenage depression and ethnic violence'.[64] This revelation came on the back of numerous earlier indiscretions on the part of Facebook employees that had, over the years, reinforced the public feeling that the image Facebook presented to the world did not reflect the real dangers posed by the social network. The establishment of an 'Oversight Board' (OB) by Facebook in 2019–2020 may thus be viewed as a response to these developments. Should the setting up of the OB, which has been likened to a 'supreme court' for Facebook,[65] be seen as a significant step

[63] Teubner, *Constitutional Fragments*, at 75–88.

[64] 'Whistle While You Work. Why the Latest Series of Facebook Leaks Is More Politically Potent', *The Economist*, 7 October 2021.

[65] The first person to liken the OB to a 'supreme court' for Facebook was Mark Zuckerberg himself, in an interview on 15 November 2018. Evelyn Douek, 'Facebook's "Oversight Board": Move Fast with Stable Infrastructure and Humility' (2019) *North Carolina Journal of Law & Technology*, 21 (1), pp. 1–77, at 3. For an empirical reconstruction of how this metaphor was taken up by online media in the United States and gradually spread, see

towards institutionalising an element of voluntary self-limitation in the social network's constitution?

Looking at Facebook from the perspective of SC, it is possible to identify both constitutive and limitative constitutional functions in the company's constitution. As the world's largest social media platform, counting almost three billion monthly active users in 2022 from 100 different countries,[66] Facebook is intensely interested in developing constitutive constitutional functions and protecting its relative independence from expanding government regulation. Facebook's primary business model is to collect user data and sell it to 'attention merchants' for resale to advertisers.[67] According to Tim Wu, the resale of attention has become a global industry, with a turnover of USD 580 billion in 2017, and attention brokerage has come to constitute the primary business model for major tech companies.[68] Facebook's leading business partners are advertising companies; its product is the users who provide their data to the social network in exchange for the networking services it offers.[69] Shoshana Zuboff argues that companies like Facebook are primarily interested in maximising what she calls the 'behavioural surplus', that is the large quantities of data constantly produced by any user behaviour on the internet.[70] By employing surveillance technologies, firms such as Google, Facebook and Amazon are able to extract the behavioural surplus and optimise this data using machine power (via artificial

Josh Cowls, et al., 'Constitutional Metaphors: Facebook's "Supreme Court" and the Legitimation of Platform Governance' (2022) *New Media & Society*, 26 (5), pp. 1–25, at 10–12.

[66] Stacy Dixon, 'Number of Facebook Users Worldwide 2008–2022', *Statista*, 13 February 2023, www.statista.com/statistics/264810/number-of-monthly-active-facebook-users-worldwide/.

[67] Tim Wu, *The Attention Merchants: The Epic Scramble to Get Inside Our Heads*, New York: Alfred A. Knopf, 2016.

[68] Tim Wu, 'Blind Spot: The Attention Economy and the Law' (2019) *Antitrust Law Journal*, 82 (3), pp. 771–806, at 784–87.

[69] Wu, *The Attention Merchants*, at 325; see also John Lanchester, 'You Are the Product', *London Review of Books*, 17 August 2017.

[70] Shoshana Zuboff, *The Age of Surveillance Capitalism: The Fight for a Human Future at the New Frontier of Power*, New York: Public Affairs, 2019; for a critique, see Mariano-Florentino Cuéllar and Aziz Z. Huq, 'Economies of Surveillance' (2020) *Harvard Law Review*, 133 (4), pp. 1280–1336.

intelligence, profiling and data mining) to control (i.e. predict and manipulate) future user behaviour in order to make money.[71]

Facebook has issued internal guidelines,[72] as well as two public documents to inform users about its rules.[73] The first document, 'Terms of Service',[74] contains primarily legal information about the contract with the social network, data protection, personalisation, the company's cookie policy and dispute resolution. The second document, 'Community Standards',[75] sets out detailed rules for all users who post content on the platform, including pornography and nudity, hate speech, violence and intellectual property. Taken together, the two documents embody the platform's self-perception and aim to prove its supposed capacity to self-regulate with regard to all issues that arise when users are active on Facebook. In this way, these documents attempt to substantiate the platform's claim to put user interests first, and thereby to prevent calls for more intensive reforms of the company's decision-making processes or the imposition of state regulation.[76] Moreover, in addition to political considerations, there are compelling business reasons for Facebook to show its non-governmental stakeholders (i.e., advertisers, users and the media) that it is willing to establish speech norms which promise to strike a balance between conflicting social values.[77]

As Facebook continued to grow, so too did the problems it created, such as the spread of fake news, disinformation, propaganda and hate speech. Although the social network has been investing in improving

[71] For a similar analysis, see Mireille Hildebrandt, *Smart Technologies and the End(s) of Law: Novel Entanglements of Law and Technology*, Cheltenham, UK, and Northampton, MA: Edward Elgar, 2015.

[72] Kate Klonick, 'The New Governors: The People, Rules, and Processes Governing Online Speech' (2018) *Harvard Law Review*, 131 (6), pp. 1598–1670, at 1638–39.

[73] Tarleton Gillespie, *Custodians of the Internet: Platforms, Content Moderation, and the Hidden Decisions That Shape Social Media*, New Haven: Yale University Press, 2018, at 46.

[74] Meta, 'Facebook Terms of Service', www.facebook.com/terms (accessed 26 July 2022).

[75] Meta, 'Facebook Community Standards', https://transparency.fb.com/policies/community-standards/ (accessed 22 March 2023).

[76] Douek, 'Facebook's "Oversight Board"', at 21.

[77] Monika Bickert, 'Defining the Boundaries of Free Speech on Social Media', in Geoffrey R. Stone and Lee C. Bollinger (eds.), *The Free Speech Century*, Oxford: Oxford University Press, 2018, pp. 254–271, at 265.

content moderation to forestall demands for government regulation, neither the use of artificial intelligence nor the 15,000 content moderators that Facebook employs to enforce its Community Standards[78] can cope with the tens of millions of pieces of content that must be reviewed daily.[79] This situation is exacerbated by the fact that cases differ, contexts vary and those charged with content moderation are often 'burnt-out, time-pressured and geographically distributed contractors',[80] unable to consider each decision with sufficient diligence.[81] Against this backdrop, the establishment of the OB by Facebook promised to remedy flaws in moderation practices, with Facebook presenting the project to the world as a voluntary self-limitation on its exercise of power, by subjecting its content moderation to independent checks.[82] A charter, a trust endowed with USD 130 million (intended to fund the OB for the first six years) and the election of a group of highly respected people with diverse backgrounds as its first members were meant to ensure the OB's independence.[83]

Despite these lofty aims, a close examination of the charter of the OB[84] reveals a somewhat ambivalent document, as it not only guarantees the independence of the members of the OB but, according to Mark Zuckerberg, also ensures 'their commitment to the principles they *must* uphold'.[85] Facebook/Meta has set out all the rules that the board ought to implement in 'a unilateral manner', which raises questions about their 'democratic legitimacy'.[86] Hence, individuals who accept a position on the OB simultaneously subject themselves to fundamental values of Meta/Facebook, such as Zuckerberg's belief in the democratising power

[78] 'Autumn is Coming. As AI's Limits Become Apparent, Humans Will Add More', *The Economist*, 11 June 2020.

[79] Douek, 'Facebook's "Oversight Board"', at 10–15. [80] Ibid., at 27. [81] Ibid., at 11.

[82] Ibid., at 46.

[83] Evelyn Douek, 'What Kind of Oversight Board Have You Given Us?', *The Chicago Law Review Online*, 11 May 2020, https://lawreviewblog.uchicago.edu/2020/05/11/fb-oversight-board-edouek/.

[84] Meta, Oversight Board Charter, https://oversightboard.com/attachment/494475942886876/ (version of February 2023).

[85] Mark Zuckerberg, as quoted in Douek, 'Facebook's "Oversight Board"', at 48.

[86] Chinmayi Arun, 'The Facebook Oversight Board: An Experiment in Self-Regulation', *Just Security*, 6 May 2020, www.justsecurity.org/70021/the-facebook-oversight-board-an-experiment-in-self-regulation/.

of technology.[87] Moreover, doubts regarding the OB's ability to effectively function as a constitutional self-limitation of Facebook's power also arise from the fact that it neglects to target 'the vicious circle of monetisation of engagement and compulsion to social manipulation'.[88] Thus, the social network fails to bring under control the central mechanisms that have simultaneously enabled its unparalleled growth and imposed considerable social costs as 'collateral damage'. Indeed, tech companies like Facebook have been criticised for pushing the designers they employ to optimise social apps for compulsive use.[89] In an interview with a tech news website, Tristan Harris, a coder turned design ethicist, spoke about technologies that are designed to create addiction in users and persuade them to do things like spending time on a client's website, clicking on a link, subscribing to a newsletter or buying something.[90] This is also true of Facebook, whose purpose is to capture human attention, since this is what fuels its business.[91]

The example of Facebook shows how difficult it is in practice to induce TNCs to exercise self-restraint voluntarily. In any case, it is essential to closely monitor whether a voluntary measure – here the establishment of the OB – really has a limiting effect on the expansionist tendencies of a transnational corporation or whether it is more of a marketing strategy to tranquilise critics, regulators, the media, customers and users.

2.5 CRITIQUE AND METHODOLOGICAL IMPLICATIONS

The attempt to expand the concept of a constitution from its classical, formal interpretation grounded in the nation-state so that it covers

87 Douek, 'Facebook's "Oversight Board"', pp. 1–77, at 51.

88 Angelo Jr Golia, 'Beyond Oversight: Advancing Societal Constitutionalism in the Age of Surveillance Capitalism', *Working Paper*, 25 February 2021, Heidelberg: Max Planck Institute for Comparative Public Law and International Law, https://ssrn.com/abstract=3793219.

89 Bianca Bosker, 'The Binge Breaker', *The Atlantic*, November 2016, www.theatlantic.com/magazine/archive/2016/11/the-binge-breaker/501122/.

90 Recode Staff, 'Full Transcript: Time Well Spent Founder Tristan Harris on Recode Decode', *Recode Decode*, 7 February 2017, www.vox.com/2017/2/7/14542504/recode-decode-transcript-time-well-spent-founder-tristan-harris.

91 Wu, *The Attention Merchants.*

international, political-sociological and societal perspectives elicits somewhat ambivalent feelings.

On the one hand, this expansion of the scope of the term dilutes the established concept of a constitution, especially since the crucial aspect of legitimacy is left out. Dieter Grimm, for example, emphasises the central importance of democratic legitimacy in the nation-state for his understanding of the constitution, rejecting any broadening of the concept. He argues that democracy is a necessary principle for the legitimation of public power and that renouncing it or replacing it with an alternative 'would undermine the function of the constitution'.[92] He also rejects suggestions that two types of constitution could co-exist: a rule-of-law type and a democratic type. For Grimm, only a constitution comprising both elements can wholly fulfil the expectations of constitutionalism.[93] Moreover, he rejects SC even more fully than the extension of the concept of a constitution to the international level. The possibility to which SC lays claim, namely self-restraint by global private actors for the common good, is illusory, because no public authority is capable of enforcing such processes if it proves necessary. Grimm cautions: 'And even if existing international institutions possessed this power, how effectively would they use it without the democratic and representative element that guarantees participation of those affected by the decisions and thus enables a perception of problems beyond the institutional interests of the actors?'[94]

On the other hand, there is no doubt that the internet confronts us with questions of great socio-political urgency, to which constitutional doctrine and the classical conception of a constitution are blind, as the result of their methodological 'default settings'. The strength of SC lies in the fact that it provides a benchmark for the empirical observation of actual social developments. As a sociological theory rooted in Sciulli's work and Luhmann's systems theory, which was further elaborated by Teubner, it perceives *factual* developments on the internet as phenomena of constitutional significance, even where a classical understanding

[92] Grimm, 'The Achievement of Constitutionalism and Its Prospects in a Changed World', at 10.

[93] Ibid. [94] Ibid., at 20.

of the constitution would not expect them. Moreover, a further advantage of SC having its roots in Luhmann's systems theory is that it can be connected to legal-theoretical discussions on the emergence of normative expectations in state and non-state/societal contexts. These questions will be discussed in detail in Chapters 4 and 5.

However, SC should not be understood as a normative-legal theory, since factual developments alone cannot create legitimacy.[95] It would be naive to blindly rely on bottom-up societal dynamics in cases where state regulatory approaches remain ineffective. Even the power generated by protest movements or other forms of pressure from civil society must not be exempt from the legitimacy test. As many recent examples have shown, manipulation and algorithmic mechanisms can deceptively make bottom-up mass movements appear larger than they are.[96] I thus agree with Grimm that legitimacy can only arise from democratic processes and political representation at the nation-state level.

The upshot is that contradictions remain between state-centred and societal constitutional legitimacy. I therefore suggest introducing a distinction between normative-legal and sociological perspectives.[97] Normative-legal analysis requires a standpoint within the legal system, and legitimacy is a function of democratically grounded generalised legal procedures. Conversely, a sociological perspective focuses on the observation and description of real events, with *acceptance* being the apparent result of socially generated power.[98] Indeed, Max Weber forcefully argued that there may be acceptance *without democratic legitimation*,[99] assuming that legal subjects generally obey commands that are accepted. While democratic processes promote the acceptance of a norm,

95 Emilios Christodoulidis, 'On the Politics of Societal Constitutionalism' (2013) *Indiana Journal of Global Legal Studies*, 20 (2), pp. 629–663.

96 For an analysis of Facebook's role in the 'Cambridge Analytica' scandal, see Michael Fässler, 'Google's Privacy Sandbox Initiative: Old Wine in New Skins', *i-call Working Paper*, No. 01/2023, Zurich: University of Zurich, at 14–16, www.zora.uzh.ch/id/eprint/232978/.

97 See Graber, 'Bottom-Up Constitutionalism', at 548–549.

98 For a similar argument, see Thornhill, 'Towards a Historical Sociology of Constitutional Legitimacy', at 165.

99 Max Weber, *Economy and Society: An Outline of Interpretive Sociology*, translated by Günther Roth, Berkeley: University of California Press, 1978 (1922), at 212–216.

acceptance and democratic legitimation must nonetheless be distinguished.[100] On the theoretical level, there may be situations where the processes that produce democratic legitimation are flawed or do not sufficiently incorporate specific values that have not yet received precise normative contours. In the as-yet poorly mapped digital ecosphere, it may indeed be the case that the social values of open internet access or privacy protection – although crucial to the public interest – are not sufficiently represented in legislative processes, which are often dominated by powerful lobbies pushing for corporate interests. An SC perspective can provide a benchmark for reviewing general legal processes. Conversely, classic constitutionalism establishes a rule-of-law standard and a democratic standard for identifying and remedying failures of bottom-up, civil-society-driven dynamics. Consequently, in the following, I will consistently assume the coexistence of empirical-sociological and normative-legal levels of meaning in interpreting constitutional processes, with the result that the distinction between the social-empirical and the legal-normative perspective on internet-related constitutional developments is reintroduced into (classical) constitutional law.[101]

[100] Armin von Bogdandy, et al., *In Whose Name?: A Public Law Theory of International Adjudication*, Oxford: Oxford University Press, 2014, at 155.

[101] Re-entry is the term used in the theory of distinction to describe the re-entrance of the distinction into what it is distinguishing. Niklas Luhmann, *Die Wissenschaft der Gesellschaft*, Frankfurt: Suhrkamp, 1990 at 83–84 and 379–380.

CHAPTER 3

Transnationalism or 'Splinternet'?

Chapter 2 has shown to what extent the current debate on the concept of a constitution is shaped by theories of transnationalisation. Communication today is strongly influenced by the technical conditions of the internet, which can be provisionally defined as the complex interaction between software and hardware within globally networked computer systems. Over the last decades, the debate on internet governance has evolved in parallel with the technical development of the 'network of networks' and its growing economic and social importance. This debate is taking place in a field of tension, whose poles can be described as transnationalism and 'splinternet'.

3.1 TRANSNATIONAL OR NATIONAL STANDARDS IN INTERNET LAW

Numerous studies and academic papers have addressed the question of whether a transnationalisation of law is occurring.[1] According to Philip Jessup, who coined the term in 1956, 'transnational law' encompasses 'all law which regulates actions or events that transcend national frontiers'.[2] In the more than 65 years since it was first introduced, this concept has been extensively invoked in a variety of legal, political and sociological discussions in numerous methodological and

[1] See, e.g., the large number of articles on a variety of topics in Peer Zumbansen (ed.), *The Oxford Handbook of Transnational Law*, New York: Oxford University Press, 2021.

[2] Philip Jessup, *Transnational Law*, New Haven: Yale University Press, 1956, at 2.

analytical settings.[3] The expansion in its use paralleled burgeoning hopes in, or fears of, the effects of globalisation, with some theorists going so far as to see transnational law as mostly, or even completely, disconnected from the state. For my part, I agree with Gregory Shaffer and Terence Hallyday that such views are empirically and normatively unconvincing: empirically, this position 'is mistaken to the extent it suggests that autonomous, nonstate legal ordering is becoming predominant',[4] while it is normatively problematic insofar as it suggests that newly emerged non-state legal orders solve burning social problems, when, in fact, 'state institutions remain central for fostering social order and legitimising and enforcing social norms'.[5] In its place, a more pragmatic and down-to-earth conceptualisation of transnational law is preferable, one which sees the state as an actor that has lost influence, but that continues to decisively shape the normative order in competition or cooperation with other states and non-state corporate or civil society actors, both organised and spontaneous.

The focus of this book lies on transnationalisation issues in the field of internet governance. State law is, in many respects, challenged in this sphere by the private ordering of transnational corporations. The state's ability to govern thus often depends on cooperation with actors in international forums or civil society. Moreover, due to the increasing significance of technological infrastructure for communications, transnational law is also called upon to address fundamental questions concerning the relationship between materiality and sociality. It is thus increasingly forced to adopt interdisciplinary perspectives. Moreover, there are further methodological challenges, such as the issue that addressing the state's role in internet governance requires us to distinguish between empirical and normative perspectives. While the former

[3] Peer Zumbansen, 'Transnational Law: Theories and Applications', in Peer Zumbansen (ed.), *The Oxford Handbook of Transnational Law*, New York: Oxford University Press, 2021, pp. 2–30, at 3–7.

[4] Gregory Shaffer and Terence Halliday, 'With, Within, and Beyond the State: The Promise and Limits of Transnational Legal Ordering', in Peer Zumbansen (ed.), *The Oxford Handbook of Transnational Law*, New York: Oxford University Press, 2021, pp. 986–1006, at 988.

[5] Ibid., at 1004.

involves an attempt to observe and describe what is happening in value-neutral terms, the latter is concerned with normative judgements and calls for (more or less) transnationalisation (e.g., of fundamental rights).

3.2 DIFFERENT APPROACHES TO CONTENT AND TECHNOLOGY

If the state of transnationalisation on the internet is to be assessed empirically, it is necessary to distinguish the regulation of content from the regulation of the network infrastructure. The first years following the invention of the World Wide Web by Tim Berners-Lee in 1991[6] were dominated by a libertarian outlook that wholly denied the existence of territorial boundaries and state authority on the internet. This position is eloquently verbalised in John Perry Barlow's declaration of the independence of cyberspace. At the World Economic Forum in Davos in 1996, he solemnly declared:

> Governments of the Industrial World, you weary giants of flesh and steel, I come from Cyberspace, the new home of Mind. On behalf of the future, I ask you of the past to leave us alone. You are not welcome among us. You have no sovereignty where we gather.
>
> We have no elected government, nor are we likely to have one, so I address you with no greater authority than that with which liberty itself always speaks. I declare the global social space we are building to be naturally independent of the tyrannies you seek to impose on us. You have no moral right to rule us nor do you possess any methods of enforcement we have true reason to fear.[7]

Barlow's declaration encapsulated the dream of 'digital libertarians' of a state-free space, a thesis that was powerful enough to permeate scholarly debates about the regulation of internet speech from the very

[6] Tim Berners-Lee with Mark Fischetti, *Weaving the Web: The Original Design and Ultimate Destiny of the World Wide Web by Its Inventor*, New York: Harper Collins, 1999.

[7] John Perry Barlow, 'A Declaration of the Independence of Cyberspace', *EFF*, 8 February 1996, www.eff.org/cyberspace-independence.

beginning.[8] Already in 1997, James Boyle identified, with impressive foresight, three characteristics of the internet underpinning the thesis: 1) its technological foundation, 2) the geographic distribution of its users and 3) the digital specificities of the distributed content.[9]

Boyle, Joel Reidenberg[10] and Lawrence Lessig[11] have criticised and deconstructed the thesis of a regulation-free cyberspace, drawing attention instead to the regulatory effects of digital technology that unfold in interaction with the law. Unimpressed by this analysis, regulators in the United States and Europe opted for self-policing and 'internet exceptionalism', that is the exemption of online content from liability in light of free-speech considerations.[12] This approach is most clearly reflected in the so-called safe harbour rules in the US Communications Decency Act (CDA) of 1996.[13] In particular, Section 230 of the CDA states: 'No provider or user of an interactive computer service shall be treated as the publisher or speaker of any information provided by another information content provider.' Accordingly, internet intermediaries hosting or redistributing content provided by third-party users (hereafter, Internet Content and Service Providers (ICSPs)) have been exempted from the effects of a range of laws that would otherwise apply. The European Union, for its part, adopted horizontal liability rules in the E-Commerce Directive (ECD) of 2000,[14] foreseeing a self-regulatory 'notice and

[8] For an influential academic defence of the idea that cyberspace constitutes a uniquely new legal realm that goes beyond the State, see David R. Johnson and David Post, 'Law and Borders: The Rise of Law in Cyberspace' (1996) *Stanford Law Review*, 48 (5), pp. 1367–1402.

[9] James Boyle, 'Foucault in Cyberspace: Surveillance, Sovereignty, and Hardwired Censors' (1997) *University of Cincinnati Law Review*, 66 (1), pp. 177–205, at 178.

[10] Joel Reidenberg, 'Lex Informatica: The Formulation of Information Policy Rules Through Technology' (1998) *Texas Law Review*, 76 (3), pp. 553–593.

[11] Lawrence Lessig, *Code and Other Laws of Cyberspace*, New York: Basic Books, 1999.

[12] For the United States, see Mark Tushnet, 'Internet Exceptionalism: An Overview from General Constitutional Law' (2015) *William & Mary Law Review*, 56 (4), pp. 1637–1672; Tim Wu, 'Is Internet Exceptionalism Dead?', in Berin Szoka and Adam Marcus (eds.), *The Next Digital Decade: Essays on the Future of the Internet*, Washington DC: TechFreedom, 2010, pp. 179–188.

[13] 47 US Code.

[14] Directive 2000/31/EC of the European Parliament and of the Council of 6 August 2000 on certain legal aspects of information society services, in particular electronic

takedown' mechanism for hosting services in Article 14.[15] According to this mechanism, ICSPs are exempt from liability, provided that they did not know they were hosting illicit information or activity and that they act promptly to remove or disable access to the illegal content.[16] The ECD's approach is deemed 'horizontal' because it deals with any liability (penal, administrative, tortuous, contractual, etc.) for any kind of activity undertaken by third parties, including intellectual-property infringements, libel, unfair competition, misleading advertising, the publication or distribution of illegal content and so on. In October 2022, the novel Digital Services Act (DSA) replaced the ECD, without removing the liability 'safe harbours'.[17] Recital 16 of the DSA explains that the horizontal framework of conditional liability exemptions, laid down in the ECD, 'has allowed many novel services to emerge and scale up across the internal market', concluding '[t]hat framework should therefore be preserved'.

It is by no means the case that internet exceptionalism and content self-regulation have gone unchallenged. As cases of online abuse, voter manipulation, harassment and hate speech have increased,[18] calls have grown to move away from the current approach and to strengthen the liability of intermediaries for the content they host, cache or transmit. However, the view that the internet owes its potential as a facilitator of public discourse, 'democratic culture'[19] and thriving digital markets to

commerce, in the Internal Market (Directive on Electronic Commerce), OJ L 178, 17 July 2000.

15 Lilian Edwards, 'Articles 12–15 ECD: ISP Liability: The Problem of Intermediary Service Provider Liability', in Lilian Edwards (ed.), *The New Legal Framework for E-Commerce in Europe*, Oxford: Hart, 2005, pp. 93–136, at 112.

16 Arno R. Lodder, 'Directive 2000/31/EC on Certain Legal Aspects of Information Society Services, in Particular Electronic Commerce in the Internal Market', in Arno R. Lodder and Andrew D. Murray (eds.), *EU Regulation of E-Commerce: A Commentary*, 2nd edn, Cheltenham: Edward Elgar, 2022, pp. 18–63, paras 2.135–2.137.

17 Regulation (EU) 2022/2065 of the European Parliament and of the Council of 19 October 2022 on a Single Market for Digital Services and amending Directive 2000/31/EC (Digital Services Act), OJ L 277, 27 October 2022.

18 For documentation of this phenomenon, see Nicolas P. Suzor, *Lawless: The Secret Rules That Govern Our Digital Lives*, Cambridge: Cambridge University Press, 2019, chapter 3.

19 Jack M. Balkin, 'Digital Speech and Democratic Culture: A Theory of Freedom of Expression for the Information Society' (2004) *New York University Law Review*, 79 (1), pp. 1–55.

a hands-off regulatory approach has proved extremely vital. As a result, neither the United States nor the EU has shown any concrete intentions to move away from the existing regime. In the United States, proposals to revise Section 230 of the CDA were recently made in Congress, but none of them have been voted on in either the Senate or the House of Representatives.[20] In the EU, introducing the DSA did not do away with the mantra of content self-regulation either. Instead, the liability rules in the DSA have been copied from the ECD, mainly to ensure continuity.[21]

At the same time, the discussion about the use of 'network technology' – that is, the physical layer of the internet[22] – took a different direction at an early stage.[23] Around 1999, academics in the United States and Europe started issuing warnings about potential risks to the open internet infrastructure.[24] In 2003, Tim Wu coined the term 'net neutrality', which he understood as a political principle demanding that 'broadband carriers should not discriminate in how they treat traffic on their broadband network'.[25] Wu's intention was to articulate a principle that struck a balance between the 'inter network', where broadband operators had no authority to impose restrictions, and the local network, where they should be allowed 'to police what they own'.[26] Despite its conceptual vagueness, the principle soared to prominence in the United States, quickly becoming a crucial benchmark in civil society debates, political deliberations and the Federal

[20] See 'What Is Section 230?', *The Economist*, 20 February 2023.

[21] Folkert Wilman, 'Between Preservation and Clarification: The Evolution of the DSA's Liability Rules in Light of the CJEU's Case Law', *Verfassungsblog*, 2 November 2022, https://verfassungsblog.de/dsa-preservation-clarification/.

[22] For a distinction between the physical layer of network technology and the protocol layer, which provides the link to the content layer and the social layer of the internet, see Jonathan Zittrain, *The Future of the Internet and How to Stop It*, New Haven: Yale University Press, 2008, at 67–68.

[23] The administration of the Internet protocol layer, including IP addresses and internet domain names, will be discussed in Chapter 6.

[24] Christopher T. Marsden, *Network Neutrality: From Policy to Law to Regulation*, Manchester: Manchester University Press, 2016, at 29.

[25] Tim Wu, 'Network Neutrality, Broadband Discrimination' (2003) *Journal of Telecommunications and High Technology Law*, 2, pp. 141–179, at 171.

[26] Ibid.

Communications Commission's (FCC) regulatory efforts to shape the future of the internet's architecture.

The FCC invoked the principle for the first time, albeit without naming it, in a 2005 Statement on Internet Policy, determining that 'the Commission has jurisdiction necessary to ensure that providers of telecommunications for internet access or Internet Protocol–enabled (IP-enabled) services are operated in a neutral manner'.[27] The policy statement outlined several principles of network neutrality that aimed to encourage 'broadband deployment', as well as to preserve and promote the 'open and interconnected nature of the public internet'.[28] Based on these principles, a 2008 order issued by the FCC prohibited Comcast from throttling BitTorrent traffic when providing broadband internet access over its cable lines.[29] This represented the FCC's first attempt to turn net neutrality into a *legal* concept. However, it was unsuccessful, as the Court of Appeals for the DC Circuit overturned the FCC order on 6 April 2010, ruling that there was no legal basis in the Communications Act that would authorise the FCC to regulate Comcast's network management practices.[30] The Court recalled the FCC's still-binding 2002 Cable Modem Order, in which 'the Commission [had] ruled that cable internet service is neither a "telecommunications service" covered by Title II of the Communications Act nor a "cable service" covered by

[27] FCC, 'Appropriate Framework for Broadband Access to the Internet Over Wireline Facilities; Review of Regulatory Requirements for Incumbent LEC Broadband Telecommunications Services; Computer III Further Remand Proceedings: Bell Operating Company Provision of Enhanced Services; 1998 Biennial Regulatory Review—Review of Computer III and ONA Safeguards and Requirements; Inquiry Concerning High-Speed Access to the Internet Over Cable and Other Facilities; Internet Over Cable Declaratory Ruling; Appropriate Regulatory Treatment for Broadband Access to the Internet Over Cable Facilities', CC Docket Nos. 02–33, 01–337, 98–10, 95–20, GN Docket No. 00–185, CS Docket No. 02–52, Policy Statement, 20 FCC Rcd 14986 (2005), at 3.

[28] Ibid.

[29] FCC, 'Formal Complaint of Free Press and Public Knowledge Against Comcast Corporation for Secretly Degrading Peer-to-Peer Applications, Broadband Industry Practices; Petition of Free Press et al. for Declaratory Ruling that Degrading an Internet Application Violates the FCC's Internet Policy Statement and Does Not Meet an Exception for "Reasonable Network Management"', File No. EB–08–IH–1518, WC Docket No. 07–52, Memorandum Opinion and Order, 23 FCC Rcd 13028 (2008).

[30] *Comcast v. FCC* No. 08–1291 (DC Cir. 2010), at 3.

Title VI'.[31] In response to the court ruling, the FCC adopted the Open Internet Order on 21 December 2010,[32] which outlined three basic rules for providers of broadband services: 1) a transparency norm, 2) a prohibition against blocking lawful content and 3) a prohibition against unreasonable discrimination. The Commission reasoned that the newly adopted protections 'are grounded in broadly accepted internet norms, as well as our own prior decisions'.[33] However, the Court of Appeals found that this did not provide a sufficient legal basis for the new rules and struck down the order in *Verizon v. FCC* (14 January 2014).[34]

Drawing on the lessons of its previous defeats, the FCC issued a two-tiered order in 2015 that, first, reclassified broadband services under Title II of the Communications Act and, second, laid out new rules on net neutrality, requiring providers of fixed and wireless internet access to respect the principle of internet openness and abstain from engaging in blocking, throttling or paid-prioritisation practices.[35] The Court of Appeals upheld the decision in 2016 and confirmed that the necessary legal basis was now in place.[36] However, net-neutrality advocates could not celebrate the new, stricter rules for long, as their next defeat loomed, this time on the political front. The incoming Trump administration repealed the new rules and reclassified broadband services as private mobile services,[37] taking the debate about net neutrality in the United States back to square one. Developments since then have confirmed this stop-start dynamic. The net-neutrality rules reinstated by the FCC under the Biden presidency in January 2024 were overturned by the Court of Appeals for the Sixth Circuit on 2 January 2025. It ruled that the FCC was wrong to classify broadband internet as a telecommunications service.[38] Supporters of net neutrality are now hoping that Congress will pass

[31] Ibid., at 5.

[32] FCC, 'Preserving the Open Internet; Broadband Industry Practices', GN Docket No 09–191, WC Docket No 07–52, Report and Order, 25 FCC Rcd 17905 (2010).

[33] Ibid., at 2. [34] *Verizon v. FCC* No. 11–1355 (DC Cir. 2014).

[35] FCC, 'Protecting and Promoting the Open Internet', GN Docket No. 14–28, Report and Order on Remand, Declaratory Ruling, and Order, 30 FCC Rcd 5601 (2015), at 7–8.

[36] *US Telecom Assoc. v. FCC* No. 15-1063 (DC Cir. 2016).

[37] FCC, 'Restoring Internet Freedom', WC Docket No. 17–108, Declaratory Ruling, Report and Order, and Order, 33 FCC Rcd 311 (2018).

[38] *Ohio Telecom Association v. FCC* No. 24–3449 (6th Cir. 2025).

legislation to protect it nationwide. Given the current political balance of power, however, this seems rather unrealistic.

The history of open internet regulation in the EU is very different from its history in the United States, apparently confirming Christopher Marsden's thesis that net neutrality is 'the internet's exception to transnational law'.[39] The debate in the EU got off to a slow start for several reasons, including difficulties in framing net neutrality in an intelligible way and in mobilising civil society, the organisation of the telecom authorities and regulatory structures.[40] Eventually, however, it gained momentum[41] and led straight to the adoption of the Open Internet Regulation, a directly applicable EU legislation on access to the open internet and net neutrality.[42] The European Court of Justice (ECJ) has already concretely applied this regulation in various cases, making clear that the new set of rules has teeth (for details, see Chapter 6).

The upshot of this brief account of the history of net neutrality in the United States and the EU is that regulatory solutions have been found along national territorial lines. While the EU has adopted strict net-neutrality rules that are implemented in an effective way, the legislative process in the United States has been stuck in the political doldrums. Does this reflect a trend towards a renationalisation of the internet?

The spectre of a 'splinternet' affecting the internet's most significant unifying elements has recently been evoked in the literature.[43] When Clyde Wayne Crews, then director of studies at the Cato Institute, a libertarian think-tank, coined the term in 2001, he gave it a positive

[39] Christopher T. Marsden, 'Transnational Internet Law', in Peer Zumbansen (ed.), *The Oxford Handbook of Transnational Law,* New York: Oxford University Press, 2021, pp. 418–436, at 432.

[40] Jan Gerlach, *The Informational Ecosystem of Net Neutrality: A Comparison of Regulatory Discourses in the U.S. and the E.U.,* St Gallen: Dike, 2016, at 240–264.

[41] For a discussion, see Section 3.3.

[42] Regulation (EU) 2015/2120 of the European Parliament and of the Council of 25 November 2015 laying down measures concerning open internet access (Open Internet Regulation), OJ L 310/1, 26 November 2015.

[43] Scott Malcomson, *Splinternet: How Geopolitics and Commerce Are Fragmenting the World Wide Web,* New York and London: OR Books, 2016; Milton L. Mueller, *Will the Internet Fragment?: Sovereignty, Globalization, and Cyberspace,* Cambridge and Malden: Polity, 2017; Stacie Hoffmann, et al., 'Standardising the Splinternet: How China's Technical Standards Could Fragment the Internet' (2020) *Journal of Cyber Policy,* 5 (2), pp. 239–264.

connotation. In an article published in Forbes on 2 April 2001, Crews identified 'the Internet's nobody-owns-it, common-property status' as the main reason for the political battles raging over cyberspace regulation.[44] As a solution, he recommended making 'way for proprietary "splinternets" where pre-specified ground rules regarding privacy and other governance issues replace regulation and central planning'.[45] However, in the context of the ongoing geopolitical realignments around Russia and China, the term 'splinternet' has taken on a negatively charged meaning. In his 2016 book *Splinternet*, Scott Malcomson describes the changes in internet regulation since the turn of the millennium in terms of increasing fragmentation driven by cooperation between the public and the private sectors.[46] A critical development in this process was the US government's decision in 1998 to transfer internet policy from a Department of Defence contractor to the newly formed Internet Corporation for Assigned Names and Numbers (ICANN),[47] paving the way for the internet's transformation from a military-academic piece of infrastructure to a primarily business-oriented one.[48] In response to the threat of the increasing 'balkanisation' of the internet under the influence of authoritarian regimes,[49] the state began acting as a regulator rather than an investor.[50] Building on this analysis, Milton Mueller has asked whether geopolitics will divide cyberspace into national legal spaces.[51] Securitisation, the territorialisation of information flows and control over critical internet resources are the methods that states employ in an attempt to ensure the alignment of communications with national politics. However, he observes an 'inherent clash between alignment and the economic efficiencies and capabilities of digital technology'.[52] When it comes to China's standardisation policy, Hoffmann et al. are less optimistic, arguing that China's national strategy of using

[44] Clyde Wayne Crews, 'Pick Your Net', *Forbes*, 2 April 2001, www.forbes.com/forbes/2001/0402/036.html.

[45] Ibid. [46] Malcomson, *Splinternet*. [47] For details, see Chapter 6.

[48] Malcomson, *Splinternet*, at 133–137.

[49] Cass R. Sunstein, *#Republic: Divided Democracy in the Age of Social Media*, Princeton: Princeton University Press, 2017, at 66 and 70.

[50] Malcomson, *Splinternet*, at 183–184. [51] Mueller, *Will the Internet Fragment?*, chapter 4.

[52] Ibid., at 61.

technical standards to micromanage the internet from the top down has 'the potential to break the global, free and interoperable internet into two or 200 distinct intranets'.[53]

Against this backdrop, the EU's aim is to increase its independence vis-à-vis both the historical pacemaker in network policy (the United States) and the newly emerging pacemaker (China). In this spirit, it has recently chosen to move forward with fine-grained internet regulation, in relative independence from US strategies or multilateral perspectives, as evidenced by the Cybersecurity Act (2019), the Digital Services Act, the Digital Markets Act (2022) and the Artificial Intelligence Act (2024). These developments seemingly confirm Marsden's thesis that net neutrality is the exception to transnational law. As compelling as this thesis may seem, however, the following section presents counterarguments based on an analysis of civil society mobilisation in net-neutrality debates.

3.3 NET-NEUTRALITY DEBATES AND TRANSNATIONALISATION

One argument against Marsden's thesis and in favour of the transnational character of net neutrality is that the debate on the open internet partly took place across national borders. In the following, we will first reconstruct its origins in the United States, before showing how it was received in other regions, specifically the EU and India.

As mentioned earlier, the net-neutrality debate in the United States began around the turn of the millennium. In total, the FCC engaged in ten years of continuous attempts to establish net neutrality as a legal principle in US law. After it failed for the second time to defend an order to regulate net neutrality before the Court of Appeals, in the *Verizon* case, Tim Wu commented on the verdict in a newspaper interview, criticising the FCC for opting for the wrong strategy when 'arguing that its rules are not common carrier rules' in the sense of Title II of the US Communications Act and recommending that the FCC should now 'reclassify broadband under Title II authority'.[54] Although he agreed

[53] Hoffmann, et al., 'Standardising the Splinternet', at 252.

[54] Brian Fung, '"A FEMA-Level Fail": The Law Professor Who Coined "Net Neutrality" Lashes Out at the FCC's Legal Strategy', *The Washington Post*, 14 January 2014.

with the interviewer's remark that such a radical decision would likely trigger considerable political resistance, he nonetheless insisted that now was the time 'to get people in Congress excited about that'.[55]

Various internet advocacy and public-interest groups in the United States took Wu's recommendation to heart and launched a unique campaign to lobby for free and open internet infrastructure. Notably, the FCC had by now come to grasp the importance of civil society feedback and invited the public to comment on its new proposal for open internet rules, which was published as 'Notice of Proposed Rulemaking' on 15 May 2014.[56] The proposal and invitation for comment contained a set of suggestions for securing the 'open internet', combined with numerous questions and possible alternative strategies, such as making a distinction between fast and slow lanes. One of the most active lobbyists at this stage was Public Knowledge, a non-profit public interest organisation. On 15 May 2014, the first day of the consultation process, Public Knowledge filed detailed comments with the FCC, criticising the distinction between fast and slow lanes in the commission's proposal.[57] Public Knowledge, the Electronic Frontier Foundation, Battle for the Net and other influential internet advocates not only provided coverage of the events (similar to the mass media), but also mobilised hundreds of thousands of supporters to send comments directly to the FCC explaining what they thought a genuinely open internet architecture would look like.[58] Humorous interventions, such as a video by John Oliver, enriched the campaign and strongly motivated net-neutrality supporters.[59] Oliver,

[55] Ibid.

[56] FCC, 'Protecting and Promoting the Open Internet', GN Docket No 14–28, Notice of Proposed Rulemaking, 29 FCC Rcd 5561 (2014). The document set out the rules for submitting comments, setting 15 July and 10 September 2014 as deadlines for submitting comments and responding to comments, respectively (at 1 and 91).

[57] Public Knowledge, Benton Foundation and Access Sonoma Broadband, 'Official Comments for FCC Net Neutrality Proceeding', 15 July 2014, at 34–60, https://publicknowledge.org/policy/official-comments-for-fcc-net-neutrality-proceeding/.

[58] See Robert Faris, et al., 'Score Another One for the Internet?: The Role of the Networked Public Sphere in the U.S. Net Neutrality Policy Debate', *Berkman Center Research Publication*, No. 2015-4, February 2015, Cambridge, MA: The Berkman Center for Internet & Society, https://cyber.harvard.edu/sites/cyber.harvard.edu/files/2015_02_10_Score_Another_One_for_the_Internet_0.pdf.

[59] See ibid., at 17–18.

the host of the popular HBO weekly comedy-news programme *Last Week Tonight*, dedicated his show on 1 June 2014 to satirising net-neutrality politics.[60] He strongly criticised the FCC's plan to allow fast lanes and urged his fans to give feedback to the FCC in order to save the free and open internet. The mobilisation campaign was so successful that a massive surge in traffic caused the FCC's website to crash, forcing the Commission to extend the deadline for submitting comments.[61]

In this phase, the FCC received nearly 4 million comments, 2 million of which were filed directly through the FCC's electronic comment system. Tom Wheeler, the FCC chairman, commented on the broad public participation in the consultation: 'We heard from startups and world-leading tech companies. We heard from ISPs, large and small. We heard from public-interest and public-policy think tanks. We heard from Members of Congress, and yes, the President. Most important, we heard from nearly 4 million Americans who overwhelmingly spoke up in favor of preserving a free and open Internet.'[62]

The net-neutrality debate in the United States has witnessed the extraordinary mobilisation of millions of people commenting on the FCC's proposal by emailing the Commission, calling members of Congress or writing to the White House. As the FCC wrote in a press release accompanying its Report and Order of 26 February 2015, it was 'the nearly 4 million commenters who participated in the FCC's Open Internet proceeding' who convinced the Commission to adopt new rules on net neutrality that 'are guided by three principles: America's broadband networks must be fast, fair and open'.[63] In reclassifying broadband internet services as telecommunications services (under Title II of the Communications Act) as a first step towards the adoption of the novel

60 Gerlach, *The Informational Ecosystem of Net Neutrality*, at 87.

61 FCC, 'Wireline Competition Bureau Extends Deadline for Filing Reply Comments in the Open Internet and Framework for Broadband Internet Service Proceedings', GN Docket Nos. 14–28, 10–127, Public Notice, 29 FCC Rcd 9714 (2014).

62 FCC, 'Protecting and Promoting the Open Internet', GN Docket No. 14–28, Report and Order on Remand, Declaratory Ruling, and Order, 30 FCC Rcd 5601 (2015), at 314.

63 FCC, 'FCC Adopts Strong, Sustainable Rules to Protect the Open Internet', News Release, 26 February 2016, https://transition.fcc.gov/Daily_Releases/Daily_Business/2015/db0226/DOC-332260A1.pdf, at 1.

net-neutrality rules,[64] the FCC heeded expert advice and the extensive feedback from the public recommending such a move. When one reads the 2015 FCC Order, it is striking that throughout most of the report's 400 pages, the FCC continually refers to opinions and views received from the public. In para 114 of the Order, the FCC mentions that it abandoned its original idea of fast lanes as a result of arguments made in many of the comments.

> After consideration of the record, we reject the minimum level of access standard. Broadband providers, edge providers, public interest organizations, and other parties note the practical and technical difficulties associated with setting any such minimum level of access. For example, some parties note the uncertainty created by an indefinite standard. Other parties observe that in creating any such standard of service for no-blocking, the Commission risks jeopardizing innovation. We agree with these arguments and many others in the record expressing concern with the proposed minimum level of access standard.[65]

Public feedback thus played an instrumental role in persuading the FCC to reclassify broadband services and abandon the idea of fast and slow lanes. The FCC's explicit reference to the comments it received shows that the Commission developed and legally formalised its position on the open internet based not on the views of a few political leaders, but on a public debate that took into account a wide variety of voices, including those of experts, broadband providers, public-interest groups and other civil society stakeholders. The fact that President Obama spoke out in favour of strict net-neutrality rules on 10 November 2014 does not undermine this analysis. Although his intervention was significant for the FCC, it came relatively late in the debate, when the networked public sphere had already shown a strong preference for net neutrality.[66]

Advocates of the open internet (as well as its opponents) have used mass media and internet-based social networking to mobilise civil

[64] FCC, 'Protecting and Promoting the Open Internet', GN Docket No. 14–28, Report and Order on Remand, Declaratory Ruling, and Order, 30 FCC Rcd 5601 (2015), at 18 (para 59).

[65] Ibid., at 49 (para 114).

[66] See Faris, et al., 'Score Another One for the Internet?', at 21.

society.[67] During the consultation process, information technology and social media facilitated the extraordinary mobilisation of large numbers of people in a very short time.[68] At the same time, however, the use of digital networks casts a critical light on the reliability of the consultation, as self-selection may have led to the overrepresentation of young, internet-savvy individuals.[69] Likewise, the proliferation of response letter templates by both friends and foes of net neutrality exposed the consultation to risks of distortion. According to a 2007 survey on consultation procedures, commenters who submit form comments (rather than self-drafted ones) generally appeared to be less educated, less informed about politics and more pessimistic about the government.[70] Questions have also been raised due to the fact that, at the time of the consultation, most Americans had heard little or nothing about the planned new rules on net neutrality, with only 10 per cent having heard 'a lot' about the topic.[71] Due to the technical and economic complexity of the issue, it was difficult for consultation participants to fully understand what net neutrality meant and what the consequences of adopting the proposed rules would be.[72] More generally, the risk of fraud in online campaigns should not be underestimated: massive online lobbying occurred in relation to the FCC's 2017 decision to abolish net neutrality and deny itself regulatory jurisdiction over these issues. A 2021 report by the New York State Attorney General revealed that nearly 18 million of the more than 22 million comments the FCC received upon its Notice of Proposed

[67] See ibid., at 23. [68] See ibid., at 32.

[69] For a similar argument deriving from an analysis of a public consultation on net neutrality in the EU, see René C.G. Arnold, et al., 'All But Neutral: Citizen Responses to the European Commission's Public Consultation on Network Neutrality', in Luca Belli and Primavera De Filippi (eds.), *Net Neutrality Compendium: Human Rights, Free Competition and the Future of the Internet*, Cham: Springer International Publishing, 2016, pp. 199–210, at 209–210.

[70] David Schlosberg, et al., 'Democracy and E-Rulemaking: Web-Based Technologies, Participation, and the Potential for Deliberation' (2007) *Journal of Information Technology & Politics*, 4 (1), pp. 37–55.

[71] See Center for Political Communication, 'National Survey on Internet "fast lanes"', *University of Delaware*, 10 November 2014, at 1, https://udspace.udel.edu/server/api/core/bitstreams/63cd3265-b80f-476d-8879-bc5966edadae/content.

[72] This analysis has been confirmed by a European study on public consultations on net neutrality. See Arnold, et al., 'All But Neutral', at 203.

Rulemaking were fake.[73] These messages were either submitted under false identities or generated by computer 'bots'. According to Balla et al., 'malattribution of identities' and 'automation of comment submission' warrant attention, as a means of mitigating the dangers emanating from online public consultations.[74] Rather than renouncing online notice-and-comment rulemaking, they recommend employing new summarising and sorting technology to counter the adverse effects of mass computer-generated submissions.[75]

For various reasons, net neutrality became a political issue in the EU at a later point than in the United States. For one thing, the telecommunications sector in Europe had already been subject to detailed regulation for some time. As this approach had been quite successful, the telecom sector saw net neutrality as an American problem as late as 2008.[76] Within the framework of the comprehensive telecommunications reform of 2009 (Telecoms Package), concerns about net neutrality were taken up, but without explicitly mentioning the principle.[77] In an annex to the rules that were adopted, the Commission declared – albeit rather indecisively – that it was taking full account of the will of the co-legislators to enshrine net neutrality as a policy objective.[78] Changes to transparency requirements for broadband providers in the Telecoms Package (Articles 20 and 21 of the Universal Services Directive[79]) subsequently sparked controversy over net neutrality,[80] with public-interest groups arguing that American telecom companies had pushed for these

[73] New York State Office of the Attorney General Letitia James, 'Fake Comments: How U.S. Companies & Partisans Hack Democracy to Undermine Your Voice', 6 May 2021, https://ag.ny.gov/sites/default/files/reports/oag-fakecommentsreport.pdf.

[74] Steven J. Balla, et al., 'Responding to Mass, Computer-Generated, and Malattributed Comments' (2022) *Administrative Law Review*, 74 (1), pp. 95–160, at 98.

[75] Ibid., at 149–153.

[76] Gerlach, *The Informational Ecosystem of Net Neutrality*, at 174.

[77] Ibid., at 175–176.

[78] See Christoph B. Graber, 'Internet Creativity, Communicative Freedom and a Constitutional Rights Theory Response to "Code is Law"', in Sean Pager and Adam Candeup (eds.), *Transnational Culture in the Internet Age*, Cheltenham: Edward Elgar, 2012, pp. 135–164, at 150–151.

[79] Directive 2009/136/EC of 25 November 2009 on universal service and users' rights relating to electronic communications networks, OJ L 337, 18 December 2009; see Article 20, point 1(b) and Article 21, points 3 and 4.

[80] Monica Horten, *The Closing of the Net*, Cambridge and Malden: Polity, 2016, at 103–107.

changes with the goal of allowing broadband providers to alter the quality of their services or to discriminate between fast and slow lanes for data transport.[81] The implementation of the Telecoms Package was uneven: while many member states did not meet the two-year deadline, the Netherlands, the United Kingdom and Slovenia adopted national net-neutrality rules that were much stricter than the vague objectives outlined in the directives.[82] In the fall of 2011, a resolution of the European Parliament called on the Commission to ensure that net neutrality was adequately protected.[83] To this end, the Commission was asked 'to follow closely the adoption of any national regulations related to net neutrality', while considering 'that it would benefit all stakeholders if the Commission were to provide EU-wide guidelines'.[84] On 11 September 2013, the Commission followed suit with a proposal for the regulation of net neutrality.[85] However, during the so-called trilogue legislative process, which eventually led to the adoption of the Open Internet Regulation on 27 October 2015, civil society groups expressed frustration at the fact that the Council was ultimately able to prevail over the more net-neutrality-friendly positions of the Commission and the Parliament.[86] La Quadrature du Net complained that, during these proceedings, European legislators showed no willingness to listen to the views of European citizens.[87] Although the Commission had carried out public consultations, it had understood them as more of a fact-finding exercise than a participatory one, in marked contrast to the

[81] La Quadrature du Net, 'Protecting Net Neutrality in Europe', 11 November 2009, www.laquadrature.net/files/LaQuadratureduNet-DOSSIER_Protecting_Net_Neutrality_in_Europe.pdf.

[82] Christopher T. Marsden, 'Transnational Internet Law', at 431.

[83] European Parliament, Resolution of 17 November 2011 on the open internet and net neutrality in Europe, P7 TA (2011) 0511.

[84] Ibid., at para 9.

[85] European Commission, Proposal for a Regulation, COM (2013) 627 final, 11 September 2013.

[86] EDRI, 'Democratic Support for Net Neutrality is Clear, as Is Council's Stubbornness', 25 June 2015, https://edri.org/our-work/democratic-support-for-net-neutrality-is-clear-as-is-councils-stubbornness/.

[87] La Quadrature du Net, 'Net Neutrality: EU Member States Refuse to Hear the Voice of Citizens', 3 June 2015, www.laquadrature.net/en/2015/06/03/net-neutrality-eu-member-states-refuse-to-hear-the-voice-of-citizens/.

FCC.[88] Overall, there was little participation from civil society in the lead-up to the adoption of the Open Internet Regulation.

Somewhat surprisingly, however, the situation changed when it came time for the Body of European Regulators for Electronic Communications (BEREC) to draft guidelines for the implementation of the new rules at the member-state level. Inspired by the example of the United States, BEREC included civil society experts in the preparation and publishing of draft guidelines for public consultation on implementing new net-neutrality rules.[89] BEREC received almost half a million responses, which is of historic proportions considering that they had never received more than a hundred responses in their previous consultations.[90] Save the Internet, a transnationally active coalition of civil society advocates and internet activists, was a crucial player in this process, creating a website that provided legal analysis of the various official documents and assisted citizens with their participation in public consultations.[91] Despite Europe's fragmented linguistic landscape, through an imaginative campaign, they managed to attract considerable media attention, motivating thousands of websites to protest[92] and mobilising a large number of citizens to contact the telecom regulators directly. BEREC, for its part, claimed that the comments it received provided valuable stakeholder input and increased transparency.[93]

88 Gerlach, *The Informational Ecosystem of Net Neutrality*, at 249–250.

89 BEREC, 'BEREC Report on the Outcome of the Public Consultation on Draft BEREC Guidelines on the Implementation by National Regulators of European Net Neutrality rules', BoR (16) 128, 30 August 2016, www.berec.europa.eu/en/document-categories/berec/reports/berec-report-on-the-outcome-of-the-public-consultation-on-draft-berec-guidelines-on-the-implementation-by-national-regulators-of-european-net-neutrality-rules.

90 Christoph B. Graber, 'Bottom-Up Constitutionalism: The Case of Net Neutrality' (2016) *Transnational Legal Theory*, 7 (4), pp. 524–552, at 550.

91 See Thomas Lohninger, 'How We Saved the Internet', *Medium*, 11 December 2016, https://medium.com/@socialhack/how-we-saved-the-internet-in-europe-810d57a64e56.

92 Vlad Dudau, '7000 EU websites are protesting net neutrality loopholes, with "EU Slowdown" campaign', *Neowin*, 28 June 2016, www.neowin.net/news/7000-eu-websites-are-protesting-net-neutrality-loopholes-with-eu-slowdown-campaign/.

93 BEREC, 'Presentation at the Net Neutrality Guidelines Press Conference', BoR (16) 145, 30 August 2016, www.berec.europa.eu/en/document-categories/berec/others/presentation-at-the-net-neutrality-guidelines-press-conference.

Incorporating much of this feedback, the final guidelines clarified some of the critical provisions that had only been vaguely defined in the Regulation, such as the rules on blocking, throttling, zero-rating and optimising services for specific content or applications.[94]

Overall, the debate around the implementation of the Open Internet Regulation shows that European activists, inspired by the example of the net-neutrality debate in the United States, used similar methods to mobilise more extensive segments of civil society in support of net neutrality.

At the global level, cross-border cooperation between civil society groups in net-neutrality activism has not been limited to the relationship between the United States and Europe, as the debate in India on 'Free Basics' shows. Here, too, obscure zero-rating practices were at issue, and here, too, Save the Internet and other transnational activist groups played a decisive role in educating the public and lobbying the government regulator.

Free Basics (formerly Internet.org) is a service that Meta (formerly Facebook) launched jointly with telecom companies in 2015. It was advertised in India and other developing countries in Latin America, South-East Asia and Africa as a philanthropic project aimed at expanding internet connectivity in the Global South.[95] However, research by civil society activists revealed that, in India, Free Basics offered access only to a 'walled garden', in the sense of a select number of websites.[96] Global internet activists and Indian civil society groups launched furious protests

[94] BEREC, 'BEREC Guidelines on the Implementation by National Regulators of European Net Neutrality Rules', BoR (16) 127, 30 August 2016, at paras 40–48 and 99–127, www.berec.europa.eu/en/document-categories/berec/regulatory-best-practices/guidelines/berec-guidelines-on-the-implementation-by-national-regulators-of-european-net-neutrality-rules.

[95] Arturo J. Carillo, 'Having Your Cake and Eating It Too?: Zero-Rating, Net Neutrality, and International Law' (2016) *Stanford Technology Law Review*, 19 (3), pp. 364–429, at 380–381; Toussaint Nothias, 'Access Granted: Facebook's Free Basics in Africa' (2020) *Media, Culture & Society*, 42 (3), pp. 329–348, at 331–334.

[96] Christopher T. Marsden, 'Zero Rating and Mobile Net Neutrality', in Luca Belli and Primavera De Filippi (eds.), *Net Neutrality Compendium: Human Rights, Free Competition and the Future of the Internet*, Cham: Springer International Publishing, 2016, pp. 241–260, at 246.

targeting the Meta project.[97] In an open letter to Mark Zuckerberg, dozens of global and national advocacy groups, including Access Now, Bits of Freedom and the Center for Media Justice, criticised the zero-rating scheme that underpins Free Basics as discriminatory, declaring that Facebook's stated aim of promoting internet access for low-income people disguised a net-neutrality violation.[98] In their view, the fact that an internet access provider had the power to decide which services were privileged over others was a violation of freedom of expression. A public consultation on net neutrality held by the Telecom Regulatory Authority of India (TRAI) in 2015 coincided with the launch and marketing of Free Basics. During the consultation, civil society experts highlighted the complex techno-economic implications of the new service in a way that was clearly understandable for laypeople. Under the name 'Save the Internet', which was known from the campaigns in the United States and the EU, a handful of activists set up a new website that immediately attracted considerable attention, thanks to a video on net neutrality produced by the famous comedy group All India Bakchod,[99] which was accompanied by a call to email the TRAI and spread the word about net neutrality. Within two weeks, more than a million people had followed suit, and soon the Indian parliament was debating net neutrality.[100]

In February 2016, following the consultation, the TRAI barred telecom service providers from charging differential rates for data services,[101] thereby effectively banning Facebook's Free Basics. While the TRAI seemed inclined to permit differential pricing as late as 2015, public opinion and civil society pressure prompted it to issue a regulatory response that went in the opposite direction.[102] Nonetheless, popular opinion in India was divided on the issue, with many vocal opponents of

[97] Carillo, 'Having Your Cake and Eating It Too?', at 368. [98] Ibid., at 381.

[99] All India Bakchod, 'Save the Internet', 11 April 2015, www.youtube.com/watch?v=mfY1NKrzqi0.

[100] Rahul Bhatia, 'The Inside Story of Facebook's Biggest Setback', *The Guardian*, 12 May 2016, www.theguardian.com/technology/2016/may/12/facebook-free-basics-india-zuckerberg.

[101] TRAI, Prohibition of Discriminatory Tariffs for Data Services Regulations, 8 February 2016, http://trai.gov.in/sites/default/files/2024-09/Regulation_08022016_0.pdf

[102] Christopher T. Marsden, 'Comparative Case Studies in Implementing Net Neutrality: A Critical Analysis of Zero Rating' (2016) *SCRIPTed*, 13 (1), pp. 1–39, at 21–22.

the protest criticising the TRAI's efforts, which they saw as hamstringing a project that could boost internet access in rural areas.[103] Overall, the successful mobilisation of Indian civil society in the debate, thanks to the active support of global and national internet activists, shows the strength of transnational net neutrality advocacy.[104] Strikingly, it was not an institutionalised representative body, but a few activist groups that raised awareness and worked to mobilise the public in favour of an open internet.[105]

3.4 CONCLUDING REMARKS

Does the regulation of the open internet infrastructure at the EU and member-state levels, along with the emergence of the related case law of the ECJ, provide evidence for the renationalisation of net neutrality? There are reasons to be sceptical. Milton Mueller, for instance, argues that debates about the technical fragmentation of the internet are overblown and distract from the fact that certain governments are striving to 're-align control of communications with the jurisdictional boundaries of national states'.[106] When it comes to net neutrality, I would agree that the predominance of national regulatory approaches should not blind us to the fact that net neutrality has emerged as a goal shared by the majority of industrialised states. This confirms Luhmann's diagnosis that there exists an ambivalence between territorial and functional differentiation with regard to the systems of politics and law in world society, a finding that is supported by Thornhill's thesis that constitutionalisation processes proceed from transnational patterns to national law – and not vice versa.[107]

103 Carillo, 'Having Your Cake and Eating It Too?', at 428; Subhayan Mukerjee, 'Net Neutrality, Facebook, and India's Battle to #SaveTheInternet' (2016) *Communication and the Public*, 1 (3), pp. 356–361, at 360.

104 Mukerjee, 'Net Neutrality, Facebook, and India's Battle to #SaveTheInternet', at 360.

105 Esha Sen Madhavan, 'Internet and Social Media's Social Movements Leading to New Forms of Governance and Policymaking: Cases from India' (2016) *Glocalism: Journal of Culture, Politics and Innovation*, 1, pp. 1–32, at 21–22.

106 Mueller, *Will the Internet Fragment?*, at 17.

107 Chris Thornhill, 'Transnational Constitutional Law', in Peer Zumbansen (ed.), *The Oxford Handbook of Transnational Law*, New York: Oxford University Press, 2021, pp. 134–156, at 142 and 149.

The overview of the debates on net neutrality in the United States, the EU and India presented in this chapter has shown that this conversation transcends national frontiers, mainly thanks to civil society organisations that are active at the global level and the cross-border influence of their campaigns. Humorous interventions by satirists and comedians, who were able to instantaneously reach a mass audience with their videos, often acted as accelerators. The participants were thus provided with information in a comprehensible form that enabled them to understand, at least to some extent, the stakes of net neutrality. Moreover, the net activists skilfully appealed to a tech-savvy young audience and convinced them to email regulators, parliaments and governments to persuade them to take net neutrality seriously. At the same time, issues related to self-selection and the widespread use of pre-created forms weaken the legitimacy of such 'plebiscites'. In general, caution should be exercised with regard to electronic consultation procedures, following reports of mass fraud by lobbyists to influence public authorities' decision-making. Although the regulatory decisions were made at the national level, they were ultimately driven by transnationally organised activism. Marsden's thesis is thus at least partially refuted.

Thornhill characterised the process of transnational law production as the judiciary-driven incremental penetration of national law by international legal norms.[108] However, this is not how global activism functions. The expectations about net neutrality that are gradually becoming entrenched have their roots in a small part of civil society that is young, fluent in English and interested in digital technology. However, this process does not, in itself, confer political legitimacy. Instead, these expectations about net neutrality, which have their origin in a transnational discourse, were eventually formalised by national legislators and regulators and, at least in Europe, have been made the basis of legal decisions by national courts.

[108] Chris Thornhill, 'The Mutation of International Law in Contemporary Constitutions: Thinking Sociologically About Political Constitutionalism' (2016) *The Modern Law Review*, 79 (2), pp. 207–247, at 224–225.

CHAPTER 4

Network Technology and the Law

Broadening Our Perspective

It has been argued that both legal doctrine and the courts are blind to the relationship between law and technology in digital society, meaning they are unable to comprehensively address issues of free speech online. The aim of Chapters 4 and 5 is to clarify how this argument is substantiated and to spell out why technology represents a blind spot for the law and what the law can do to better respond to struggles related to network technology. How is the law capable of learning in a society of computer networks? In order to answer this question, it is necessary to clarify how law is conceptualised in the twenty-first century.

4.1 THE TECHNOLOGICAL BLINDNESS OF JURISTS

When courts deal with free-speech issues, the technical medium through which an opinion is disseminated plays little role. To be sure, in its case law on freedom of expression (Article 10 of the European Convention on Human Rights (ECHR)), the European Court of Human Rights (ECtHR) does make a distinction between whether an opinion is expressed in print, through a broadcasting medium or on the internet. Historically speaking, the technical characteristics of broadcasting have been considered the reason that states are entitled, according to the third sentence of Article 10(1) ECHR, to regulate the way in which broadcasting is organised on their territory. The scarcity of frequencies available for broadcasting programmes remained the primary justification for a public-broadcasting monopoly until 1993. In *Informationsverein Lentia v. Austria*, which marked the turning point, the ECtHR wrote that '[a]s a result of the technical progress made over the last decades', a justification for a public-broadcasting monopoly 'can no longer today be found in considerations relating to the number of frequencies and channels available'.[1] When highlighting the critical role played by audio-visual media in a democratic society, the Court repeatedly pointed out significant differences with print media: 'Because of their power to convey messages through sound and image, [audio-visual media] have more immediate and pervasive effects than print media.'[2] With regard to the internet, the ECtHR has maintained that, in virtue of 'its accessibility and its capacity to store and communicate vast amounts of information', it plays 'an important role in enhancing the public's access to news and facilitating the dissemination of information in general'.[3] In the context of social media, the Court speaks of internet 'tools' which enable participation in public debates.[4] However, the example of YouTube shows that the relationship between technology and communication on social media is more complex than that, since YouTube's algorithm is not limited to recommending videos to users, but also influences the type of content that is shared via the platform and how it is presented. In order to attract more attention, content producers adapt their strategies to the expected preferences of the algorithm, while users' perceptions and beliefs are influenced by the algorithm's recommendations.

In *Autronic AG v. Switzerland*, a judgment from 1990, the ECtHR addressed for the first time the relevance of technology as a condition for free speech. In the Court's view, the Swiss government's attempt to prohibit a private company from receiving information from a satellite without the broadcaster's prior consent violates Article 10 ECHR. The ECtHR wrote, 'Article 10 applies not only to the content of information

[1] *Informationsverein Lentia v. Austria* App. nos 13914/88; 15041/89; 15717/89; 15779/89; 17207/90 (ECtHR, 24 November 1993), at para 39.

[2] *Schweizerische Radio- und Fernsehgesellschaft and publisuisse SA v. Switzerland* App. no. 41723/14 (ECtHR, 22 December 2020), at para 85, with references (translation by the author from French).

[3] *Delfi AS v. Estonia* App. no. 64569/09 (ECtHR (GC), 16 June 2015), at para 133.

[4] *Cengiz and Others v. Turkey* App. nos 48226/10 and 14027/11 (ECtHR, 1 December 2015), at para 49.

but also to the means of transmission or reception since any restriction imposed on the means necessarily interferes with the right to receive and impart information'.[5]

Compared with the extensive ECtHR case law on Article 10 ECHR, these isolated references to the specificities of a distribution medium for expressing opinions appear marginal. Moreover, the Court's reasoning regarding the impact of a specific dissemination technology on free speech remains superficial. While certain dissemination technologies (e.g. print media, electronic media, the internet) are distinguished and some of their media-specific features identified, the technology itself is treated like a 'black box', and there is a lack of in-depth analysis. We find a similar situation in the legal literature explaining the functionality of the internet, for instance, *The Max Planck Encyclopedia of Public International Law* (MPIL), a standard legal work. The entry for 'Internet' in the MPIL defines it as 'physically the entirety of the global interconnected computer networks, which colloquially is equated with the information, communication, and other services available therein'.[6]

In practice, legal disputes are generally resolved within the framework of specific legal categories. That is, legal questions relating to networked digital technologies are often assigned to a specific category, such as telecommunications law, intellectual-property law, data-protection law, competition law, penal law, contract law or tort law, and then resolved by appealing to the doctrines applied within that category. The result of this approach is that novel technologies are often squeezed into pre-existing doctrinal boxes,[7] inevitably producing unsatisfactory results. Take, for example, the furore over copyright-infringement claims made against Google in Germany.[8] These disputes

[5] *Autronic AG v. Switzerland* App. no. 12726/87 (ECtHR, 22 May 1990), at para 47.

[6] Johann-Christoph Woltag, 'Internet', in Rüdiger Wolfrum (ed.), *The Max Planck Encyclopedia of Public International Law*, 2nd edn, Oxford: Oxford University Press, 2013, at para 1.

[7] Frank Pasquale and Arthur J. Cockfield, 'Beyond Instrumentalism: A Substantivist Perspective on Law, Technology, and the Digital Persona' (2018) *Michigan State Law Review*, pp. 821–868, at 829.

[8] See, e.g., Matthias Leistner, 'The German Federal Supreme Court's Judgment on Google's Image Search: A Topical Example of the "Limitations" of the European

arose from the functionality of search engines, such as Google Images, which display thumbnails of images available on the internet in response to a specific search query made by a user. If German copyright doctrine were to be applied literally, Google Images would have to be shut down. To circumvent such severe restrictions on internet free speech, the German Federal Court of Justice (Bundesgerichtshof, BGH), without further ado, invented a novel privilege for search engines. The Court based this move on the assumption that a rights holder who has not taken any special technical measures to prevent search engines from indexing images has tacitly consented to having her works reproduced as thumbnails.[9] In an act of evolutionary interpretation, the BGH decided to depart from the framework of the prevailing interpretation of copyright law, in order to ensure the protection of freedom of expression, a solution that has been criticised by various voices in the literature as an attack on the systematic coherence of German copyright doctrine.[10]

The overall impression that such manoeuvring gives is of a legal practice struggling in cases where there is a tension between law, technology and society, since the law lacks an adequate understanding of technology and its broader societal implications. The effects of such *technological blindness* are ad hoc decisions that go beyond established doctrine, as in the BGH's Google Thumbnails judgments, as well as decisions that do not sufficiently consider potential conflicts with other areas of the law or primary constitutional values. What causes the law to be so blind with regard to technology? One answer is the dominance of *instrumental approaches to technology* in legal practice.[11] According to Andrew Feenberg, an instrumental theory of technology is rooted in the idea 'that technologies are "tools" standing ready to serve the

Approach to Exceptions and Limitations' (2011) *IIC-International Review of Intellectual Property and Competition Law*, 42 (4), pp. 417–442.

[9] BGH, *Thumbnails II*, I ZR 140/10, 19 October 2011, at para 49.

[10] For an overview, see Christophe Geiger and Elena Izyumenko, 'Towards a European "Fair Use" Grounded in Freedom of Expression' (2019) *American University International Law Review*, 35 (1), pp. 1–74, at 15–17.

[11] Arthur Cockfield and Jason Pridmore, 'A Synthetic Theory of Law and Technology' (2007) *Minnesota Journal of Law, Science & Technology*, 8 (2), pp. 475–513, at 497.

purpose of their users. Technology is deemed "neutral", without valuative content of its own'.[12] Conceiving of technology as a neutral tool implies, among other things, an indifference to the variety of ends that it can achieve, as well as to its broader social, political and legal impacts.[13] It is common to encounter instrumentalist positions in discussions of the legal regulation of the internet, as analyses often hastily focus on specific goals the technology ought to fulfil.[14] Since, among other things, the term 'net neutrality' could be semantically linked to instrumentalism, it seems particularly urgent to clarify the meaning of the concept of technology as a precondition for regulating the open internet.

For Feenberg, the antithesis of technological instrumentalism consists in *substantive theories*, such as the philosophies of technology developed by Jacques Ellul and Martin Heidegger.[15] In contrast to the technological neutrality of instrumentalism, substantive theories of technology ascribe essential values to technology. They seek to explain how historically developed technologies create or constrain human agency.[16] Heidegger teaches that asking the question 'What is technology?' leads us to seek out the essence of technology. We cannot find the essence of technology 'when we regard [technology] as something neutral; for this conception of it, to which today we particularly like to pay homage, makes us utterly blind to the essence of technology'.[17] A shared feature of Heidegger's and Ellul's theories of technology is their pessimism,[18] which is expressed in

[12] Andrew Feenberg, *Transforming Technology: A Critical Theory Revisited*, New York: Oxford University Press, 2002, at 5.

[13] Ibid., at 5–6; see also Cockfield and Pridmore, 'A Synthetic Theory of Law and Technology', at 476.

[14] Pasquale and Cockfield, 'Beyond Instrumentalism', at 838.

[15] Feenberg, *Transforming Technology*, at 6–7.

[16] Karl Rogers, *Participatory Democracy, Science and Technology: An Exploration in the Philosophy of Science*, London: Palgrave Macmillan, 2008, at 40.

[17] Martin Heidegger, 'The Question Concerning Technology [1954]', in *The Question Concerning Technology and Other Essays*, translated by William Lovitt, New York: Harper Collins, 2013, pp. 3–35, at 4.

[18] For a critical discussion, see Kurt C. M. Mertel, 'Heidegger, Technology and Education' (2020) *Journal of Philosophy of Education*, 54 (2), pp. 467–486; Gordon Oyer, 'Thomas Merton and the "Pessimism" of Jacques Ellul' (2017) *The Merton Annual*, 30, pp. 131–144.

Ellul's statement that 'technique has become autonomous'[19] and his fears that technology will create a totalitarian society:[20] '[Technique] makes men happy in a milieu which normally would have made them unhappy, if they had not been worked on, molded, and formed for just that milieu. What looks like the apex of humanism is in fact the pinnacle of human submission.'[21] Pessimism is also apparent in Heidegger's diagnosis that humans and the entire world are being degraded to raw material ('standing reserves')[22] in the service of technical processes.[23]

While Ellul and Heidegger offer no solution beyond a reversion to pre-modern traditions and simplicity, spirituality or fatalistic resignation, Feenberg places hope in a *critical theory of technology*, a synthesis of instrumental and substantive theories.[24] A critical theory of technology, Feenberg argues, unfolds within an analytical framework provided by science and technology studies (STS), while adding an element of critique.[25] By incorporating the ideals of the Enlightenment and the insights of the Frankfurt School of Social Research into STS, his work enables us to think critically about technology, seeing it *not* as something to be fatalistically accepted, but as something that is flexible in multiple respects and that we can participate in shaping.

STS emerged in the 1970s as a new field of sociological research. Since then, it has produced sophisticated theories about the interaction of technology and society in myriads of case studies covering various social sectors. Inspired by Feenberg's synthetic methodology, I would like to explore in what follows the extent to which knowledge produced in STS could be imported into jurisprudence to cure the law's technology blindness.

19 Jacques Ellul, *The Technological Society*, translated by John Wilkinson, New York: Knopf, 1964 (1954), at 348.

20 Rogers, *Participatory Democracy, Science and Technology*, at 57–58.

21 Ellul, *The Technological Society*, at 348.

22 Heidegger, 'The Question Concerning Technology [1954]', at 17.

23 Feenberg, *Transforming Technology*, at 7; Rogers, *Participatory Democracy, Science and Technology*, at 54.

24 Feenberg, *Transforming Technology*, at 8.

25 Andrew Feenberg, 'A Critical Theory of Technology', in Ulrike Felt, et al. (eds.), *The Handbook of Science and Technology Studies*, Cambridge, MA, and London: The MIT Press, 2017, pp. 635–663, at 637.

4.2 STS AND THE LAW

STS is a field of interdisciplinary research that took shape in the 1970s, mainly in Europe and Northern America.[26] Today, it is thriving, having successfully institutionalised itself with specialised chairs at prestigious universities. The acronym STS stands for 'science and technology studies', but it has sometimes also been used as a collective term for the entire field of science, technology and society. By adopting a broadly social constructivist research method,[27] STS has distanced itself from classical positions and positivist premises in the theory and sociology of science.[28]

Scientific positivists were convinced that 'collecting accurate data, generating logical generalisations which explain that data, and testing those data'[29] was the key characteristic of the scientific method. STS scholars, in contrast, are more interested in studying 'how science (and technology) work in practice'.[30] This focus on practice is shared by the essential dynamics within the broader STS framework, including SSK (sociology of scientific knowledge), SCOT (social construction of technology), ANT (actor-network theory) and many feminist technoscience studies.[31] Rather than adopting the positivist line, STS argues that 'technoscience practices are methods that shape and reproduce the social world'.[32] Just as social constructivism is a general feature of STS,

[26] See Sergio Sismondo, *An Introduction to Science and Technology Studies*, 2nd edn, Chichester: Wiley-Blackwell, 2010, at 10.

[27] Andrew Feenberg, *Technosystem: The Social Life of Reason*, Cambridge, MA: Harvard University Press, 2017, at 38–40, considers social constructivism and actor–network theory (ANT) as two main currents of STS.

[28] John H. Zammito, *A Nice Derangement of Epistemes: Post-positivism in the Study of Science from Quine to Latour*, Chicago: University of Chicago Press, 2004; see Ronald Giere, 'What Everyone Should Know About STS' (2006) *Social Studies of Science*, 36 (3), pp. 489–493.

[29] John Law, 'STS as Method', in Ulrike Felt, et al. (eds.), *The Handbook of Science and Technology Studies*, Cambridge, MA, and London: The MIT Press, 2017, pp. 31–57, at 32.

[30] Ibid., at 31.

[31] John Law and Vicky Singleton, 'Performing Technology's Stories: On Social Constructivism, Performance, and Performativity,' (2000) *Technology and Culture*, 41 (4), pp. 765–775, at 766.

[32] John Law, 'STS as Method', at 31.

scientific truth and technical artefacts are viewed as being produced by social practices in specific contexts.[33]

Alongside antipositivism, *antideterminism* is another characteristic of social constructivism and STS.[34] In the past, theorists of anarchism and Marxism tended to take technological determinism as the basis for explaining the present situation and how to achieve an egalitarian and rational society.[35] On a determinist view, 'the development of technology proceeds in an autonomous manner, determined by an internal logic independent of social influence'.[36] This position, reminiscent of Ellul's diagnosis of autonomous technology, has been widely criticised in the literature,[37] and nowadays it is difficult to find theorists who would explicitly support it.[38] Rejecting technological determinism, social-constructivist versions of STS claim that society can influence or shape technology, objecting to the view that a designer of an artefact determines the range of its potential uses. Social constructivism correspondingly insists on the possibility that users will respond flexibly to the original design. Technologies are perceived as underdetermined[39] or 'multistable', to use Don Ihde's term.[40] Ihde, who is a proponent of postphenomenology, one of the most influential schools of thought within the philosophy of technology, calls technology 'multistable' to express the view that technologies are neither neutral nor autonomous,

[33] Wiebe E. Bijker, 'Technology, Social Construction Of', in James D. Wright (ed.), *International Encyclopedia of the Social & Behavioral Sciences,* 2nd edn, Oxford: Elsevier, 2015, pp. 135–140, at 135; Trevor J. Pinch and Wiebe E. Bijker, 'The Social Construction of Facts and Artefacts: Or How the Sociology of Science and the Sociology of Technology Might Benefit Each Other' (1984) *Social Studies of Science,* 14 (3), pp. 399–441, at 419–421.

[34] Feenberg, 'A Critical Theory of Technology', at 637.

[35] Rogers, *Participatory Democracy, Science and Technology,* at 41.

[36] Ronald R. Kline, 'Technological Determinism', in James D. Wright (ed.), *International Encyclopedia of the Social & Behavioral Sciences,* 2nd edn, Oxford: Elsevier, 2015, pp. 109–112, at 109.

[37] See, e.g., Cockfield and Pridmore, 'A Synthetic Theory of Law and Technology', at 489–494.

[38] Keith Grint and Steve Woolgar, *The Machine at Work: Technology, Work and Organization,* Cambridge: Polity, 1997, at 7.

[39] Feenberg, *Technosystem,* at 46.

[40] Don Ihde, *Technology and the Lifeworld: From Garden to Earth,* Bloomington and Indianapolis: Indiana University Press, 1990, at 144.

but structurally ambiguous. This ambiguity stems from the fact that technologies can be variably embedded. As he puts it, 'the "same" technology in another cultural context becomes quite a "different" technology'.[41] By way of illustration, he gives the example of a drawing of a cube, which, after a 'gestalt switch', appears to be a six-legged insect.[42] The earliest example of a 'gestalt switch' is Ludwig Wittgenstein's famous rabbit/duck puzzle picture,[43] which, as he explains, 'can be seen as a rabbit's head or as a duck's'.[44] Once the observer has understood that the drawing is of a duck *and* a rabbit, the perceptual ambiguity will be inescapable. It will no longer be possible to see the rabbit without being irritated by the image of the duck and vice versa. For Feenberg, Ihde's multistability is a version of underdetermination.[45] Both terms emphasise that an artefact leaves room for interpretation, a thesis to which not only Feenberg himself, but STS scholarship more generally, attaches great importance.[46] This thesis has also been expressed in the context of analyses of the underdetermination of information technology.[47] There is interpretive flexibility not only when the artefact or technological system is designed but also in its subsequent uptake.[48]

Some STS scholars have defended a radical constructivist perspective on technology.[49] In its most extreme form, social constructivism claims that 'technology does not have any influence which can be gauged independently of human interpretation'.[50] In other words, technology

[41] Ibid. [42] Ibid., at 145–146.

[43] Ludwig Wittgenstein, *Philosophical Investigations, The German text, with an English translation by G. E. M. Anscombe, P. M. S. Hacker and Joachim Schulte,* 4th edn, Oxford: Wiley-Blackwell, 2009 (1953), at 204–207.

[44] Ibid., at 408. [45] Feenberg, *Technosystem,* at 115.

[46] Sismondo, *An Introduction to Science and Technology Studies,* at 6; see also Steve Woolgar and Geoff Cooper, 'Do Artefacts Have Ambivalence?: Moses' Bridges, Winner's Bridges and Other Urban Legends in S&TS' (1999) *Social Studies of Science,* 29 (3), pp. 433–449, at 443–444.

[47] See Neil F. Doherty, et al., 'A Re-conceptualization of the Interpretive Flexibility of Information Technologies: Redressing the Balance Between the Social and the Technical' (2006) *European Journal of Information Systems,* 15 (6), pp. 569–582.

[48] Pinch and Bijker, 'The Social Construction of Facts and Artefacts', at 421; Feenberg, *Technosystem,* at 154–157.

[49] See Bijker, 'Technology, Social Construction Of', at 135.

[50] Grint and Woolgar, *The Machine at Work,* at 10.

is essentially social:[51] 'it is a construction rather than a reflection of the machine's capabilities'.[52] By contrast, other approaches to STS have objected to such an absolutisation of society. Criticising the overemphasis on human intention in radical constructivism, Bruno Latour's version of ANT argues for a symmetry between human and non-human actors, who are linked together in hybrid networks.[53] His book *We Have Never Been Modern* postulates a 'symmetry between the two branches of government, that of things – called science and technology – and that of human beings'.[54] In *Politics of Nature,* Latour attributes agency to new types of 'actants' that are not human actors.[55] He uses the adjective 'hybrid' to refer to the dissolution of the distinction between things and humans or nature and society.[56] For Latour, nature and human beings are inextricably intertwined in hybrid 'sociotechnological networks',[57] leading him to argue for an 'essential connection between technology and society', as articulated in a process of co-production.[58] Since co-production is a straightforward concept that helps us understand the relationship between society and technology,[59] it will inform the arguments developed below.

[51] For an early account, see Pinch and Bijker, 'The Social Construction of Facts and Artefacts', at 410–419.

[52] Grint and Woolgar, *The Machine at Work*, at 10.

[53] Feenberg, 'A Critical Theory of Technology', at 640. See also Edwin Sayes, 'Actor–Network Theory and Methodology: Just What Does It Mean to Say That Nonhumans Have Agency?' (2014) *Social Studies of Science*, 44 (1), pp. 134–149, at 136; Peter-Paul Verbeek, 'Artifacts and Attachment: A Post-script Philosophy of Mediation', in Hans Harbers (ed.), *Inside the Politics of Technology: Agency and Normativity in the Co-Production of Technology and Society*, Amsterdam: Amsterdam University Press, 2005, pp. 125–146, at 129–130.

[54] Bruno Latour, *We Have Never Been Modern*, translated by Catherine Porter, Cambridge, MA: Harvard University Press, 1993 (1991), at 138.

[55] Bruno Latour, *Politics of Nature: How to Bring the Sciences into Democracy*, translated by Catherine Porter, Cambridge, MA: Harvard University Press, 2004 (1999), at 62–70; Bruno Latour, *Science in Action: How to Follow Scientists and Engineers Through Society*, Harvard: Harvard University Press, 1987, at 84.

[56] Latour, *We Have Never Been Modern*, at 10–11.

[57] Ibid., at 91.

[58] Feenberg, *Technosystem*, at 75.

[59] Sheila Jasanoff, 'The Idiom of Co-Production', in Sheila Jasanoff (ed.), *States of Knowledge: The Co-Production of Science and Social Order*, London: Routledge, 2004, pp. 1–12.

What does STS have to say about the law? Some STS scholars, especially Sheila Jasanoff and Michael Lynch, have made important contributions to analysing the interrelation between science, technology and law. These writings are mainly concerned with micro-sociological studies, in the sense of small-scale sociological analyses of the behaviour of individuals in one-on-one social interactions and small groups.[60] This methodology is a distinctive feature of STS constructivism,[61] and the goal of these studies is to understand what people think, say or do in different cases, invoking issues related to law, science and technology. They include questions raised by the use of science and technology in courtrooms[62] or by analyses of the relationships between law and technology in intellectual property,[63] environmental regulation[64] and other areas of law.[65] While the large number and variety of law-related studies mentioned could give the impression that STS scholarship displays a

[60] Karin Knorr-Cetina, 'Introduction: The Micro-Sociological Challenge of Macro-Sociology: Towards a Reconstruction of Social Theory and Methodology', in Karin Knorr-Cetina and Aaron Cicourel (eds.), *Advances in Social Theory and Methodology: Toward an Integration of Micro- and Macro-Sociologies*, London: Routledge, 1981, pp. 1–47.

[61] Zammito, *A Nice Derangement of Epistemes*, at 151–182.

[62] See, e.g., Sheila Jasanoff, *Science at the Bar: Law, Science, and Technology in America*, Cambridge, MA: Harvard University Press, 1995; Sheila Jasanoff, 'Law's Knowledge: Science for Justice in Legal Settings' (2005) *American Journal of Public Health*, 95, pp. 49–58; Sheila Jasanoff, 'Just Evidence: The Limits of Science in the Legal Process' (2006) *Journal of Law, Medicine & Ethics*, 34 (2), pp. 328–341; Sheila Jasanoff, 'Making Order: Law and Science in Action', in Edward J. Hackett, et al. (eds.), *The Handbook of Science and Technology Studies*, 3rd edn, Cambridge, MA: The MIT Press, 2008, pp. 761–786; Michael Lynch and Simon Cole, 'Science and Technology Studies on Trial' (2005) *Social Studies of Science*, 35 (2), pp. 269–311; Michael Lynch, et al., *Truth Machine: The Contentious History of DNA Fingerprinting*, Chicago: University of Chicago Press, 2010.

[63] See, e.g., Mario Biagioli and Marius Buning, 'Technologies of the Law/Law as a Technology' (2019) *History of Science*, 57 (1), pp. 3–17.

[64] Alain Pottage, 'Biotechnology as Environmental Regulation', in Andreas Philippopoulos-Mihalopoulos (ed.), *Law and Ecology: New Environmental Foundations*, Oxford: Routledge, 2011, pp. 105–125; Sheila Jasanoff, 'Between Risk and Precaution: Reassessing the Future of GM Crops' (2000) *Journal of Risk Research*, 3 (3), pp. 277–282; Sheila Jasanoff, 'Science and Judgment in Environmental Standard Setting' (1998) *Applied Measurement in Education*, 11 (1), pp. 107–120.

[65] See Emilie Cloatre and Martyn Pickersgill, 'Introduction', in Emilie Cloatre and Martyn Pickersgill (eds.), *Knowledge, Technology and Law*, London and New York: Routledge, 2015, pp. 1–14, at 2.

comprehensive understanding of the law, this impression must be qualified in several respects.

To begin with, law-related STS scholarship is the exception rather than the rule. For example, in Lynch's encyclopaedic compilation of the seventy seminal conceptual articles in the history of STS, only one relates directly to law.[66] Second, STS has not developed a more generalised theory of law in scientific and technological contexts, a fact that can be partly explained by its primary focus on case studies.[67] The use of a case-study methodology and the particularities of the micro-sociological perspective make it difficult to grasp legal normativity and the law's function within the overall structure of society. Third, in focusing on technology as a modality of regulation (regulation by design), STS has worked towards opening up and relativising the concept of law. By clarifying how science and technology can influence the operation of the law – for example in forensics, legislation or social ordering more broadly – STS has contributed to relativising the state-centred understanding of the law that still prevails among legal practitioners. It has thus injected a dimension of materiality into the discussion of legal pluralism that has been ongoing in sociological jurisprudence since the beginning of the twentieth century.[68] At the same time, imagining law as something 'co-constituted rather than presupposed'[69] has raised the question of the 'dissolution of law as a social instance'.[70] Referring to the law as a 'fluid notion'[71] and stressing the technology-driven erosion of the boundaries of the legal space suggests that the social scientists working in STS cannot understand the law's proprium, which is normativity.[72] The reason for

[66] Michael Lynch (ed.), *Science and Technology Studies: Critical Concepts in the Social Sciences*, London and New York: Routledge, 2012. The article in question is Barbara Herrnstein Smith, 'The Unquiet Judge: Activism Without Objectivism in Law and Politics'.

[67] John Law, 'STS as Method', at 32.

[68] Alex Faulkner, et al., 'Introduction: Material Worlds: Intersections of Law, Science, Technology, and Society' (2012) *Journal of Law and Society*, 39 (1), pp. 1–19, at 6–8.

[69] Cloatre and Pickersgill, 'Introduction', at 8.

[70] Alain Pottage, 'The Materiality of What?' (2012) *Journal of Law and Society*, 39 (1), pp. 167–183, at 180.

[71] Cloatre and Pickersgill, 'Introduction', at 9.

[72] Simon A. Cole and Alyse Bertenthal, 'Science, Technology, Society, and Law' (2017) *Annual Review of Law and Social Science*, pp. 351–371.

this lies in STS's viewpoint, which stands *outside the law.* However, as we have known since Max Weber and H. L. A. Hart, and as will be argued below, the essence of legal normativity can only be understood from a perspective *inside the law.*

I hasten to add that the distinction between inside and outside perspectives has, of course, been an issue in the emics versus etics debates in anthropology.[73] Given the many methodological overlaps between STS and anthropology,[74] a brief comment on that debate seems necessary. It originated in linguistics, where, in the 1960s, Kenneth Pike distinguished between phon*emic* and phon*etic* concepts:[75] 'phonemic' refers to rules about sound contrasts in a language that native speakers have in their heads (internal view), while 'phonetic' refers to distinctions linguists apply in order to observe how native speakers use such sounds in their speech (external view).[76] This distinction between internal and external perspectives subsequently found its way into anthropological research, where 'etic' refers to the observation of cultures from the outside and 'emic' refers to a perspective gained through the researcher's immersion into a culture or group.[77] Emic studies go beyond mere data-gathering, often providing more detailed and culturally rich information, as well as a deeper understanding of a group's interactions.

When applied to STS and the law, an *etic* perspective would, for example, allow a scholar to describe regular correspondences between specific technologies and the practice of law-creating and law-applying agencies.[78] In contrast, an *emic* approach to STS would require a

[73] Thomas N. Headland, 'Introduction: A Dialogue Between Kenneth Pike and Marvin Harris on Emics and Etics', in Thomas N. Headland, et al. (eds.), *Emics and Etics: The Insider/Outsider Debate*, Newbury Park: SAGE Publications, 1990, pp. 13–27.

[74] For an overview, see Sismondo, *An Introduction to Science and Technology Studies*, chapter 10. See also Marisol de la Cadena, et al., 'Anthropology and STS' (2015) *HAU: Journal of Ethnographic Theory*, 5 (1), pp. 437–475.

[75] Kenneth L. Pike, *Language in Relation to a Unified Theory of the Structures of Human Behavior*, 2nd edn, The Hague: Mouton, 1967.

[76] Numa Markee, 'Emic and Etic in Qualitative Research', in Carol A. Chapelle (ed.), *The Encyclopedia of Applied Linguistics*, Malden: Wiley-Blackwell, 2013, pp. 1–4.

[77] Till Mostowlansky and Andrea Rota, 'Emic and Etic', in Joel Robbins, et al. (eds.), *The Cambridge Encyclopedia of Anthropology*, University of Cambridge, 2020, pp. 1–16.

[78] Cole and Bertenthal, 'Science, Technology, Society, and Law', at 361.

researcher to immerse herself in a particular customary practice. In his ethnographic work, Latour has applied such a perspective to the study of the law. Thus, in *The Making of Law*, he seeks to define the law based on an ethnography of the French Conseil d'État.[79] This book represents an attempt to explain what goes on in this court-like institution from the point of view of an observer who has access to all the rooms, who sees the computers and other equipment being used, who observes documents being exchanged between judges and their secretaries and who overhears conversations at the coffee machine or in the canteen. Despite its participatory perspective, however, the book does not provide an account of the legal doctrine applied by the Conseil or the reasoning justifying its decisions. It is worth noting that Latour, like most STS scholars, is not a trained jurist, although Sheila Jasanoff is a prominent exception. For this reason, these scholars lack the practical and doctrinal expertise necessary to understand legal practices and procedures, and especially the meaning of legal normativity. This shortcoming can be seen in Latour's definition of the law as 'strategically positioned networks' which 'connect and bind disparate and seemingly unrelated things, documents, and people',[80] a definition that fails to fully capture the nature of legal normativity and the distinguishing feature of norms that are voluntarily accepted by their addressees.[81]

Consequently, emic perspectives in STS cannot adopt the lawyer's habitual perspective and ask the questions about normativity that Weber associated with the *law's internal point of view*, namely: 'What is intrinsically valid as law? That is to say: What significance or, in other words, what *normative* meaning ought to be attributed in correct logic to a verbal pattern having the form of a legal proposition?.'[82] Generally

[79] Bruno Latour, *The Making of Law: An Ethnography of the Conseil d'État*, translated by Marina Brilman and Alain Pottage, Cambridge: Polity, 2010 (2002). For a discussion, see Pottage, 'The Materiality of What?'.

[80] Cole and Bertenthal, 'Science, Technology, Society, and Law', at 361.

[81] Ron Levi and Maria Valverde, 'Studying Law by Association: Bruno Latour Goes to the Conseil d'État' (2008) *Law & Social Inquiry*, 33 (3), pp. 805–825.

[82] Max Weber, *Economy and Society: An Outline of Interpretive Sociology*, translated by Günther Roth, Berkeley: University of California Press, 1978 (1922), at 311 (emphasis in the original).

speaking, the distinction between external and internal perspectives on the law is a central topic of socio-legal theory. According to Hart, an 'external' observer cannot understand what 'constitutes the normative structure of society'.[83] Following Hart's concept of law, a distinction must be made between 'being obliged' to do something and 'having an obligation' to do something.[84] Whereas being obliged describes a factual constraint, determining whether someone has an obligation refers to the essence of legal normativity.

This distinction is also relevant in a digital environment, since the coercive effects of a given technology need to be distinguished from normative structures and law. For example, the user of an ebook that is protected by a digital rights management (DRM) system is correct to say that she *is obliged* by the technology on the condition that the DRM imposes a factual restriction on her use of the book. This would be the case, for instance, if the DRM were to employ a technical mechanism to prevent her from saving a copy of the ebook on her computer, notwithstanding the fact that the copyright statute confers on users the right to make a copy for personal use. However, the user would be wrong if she were to claim that she *has an obligation* to follow the DRM rule, since the DRM lacks legal legitimacy and acceptance. For Hart, the question of whether someone has an obligation is a question that bears on the 'internal aspect of rules',[85] that is, how legal subjects themselves observe the rules, whether they accept them and whether they consider the rules legitimate. The distinction between the internal and external perspectives on the law is very important: only from the internal perspective can one recognise the normative structure of a society, that is the rules that ego expects alter to follow.[86]

In addition to the deficient grasp of legal normativity displayed by STS scholarship, the lack of a socio-critical dimension in STS analyses also needs to be mentioned, since it plays an important role, especially when the horizon of investigation is expanded from legal-doctrinal issues to

[83] H. L. A. Hart, *The Concept of Law*, Oxford: Clarendon Press, 1961, at 86.
[84] Ibid., at 79–86. [85] Ibid., at 86. [86] Ibid., at 89.

socio-political ones.[87] Feenberg asserts that STS's turn towards case studies has led it to lose sight of broader social and political concerns, due to a 'decreased emphasis on the contradiction between political agency and technocratic rationality'.[88] As evidence for this point, he refers to STS proponents such as Wiebe Bijker, who have justified STS's lack of engagement with political controversies as a necessary step in the process of establishing the field within the social sciences.[89] At the same time, Langdon Winner has criticised STS scholarship for almost completely ignoring the social consequences of technological choices:

> One tries to show why it is that particular devices, designs, and social constituencies are the ones that prevail within the range of alternatives available at a given time. But the consequences of prevailing are seldom a focus of study. What the introduction of new artifacts means for people's sense of self, for the texture of human communities, for qualities of everyday living, and for the broader distribution of power in society – these are not matters of explicit concern.[90]

Winner accuses STS of being more concerned with the purity of social research than with adopting a theoretical position vis-à-vis technological and social change. Due to its narrow focus on the interests, problems and solutions of specific social groups, its practitioners fail to recognise the need to critically reflect on deeper social dynamics related to technology.[91] Along similar lines, Geoffrey Bowker criticises Latour's work for neglecting to develop a theory that would enable things to be understood from a critical distance, instead of concentrating solely on methods,[92] while Nick Couldry laments the 'abandonment of

[87] For a broader perspective on digital technology, see Nick Couldry, 'Recovering Critique in an Age of Datafication' (2020) *New Media & Society*, 22 (7), pp. 1135–1151.

[88] Feenberg, *Technosystem*, at 39.

[89] Wiebe E. Bijker, *Of Bicycles, Bakelites, and Bulbs: Toward a Theory of Sociotechnical Change*, Cambridge, MA: The MIT Press, 1995, at 5.

[90] Langdon Winner, 'Upon Opening the Black Box and Finding It Empty: Social Constructivism and the Philosophy of Technology' (1993) *Science, Technology & Human Values*, 18 (3), pp. 362–378, at 368.

[91] Ibid., at 370–372.

[92] Geoffrey C. Bowker, 'The Theory/Data Thing Commentary' (2014) *International Journal of Communication*, 8, pp. 1795–1799, at 1796.

deconstructive critique and critical theory'.[93] Feenberg, for his part, does not seek to remedy the shortcomings he identifies by integrating critical perspectives into STS, but instead adopts an approach that starts from a reformed version of critical theory and incorporates some central aspects of STS, primarily its antipositivism and antideterminism.[94]

4.3 MEDIA THEORY AND THE LAW

The discussion of STS research and its relationship to the law has highlighted the strengths and limitations of this perspective. Its strength lies in its capacity to conceive of the relationship between society and technology in terms of co-production. However, due to its narrow focus on specific groups in specific cases, STS is unable to see the bigger picture. Moreover, since it does not seek to frame internal aspects of the law, it is also unable to grasp the essence of legal normativity. What is therefore needed is a socio-legal theory whose observational standpoint lies within the law, but that is nevertheless able to analyse the interaction between law and technology. In response to this challenge, the German jurists and legal theorists Thomas Vesting and Karl-Heinz Ladeur have proposed an approach to the law that is rooted in cultural science and media theory. Could this be the theoretical framework that we are looking for?

Over the last decade, Vesting and Ladeur have contributed to developing a cultural theory of the law that reconstructs the relationship between materiality and the law from the perspective of media theory. Because most of their publications are in German, their work has attracted little attention outside the German-speaking world, although it has influenced the legal debate on law and technology in Germany. In this section, I will introduce and engage critically with their most recent writings about the law in the age of computer networks.

With *Legal Theory and the Media of Law,* Vesting produced a groundbreaking work on law and media.[95] Published in 2018, this is an English

[93] Couldry, 'Recovering Critique in an Age of Datafication', at 1137.

[94] Feenberg, *Technosystem,* at 39.

[95] Thomas Vesting, *Legal Theory and the Media of Law,* translated by James C. Wagner, Cheltenham, UK, and Northampton, MA: Edward Elgar Publishing, 2018.

translation in one volume of four separate volumes that originally appeared in German between 2011 and 2015. Typically, a treatise on media law considers different media, such as newspapers, books, films, radio, television and the internet, as objects of law and then deals with legal issues specific to one or more of them. However, it is not these practical legal issues that attracted Vesting's attention. Instead, the four parts of his work are dedicated to 'language and speech', 'writing', 'printing' and 'computer networks'. Nor is he interested in their practical use as different channels for conveying legal knowledge. His approach is a decidedly theoretical one: turning the usual approaches to media law on their head, he studies media as conditions of possibility of the law in specific historical contexts, treating their materiality as a means of pre-structuring and co-shaping the creation of law.

For Vesting, computer networks are the dominant media of the twenty-first century.[96] His notion of media is informed by Marshall McLuhan's theory, according to which media become 'extensions of man' through their materiality.[97] According to Vesting, McLuhan's famous thesis that 'the medium is the message'[98] is the key to understanding the concept of media. However, since this formulation has often been misinterpreted, Vesting refers to an interview where McLuhan clarified its meaning as follows: 'The medium is hidden, the message is obvious. But the real effect comes from the hidden ground, not from the content, not from the figure.'[99] In order to comprehend a message, it is necessary to consider the medium used to disseminate it. While the message is manifest, the medium stays invisible. Although the medium is the 'hidden ground', it occupies the foreground of McLuhan's theory. According to Sybille Krämer, a media philosopher: 'The strategic goal of McLuhan's identification of the medium with the message was to take away the transitory transparency and neutrality of the media and make visible their autonomous opacity and instrumental

[96] Ibid., part IV.

[97] Marshall McLuhan, *Understanding Media: The Extensions of Man*, Cambridge, MA: The MIT Press, 1994 (1964).

[98] See McLuhan, *Understanding Media*, at 7.

[99] McLuhan in an interview as quoted by Vesting, *Legal Theory and the Media of Law*, at 442.

shaping power.'[100] Unlike philosophers who focus on content and its meaning, McLuhan is more interested in the materiality of the medium and how it shapes content. For McLuhan, the content of any medium 'is always another medium': 'The content of writing is speech, just as the written word is the content of print, and print is the content of the telegraph.'[101] Seconding Krämer, who emphasises McLuhan's pioneering role in the 'medial turn' in cultural studies,[102] Vesting observes the existence of an 'overlapping between media theory and cultural science'.[103] Cultural studies views the law broadly, as a cultural phenomenon in time and space, rather than focusing on the law's normative characteristics and its effects.[104] For Vesting, the media's materiality must be at the centre of media theory, not least because technology underpins the communicability of the message.[105] He claims that the strict separation of the sphere of meaning from the sphere of the organic or physical components of communication must be abolished.[106] According to Vesting, language is dependent on the materiality of the medium. This is evident in the case of writing, but it also applies to other media, including telecommunication, television and the internet.[107]

Rather than overemphasising the impact of technology as a determining factor, Vesting's media theory conflates the technical and the social. This is most obvious in his conceptualisation of the computer network, which appears as a hybrid sociotechnical construct. Quoting the work of Dirk Baecker, Manuel Castells, Ladeur and others, Vesting refers to the massive cultural and social effects produced by the spread of networked computers since the 1960s.[108] According to Vesting, '[t]he crucial change that must be accounted for is the transition from a hierarchical/centralized culture to a heterarchical/acentric one'.[109] As he sees it,

[100] Sybille Krämer, *Medium, Messenger, Transmission: An Approach to Media Philosophy*, Amsterdam: Amsterdam University Press, 2015, at 28.

[101] McLuhan, *Understanding Media*, at 8.

[102] See Krämer, *Medium, Messenger, Transmission*, at 28.

[103] Vesting, *Legal Theory and the Media of Law*, at 442.

[104] Paul W. Kahn, *The Cultural Study of Law: Reconstructing Legal Scholarship*, Chicago: University of Chicago Press, 1999, at 40–77.

[105] Vesting, *Legal Theory and the Media of Law*, at 443.

[106] Ibid., at 79–80.

[107] Ibid., at 86–87.

[108] Ibid., at 446.

[109] Ibid.

the idea of the network must not be reduced to a purely technical grid, but should rather be conceived as a hybrid construct with multiple intersections between material and social structures in the society of computer networks.[110] The 'material turn' in Vesting's theory has an impact on the relationship between media and the law. According to Vesting, the media-indifferent view of legal communication, which prevails in court practice, should be replaced by an understanding of legal communication that always carries the 'trace of the media that it uses'.[111] Hence, the mediality of legal communication[112] – that is, the question of how differences in the medial form change legal communication – takes centre stage in Vesting's media theory of law.

Ladeur agrees with Vesting's emphasis on the materiality of media and its impact on social and legal evolution.[113] Against this background, he has reconstructed the development of society in Western Europe since the end of the nineteenth century, tracing a process of societal development which is driven by media, leading from the 'society of individuals' to the 'society of organisations' and finally to the 'society of networks'.[114] In the society of individuals, intersubjective coordination (between neighbours) creates a basis of normality and experience upon which normative expectations can build.[115] In the society of organisations, it is the task of mass media and political parties to mediate between the private-individual and the public-governmental sphere, thus prestructuring the reproduction of normative expectations.[116] In the society of networks, a governance model defined by new technologies

[110] Ibid., at 447. [111] Ibid., at 87.

[112] On mediality in the context of law, see Stefan Geyer, *Die Unterwerfung der Zeichen: Zur 'Konstitution' von Herrschaftsrecht durch das Krönungszeremoniell im späten Mittelalter am Beispiel der Krönung in den Königreichen Aragon und Frankreich*, Zurich: Chronos, 2020, at 32–34. See also Andreas Thier, 'Recht, Rechtswissenschaft und Medialität' (2014) *NCCR Mediality Newsletter*, 1, pp. 7–15.

[113] Karl-Heinz Ladeur, 'Warum nach den Medien des Rechts fragen?' (2012) *Ancilla Iuris*, pp. 105–110.

[114] Karl-Heinz Ladeur, 'Die Netzwerke des Rechts und die Evolution der "Gesellschaft der Netzwerke"', in Michael Bommes and Veronika Tacke (eds.), *Netzwerke in der funktional differenzierten Gesellschaft*, Wiesbaden: VS Verlag, 2011, pp. 143–171.

[115] Karl-Heinz Ladeur, 'Die Zukunft der Medienverfassung', in Karl-Heinz Ladeur, et al. (eds.), *Die Zukunft der Medienverfassung*, Tübingen: Mohr Siebeck, 2021, pp. 17–89, at 20.

[116] Ibid., at 27.

fundamentally alters the conditions of possibility of individual action and autonomy,[117] leading to a transformation of the individual subject. In the society of networks, Ladeur argues, the individual must discover experimental thinking and new developments. The creation and renewal of knowledge are linked to a distributed heterarchical network that operates without any central mediating instance.

For Ladeur, the theoretical focus ought to be placed on the impact that media change has on the relationship between societal actors. Ladeur conceives of historical media as specific means by which to shape communication in society. Like Vesting, Ladeur perceives the computer network as a *hybrid* sociotechnical construct.[118] The computer facilitates the development of new hybrid models to interconnect knowledge and provide access to information.[119] The computer network creates the primary space within which the 'relational subjects' of the society of networks constantly configure and reconfigure their mutual relationships.[120] Ladeur believes that, in the society of networks, the relationship between cognitive and normative expectations – the two basic categories of behavioural expectation – is undergoing change. Unlike cognitive expectations, which are altered in the event of disappointment, normative expectations will not be abandoned even if they are violated by interaction partners. Ladeur states that 'the mobilisation and hybridisation of the relationship between cognitive and normative components of the law can globally be identified as the preeminent feature of the law of the society of networks'.[121]

[117] Ibid., at 31. See also Lars Viellechner, 'The Network of Networks: Karl-Heinz Ladeur's Theory of Law and Globalization' (2009) *German Law Journal*, 10 (4), pp. 515–536.

[118] Karl-Heinz Ladeur, 'Toward a Network-Oriented Law of the Internet!: The Necessity to Find a New Balance Between Risk and Opportunity in Network Communication' (2009) *German Law Journal*, 10 (9), pp. 1201–1214, at 1214.

[119] Ladeur, 'Die Netzwerke des Rechts und die Evolution der "Gesellschaft der Netzwerke"', at 153.

[120] Karl-Heinz Ladeur, 'Die Gesellschaft der Netzwerke und ihre Wissensordnung: Big Data, Datenschutz und die "relationale Persönlichkeit"', in Florian Süssenguth (ed.), *Die Gesellschaft der Daten: Über die digitale Transformation der sozialen Ordnung*, Bielefeld: transcript, 2015, pp. 225–252. See also Vesting, *Legal Theory and the Media of Law*, at 459–468.

[121] Ladeur, 'Die Netzwerke des Rechts und die Evolution der "Gesellschaft der Netzwerke"', at 160 (translation by the author).

Ladeur's position is quite radical, since the law has classically been seen as the place in society where normative expectations are stabilised.[122] By conceptualising the boundaries between cognitive and normative expectations as fluid, Ladeur questions the social relevance of the law. When he claims that cognitive forms of coordination are gaining importance within the society of networks, he is saying that normative expectations are losing ground.[123]

The question posed at the outset of this section was whether Ladeur and Vesting's media theory of law could provide a framework for conceptualising the relationship between law and technology that would neutralise the shortcomings of STS that have been identified in relation to the field of law. This question can be answered in the affirmative, insofar as Ladeur and Vesting are theorists who are also fully trained jurists, and thus familiar with the doctrines of the law and the practice of the relevant courts. At the same time, when they analyse current technological developments in society and the law, they do so from the outside perspective of cultural studies and media theory. Vesting and Ladeur's media theory mostly consists of a historical reconstruction of societal and legal evolution. Their goal is to design a general theory of the mediality of the history of the law, an approach that enables the impact of media and materiality on human actors and legal processes to be assessed in a general way, rather than, as in STS, on a case-by-case basis. Indeed, the two scholars clearly have as an ambition to formulate a grand theory of law in a world shaped by media.

Nonetheless, Ladeur and Vesting's theory is similar to STS in that it also lacks a critical standpoint. Media theory of law reconstructs cultural artefacts and tools as 'archaeological sediments', as is characteristic of a cultural studies perspective. The theory's focus on legal communications as cultural phenomena carries the risk of excessive deference to technological change. Rather than critically insisting on the significance of normative positions protecting fundamental rights, for example, or

[122] Niklas Luhmann, *Law as a Social System*, translated by Klaus Alex Ziegert, Oxford and New York: Oxford University Press, 2004 (1993), at 147–150.

[123] Ladeur, 'Die Netzwerke des Rechts und die Evolution der "Gesellschaft der Netzwerke"', at 157–158. See also Viellechner, 'The Network of Networks', at 521.

socio-political claims for resistance or regulatory response, media legal theory is primarily affirmative. Ladeur's narrow focus on cognitive expectations and adaptive behaviour neglects normative structures and the law in digital society. Furthermore, while Ladeur is right to highlight the crucial importance of individuals' learning in the digital ecosphere, the media theory of law underestimates the role of normative expectations and the law. The theory fails to consider how the law can learn under conditions shaped by computer networks and how it can stimulate reactions to the socio-political changes caused by new technologies.

In another respect, namely in its conceptualisation of networks, media legal theory is less convincing than STS. It argues that the society of networks has radically changed the way individuals experience the world and interact with each other and that the ability to adapt behavioural expectations to new developments has become paramount. The computer network has become the dominant medium for disseminating information in the twenty-first century. It is perceived as a *hybrid construct* intermingling the material and the social. However, the conception of the network as a sociotechnical hybrid does away with the separation between intentional human action and technological causality. According to the philosopher John R. Searle, 'intentionality' is 'the capacity of the mind to represent objects and states of affairs in the world other than itself'.[124] Machines, such as computers (both hardware and software), are not capable of developing intentions, but they are subject to the laws of technical causality. Even in cases where we understand machines as agents to which intentions can be ascribed, this intentionality is only derivative, in the sense that we are able to interpret the operations of a computer.[125] Vesting and Ladeur's conceptualisation of the internet as a hybrid blinds them to the independent significance of its material and social components. As a result, their theory once again misses the chance to adopt a critical stance towards technological development and propose emancipatory solutions to its social costs.

[124] John R. Searle, *The Construction of Social Reality*, London: Penguin, 1995, at 6–7.

[125] Searle presented this argument for the first time in his 1980 article 'The Chinese Room Argument' and has since revised it several times. Edward N. Zalta and Uri Nodelman (eds.), *The Stanford Encyclopedia of Philosophy* (Summer 2023 Edition), https://plato.stanford.edu/archives/sum2023/entries/chinese-room/, at para 5.2.

In comparison, the STS approach to conceptualising the computer network, which is based on the idea of a process of co-production involving both the material and the social elements, appears more fruitful, as it allows for a precise distinction to be made between the physical, the symbolic and their interaction.

Building on this critique, Chapter 5 proposes an alternative way of conceptualising the relationship between technology and law, based on a combination of systems-theory-informed legal sociology and elements of STS.

CHAPTER 5

Affordances of Technology

Locating Technology in Systems Theory

Chapter 4 gave an overview of two dominant perspectives on the relationship between technology, society and law. The first approach, science and technology studies (STS), undertakes sophisticated analyses of the complex interactions between society and materiality, with the concept of co-production helping us to understand the mutual interdependencies between technology designers and social response. However, STS's limitations can be seen in how it approaches the law: because it observes the law from the outside, it cannot capture the proprium of legal normativity. The fact that its adherents lack legal expertise prevents them from properly understanding the mechanisms of legal doctrine and practice. In contrast, the second approach, media theory of law, has developed a general account of the impact on the law of the historically dominant dissemination media. The two main downsides of this perspective are that it conceptualises the computer network as a sociotechnical hybrid (implying an uncritical view of technology) and underestimates the importance of normative social structures in the digital environment. The result is that a one-sided focus on how 'relational subjects' learn overshadows the learning undertaken by the law. Excessive deference towards technological change prevents the adherents of this approach from adopting a critical stance.

This chapter proposes a strategy to address these shortcomings by combining STS and legal sociology. In contrast to the existing law-and-society literature that draws on STS,[1] the legal sociology approach

[1] For a comprehensive literature review, see Simon A. Cole and Alyse Bertenthal, 'Science, Technology, Society, and Law' (2017) *Annual Review of Law and Social Science*, 13,

adopted here distinguishes a legal definition of the law from a sociological one. The sociological definition conceives of law as an autonomous social system, which enables fundamental rights to be reconceptualised as social rather than legal institutions. It provides the starting point for the discussion in Chapters 6 and 7 of the extent to which technological means have been recognised as independent aspects of the freedom of expression as a fundamental right.

5.1 INTRODUCTION TO LEGAL SOCIOLOGY AND SYSTEMS THEORY

What is legal sociology? The easiest approach to answering this question is to begin by specifying what legal sociology is *not*. First, it is not the same as legal *doctrine*. Legal doctrine is preoccupied with how things 'should' be; it is also fundamentally concerned with the *form* of the law, that is the systematic relationship between various abstract principles which can be used to reach logical decisions in concrete cases.[2] Eugen Ehrlich and Roscoe Pound, two pioneers of sociological jurisprudence, had already called for the formalist view of law to be abandoned at the beginning of the twentieth century.[3] They criticised as unscientific the prevailing understanding of law in legal doctrine as a closed and self-sufficient field, arguing that law in action, rather than law as it is presented in books, should be the focus of legal *science*.[4] They also argued that the necessary scientific standards could only be achieved through a study of law anchored in *sociology*. Since Ehrlich and Pound, we know that 'the divergence between law in books and law in action is more acute in some

pp. 351–371. See also Alex Faulkner, et al., 'Introduction: Material Worlds: Intersections of Law, Science, Technology, and Society' (2012) *Journal of Law and Society*, 39 (1), pp. 1–19.

[2] Christoph B. Graber, 'Legal Sociology', in Marc Thommen (ed.), *Introduction to Swiss Law*, 2nd edn, Zurich: sui generis, 2022, pp. 91–112, at 94–96.

[3] Eugen Ehrlich, *Fundamental Principles of the Sociology of Law*, translated by Walter L. Moll, New Brunswick, NJ: Transaction Publishers, 2002 (1913), at 25; Roscoe Pound, 'The Scope and Purpose of Sociological Jurisprudence: Part I' (1911) *Harvard Law Review*, 24 (8), pp. 591–619, at 594.

[4] Roscoe Pound, 'Law in Books and Law in Action' (1910) *American Law Review*, 44 (1), pp. 12–36.

periods of legal history than in others'.[5] This phenomenon is particularly pronounced in times like the present, when speedy technological development is leading to profound social transformation. In the twenty-first century, the law has tried to adapt to rapidly shifting social conditions by means of increased judicial or regulatory action. Conflicts often arise when a satisfactory or 'just' solution cannot be found in the applicable law, as a result of the failure of legal doctrine to keep pace with social and technological change.

The problem with conceiving of legal science as a sub-domain of sociology is that it overlooks the fundamental difference between 'is' and 'ought'. The statement that something 'is' the case describes observed facts. It is distinct from saying that something 'ought' to be the case, which bears on a legal proposition's prescriptive or normative aspects.

If legal sociology does not belong to the formally closed field of legal doctrine and is not limited to objectively describing legal facts, what is it? Although legal sociology is *not the same* as sociology or law, it combines them, especially in the two-step methodology it employs.

The first step involves temporarily shifting the vantage point of research from the law to the social sciences. From such an *external perspective*, the law can be described as a social fact and theories about what the law 'is' can be developed. The aim is to undertake an empirical observation and description of real legal problems and an analysis of their cause from the perspectives of social science and social theory. This approach is decidedly objectivist: its aim is the value-free observation and description of law-related facts, without letting normative preconceptions dictate the outcome. In order to achieve this goal, qualitative or quantitative social research methods can be employed. Seen from the perspective of social science, a legal conflict appears in a new light, with connections suddenly becoming visible that explain why the law was unable to find an adequate solution.

The second step consists of an attempt to re-import the insights arrived at through the external observation of the law back into the legal system. The goal is to improve the law and to adapt legal doctrine so as to

[5] Ibid., at 22.

ensure that the law functions better. Notably, the second step requires a change of perspective from describing social facts (external view) to prescribing normative ends (internal view). The transfer of knowledge from the social sciences to the law is a very demanding undertaking. Given the marked differences between external and internal observation of the law, there is no linear causality in this process, and a copy-paste type of knowledge transfer is excluded. Instead, it is a matter of reformulating the findings of social science in the language of law and studying, by trial and error, what happens when certain changes are made to the law.

The present book proposes an approach to legal sociology inspired by Niklas Luhmann's theory of *autopoietic systems*. Luhmann, who has written extensively on the law, is one of the most influential sociologists of the twentieth century. Between the 1960s and his death in 1998, he laid out a comprehensive theory of society and its main sub-systems, including the system of law. Before turning to sociology, he had trained and practised as a lawyer, which explains the exceptional quality of his writings on the sociology of the law.

Autopoiesis means self-production and self-organisation. Luhmann conceives society as an autopoietic system, autonomously reproducing communication from current communication.[6] On this view, the elements of a social system are communications, rather than humans or the actions of humans or of other agents.[7] This does not mean that autopoiesis theory is dehumanised or post-human, as some of Luhmann's critics have implied,[8] but merely that humans cannot be reduced to communication.[9] For Luhmann, a human being is a structural coupling of phenomenologically different systems. Her body (including her brain) is a

[6] Niklas Luhmann, *Social Systems*, translated by John Bednarz with Dirk Baecker, Stanford: Stanford University Press, 1995 (1984), at 37.

[7] Christoph B. Graber, 'Freedom and Affordances of the Net' (2018) *Washington University Jurisprudence Review*, 10 (2), pp. 221–256, at 232.

[8] Oliver Lepsius, *Steuerungsdiskussion, Systemtheorie und Parlamentarismuskritik*, Tübingen: Mohr Siebeck, 1999; Matthias Mahlmann, *Rechtsphilosophie und Rechtstheorie*, 4th edn, Baden-Baden: Nomos, 2017, at 241.

[9] Hugh Baxter, 'Niklas Luhmann's Theory of Autopoietic Legal Systems' (2013) *Annual Review of Law and Social Science*, 9, pp. 167–184, at 176. See also Hans-Georg Möller, *The Radical Luhmann*, New York: Columbia University Press, 2012, at 23.

biological system, her consciousness a psychic system, and human communications are components of the social system.[10] By placing communication at the centre of his theory, Luhmann does even greater justice to humans than methodologically individualistic approaches. This is because he works with much more complexity, taking into account the biological and psychological aspects of human existence in addition to communicative ones.

Not only human beings and brains, but also material objects are excluded from society.[11] This is one of the reasons why media theorists find Luhmann's theory ill-equipped to analyse the technological challenges facing contemporary society[12] and why law-and-society scholars believe that technology represents Luhmann's blind spot.[13] For Luhmann, communication is the only genuinely social operation, and only communications communicate.[14] Communication is defined as the synthesis of three selections that involve combinations of 'utterance', 'information' and 'understanding'.[15] Utterance is an act of expression, while information refers to the distinction between the act and its content. In a communicative process, the distinctions between utterance and information in a first communication are understood by a second one.[16] However, the selection of information in the first communication involves a decision about the meaning of the selected utterance. Hence, information does not pre-exist as a complete unit in the world,

[10] See Dirk Baecker, 'Digitalisierung als Kalkül', in Dirk Baecker, et al. (eds.), *Post-digitales Management*, Wiesbaden: Springer VS, 2023, pp. 23–37, at 26–27.

[11] Niklas Luhmann, *Theory of Society*, translated by Rhodes Barret, vol. 1, Stanford: Stanford University Press, 2012 (1997), at 28; Niklas Luhmann, *Law as a Social System*, translated by Klaus Alex Ziegert, Oxford and New York: Oxford University Press, 2004 (1993), at 67.

[12] Geoffrey Winthrop-Young, 'Silicon Sociology, or, Two Kings on Hegel's Throne?: Kittler, Luhmann, and the Posthuman Merger of German Media Theory' (2000) *Yale Journal of Criticism*, 13 (2), pp. 391–420, at 409–412.

[13] Vagias Karavas, 'The Force of Code: Law's Transformation Under Information Technological Conditions' (2009) *German Law Journal*, 10 (4), pp. 463–481, at 464.

[14] Luhmann, *Theory of Society*, vol. 1, at 42.

[15] Niklas Luhmann, 'The Autopoiesis of Social Systems', in R. F. Geyer and Johannes van der Zouwen (eds.), *Sociocybernetic Paradoxes: Observation, Control, and Evolution of Self-Steering Systems*, London and Beverly Hills: SAGE Publications, 1986, pp. 172–192, at 175.

[16] Niklas Luhmann, 'The Form of Writing' (1992) *Stanford Literature Review*, 9 (1), pp. 25–42, at 27.

but is internally constructed within the communication process as the result of a selection. Understanding, the third selection, synthesises the previous two selections and puts the information of the first communication into a new form. Understanding is a process that takes place *within* a social system. It is the result of applying the social system's own criteria for selection.

For Luhmann, there is no input or output of components into the social system, nor is there any transmission of information, unlike in most communication theories, which assume a sender/receiver model.[17] Between social systems, there exists a circular relationship of 'double contingency': 'The basic situation of double contingency is then simple: two black boxes, by whatever accident, come to have dealings with one another.'[18] This is Luhmann's way of saying that the complexity of communication between social systems prevents the systems involved from fully understanding each other.[19]

Under conditions so heavily influenced by contingency, successful communication is seen as very unlikely to happen. In the course of its evolution, society has reacted to this situation by developing *media* that neutralise these difficulties and 'transform what is improbable into what is probable'.[20] Luhmann distinguishes three types of media: 1) spoken language, 2) distribution media and 3) symbolically generalised communication media (success media).[21] Spoken language helps us to understand communication in a way that goes beyond mere perception, distribution media (e.g., writing, printing, broadcasting and networked computers) ensure access to communication beyond spatial and temporal constraints and success media (e.g., meaning, law, truth, power and money) provide powerful motivations to increase the chances of successful communication.[22]

[17] Lars Qvortrup, *The Hypercomplex Society*, New York: Peter Lang, 2003, pp. 126–132.

[18] Luhmann, *Social Systems*, at 109.

[19] See Raf Vanderstraeten, 'Parsons, Luhmann and the Theorem of Double Contingency' (2002) *Journal of Classical Sociology*, 2 (1), pp. 77–92, at 85.

[20] Luhmann, *Social Systems*, at 160.

[21] Ibid., at 160–161; Luhmann, *Theory of Society*, vol. 1, at 120–123.

[22] Luhmann, *Theory of Society*, vol. 1, at 122.

Luhmann distinguishes four categories of systems: social systems, biological systems (including brains), psychic systems and machine systems.[23] Although computers and brains do not themselves communicate, they are essential means of communication, especially since they enable 'structural couplings'[24] between consciousness and communication.[25] Moreover, on the level of society, meaning is the most critical success medium, since both psychic and social systems rely on meaning in order to reproduce themselves. As machines, computers do not belong to the sphere of symbols and thus do *not reproduce* meaning, but they are essential means for *distributing* meaning. Just as writing, printing, the telegraph, the telephone and electronic media shaped communication in earlier eras, the computer has become the leading distribution medium of the twenty-first century.

How does systems theory conceive of the internet? The truth is that the internet was not a central object of enquiry for Luhmann, and he only commented on it in passing. However, it would be wrong to conclude on this basis that systems theory is incapable of integrating the internet into its conceptual framework. The considerations outlined above suggest that the internet cannot be reduced to either a social system[26] or a machine. It is not merely a social system because it is not concerned with reproducing meaning. The reproduction of meaning is the responsibility of the various sub-systems of society, each with its own specialisation, such as law, politics, economics, science and art. At the same time, the internet is not just a machine because the technology that keeps it running also, to some extent, shapes the content that is distributed through it.[27] For example, YouTube's underlying technology (its recommendation algorithm) does more than just mechanically recommend videos, since it actively shapes the kind of content that is produced, promoted and consumed on the platform. Content creators adjust their

[23] Luhmann, *Social Systems*, at 2. [24] For a definition, see n. 30 and surrounding text.

[25] Luhmann, *Theory of Society*, vol. 1, at 65–66.

[26] For an opposing view, see Peter Bøgh Anderson, 'WWW as Self-Organizing System' (1998) *Cybernetics & Human Knowing*, 5 (2), pp. 5–41.

[27] See Nick Couldry, et al., 'Real Social Analytics: A Contribution towards a Phenomenology of a Digital World' (2016) *The British Journal of Sociology*, 67 (1), pp. 118–137, at 121–122; Baecker, 'Digitalisierung als Kalkül', at 28.

strategies based on the algorithm's preferences, and users' perceptions and beliefs can be influenced by what the algorithm chooses to show them. Thus, the technology underpinning the platform plays an essential role in shaping its culture and content.

What is distinctive about the internet is that it combines the functions of a distribution medium with those of a success medium. The material sphere and the symbolic sphere of communication are integrated into a single infrastructure,[28] and the two spheres interact without either of them being able to determine the other. It is clear from Luhmann's writings that such a relationship of 'dependent independence' is best captured by the concept of structural coupling,[29] which he generally defines in terms of a system presupposing certain features in its environment.[30] In the case of *social* systems, one can speak of structural coupling as a situation involving co-evolution through reciprocal observation. For the systems involved, such observations are communicative events that may trigger structural adaptions within a system according to the evolutionary process of variation, selection and stabilisation. Luhmann has clarified that the concept of structural coupling is not restricted to describing the co-evolution of meaning-reproducing systems, but may also apply when characterising a relationship of spatiotemporal proximity between the sphere of meaning and the physical world, including computer technology.[31]

> The sole alternative to the consciousness/communication structural coupling that is emerging – with unpredictable consequences – is the computer. There are already computers in use whose operations are accessible to neither consciousness nor communication, neither simultaneously

[28] For a broad interpretation of 'infrastructure' as combining material and social elements, see Geoffrey C. Bowker, et al., 'Toward Information Infrastructure Studies: Ways of Knowing in a Networked Environment', in Jeremy Hunsinger, et al. (eds.), *International Handbook of Internet Research*, Dordrecht: Springer Netherlands, 2010, pp. 97–117. See also Christian Sandvig, 'The Internet as Infrastructure', in William H. Dutton (ed.), *The Oxford Handbook of Internet Studies*, Oxford: Oxford University Press, 2014, pp. 86–106.

[29] Dan Wielsch, *Zugangsregeln: Die Rechtsverfassung der Wissensteilung*, Tübingen: Mohr Siebeck, 2008, at 236–238.

[30] Luhmann, *Theory of Society*, vol. 1, at 49–68.

[31] Ibid., at 322.

> nor reconstructively. Although they are manufactured and programmed machines, such computers function nontransparently for consciousness and for communication; their operations nevertheless affect consciousness and communication through structural coupling.[32]

Digital media play a critical role in this regard. According to Dirk Baecker:

> [They belong] to those mechanisms of structural coupling that one summarises under the title 'technology' and describes as forms of access to causality. They create an interface between the body, consciousness and communication (each differently) on the one hand and computers (hardware, software, algorithms, networks) on the other.[33]

However, Vesting and Ladeur reproach sociological systems theory for failing to adequately conceptualise the network,[34] finding particular fault with Luhmann's separation of the physical sphere of media from the sphere of meaning.[35] In Chapter 4, we saw that they prefer to conceive of the network as a hybrid socio-technical construct, and as the discussion of Luhmann's distinction between 'distribution media' and 'success media' shows, he does indeed separate the social from the material. Rather than denouncing this as a deficiency, I see it as a strength of Luhmann's theory. It offers the possibility to overcome some of the shortcomings identified in Vesting and Ladeur's media theory of law, because only when the two spheres are separated can the law develop a normative standpoint with regard to a given technology. To be sure, Luhmann never claimed to fully conceptualise the place of technology or the internet within his communication theory. However, he did show how the interface between the communicative and material components of the internet can be reconstructed as a structural coupling.[36] Hence, Luhmann not only separates distribution media and symbolically

[32] Ibid., at 66. [33] Baecker, 'Digitalisierung als Kalkül', at 25 (translation by the author).

[34] Thomas Vesting, *Legal Theory and the Media of Law*, translated by James C. Wagner, Cheltenham, UK, and Northampton, MA: Edward Elgar Publishing, 2018, at 447–448.

[35] Karl-Heinz Ladeur, 'Warum nach den Medien des Rechts fragen?' (2012) *Ancilla Iuris*, pp. 105–110, at 110.

[36] Luhmann, 'The Autopoiesis of Social Systems', at 174.

generalised communication media but also understands the relevance of their mutual interdependencies.[37]

At this juncture, a sceptical reader might object that Luhmann's concept of structural coupling is excessively vague. In reality, however, Luhmann defined the contours of the term more clearly in concrete contexts. In law, for example, structural coupling has been elaborated on in detail in relation to the concepts of statute, contract and constitution.[38] The fact that something similar has not yet been done in the case of materiality and sociality on the internet does not mean that it is impossible to do so. Baecker, who completed his PhD and *habilitation* under Luhmann's supervision, took it upon himself to develop his teacher's theory in the digital space. Baecker starts by explaining what structural coupling does: 'Mechanisms of structural coupling allow a system to orient its own operations towards structures that are constructed as facts of the environment or structures of other systems, even if their connection value for further operations is different in each system.'[39]

In order to understand how the structural coupling of psychic, biological and social systems with digital media works, the concept of a *calculus of digitisation* is of crucial importance. In human interactions, each of the biological, psychic and social systems involved is an actor 'carrying out distinctions that extract a discretely processable reality from an analogue world'.[40] What enables phenomenologically distinct systems to act on each other is the digitalisation of analogue processes. The digital form is the prerequisite for the mutual offsetting of the contributions of the participating systems and the digital media. It serves 'the digital media, while at the same time varying this form of its operations medially to cope with the demands made by a digital medium'.[41]

Baecker calls digitisation a *calculus*, because every response causes variation in every other response. As a result, the form is constantly being transformed into another form of itself: 'Each of the system references involved confronts every other with the problem of translating a

[37] Luhmann, *Theory of Society*, vol. 1, at 193–194.

[38] See Baxter, 'Niklas Luhmann's Theory of Autopoietic Legal Systems', at 178–182; Graber, 'Legal Sociology', at 98.

[39] Baecker, 'Digitalisierung als Kalkül', at 26 (translation by the author).

[40] Ibid. (translation by the author).

[41] Ibid., at 27 (translation by the author).

continuously analogue state of affairs into a digital data format that the body and brain, consciousness and communication can read and operate according to their distinctions and in engagement with their inner environment.'[42] In other words, the calculus of digitisation makes it possible to convert, process and interpret information from different systems (biological, psychic and communicative), as well as to integrate it into the digital realm of the internet. Since both communication and computer signals are digitally encoded, digitisation gives humans who are engaged in communication access to physical causality. Hence, the calculus of digitisation describes how binary coding facilitates mutual adaptation between phenomenologically different systems in a relationship of structural coupling.

The concept of structural coupling is better suited to understanding the complex interrelations between technology and society in internet-mediated communication processes than the vague concept of a 'hybrid network'. The nature of the relationship between the sphere of the social and the sphere of the material is not hybrid, but separate. The separation of the two spheres is the prerequisite for describing the complexity of their cooperation with sufficient precision, as well as, in the context of the internet, for understanding how the systems involved in a given case of structural coupling rely on digital technology to gain access to causality. As I will argue below, this is the theoretical precondition for a *critical* view of novel technologies and their societal cost.

5.2 MARRYING SYSTEMS THEORY WITH STS THROUGH AFFORDANCES

The remarks above have shown where the interface between the social and the materiality of computers can be found in sociological systems theory. For reasons that are unclear to us, Luhmann did not elaborate on these questions. One possible explanation is that his life was simply too short, coming to an end one year after he had completed the *Theory of Society*, the summa of more than forty years of research. We can only speculate about whether, had he lived longer, he might have

[42] Ibid., at 32 (translation by the author).

increasingly turned to the world of computers and the internet, and especially to the interrelation between society and networked computers. What we do know for sure is that technology represents a gap in Luhmann's theory. In what follows, I aim to contribute to filling this gap. By taking up the thread laid down by Luhmann as best I can, I would like to show how the theory of autopoiesis can be linked to the central insights of STS. The starting point for this ambitious endeavour is the concept of 'technical affordances' taken from STS.[43] I will begin by introducing the idea and defining its specific scope. Then building on the thesis of co-production in STS, I will explain how affordances enter into a technology. This will pave the way for me to elaborate on how technical affordances can theoretically be integrated into a systems-theory-informed legal sociology.

5.2.1 TECHNICAL AFFORDANCES

The term 'affordance' lacks conceptual clarity. It was coined in 1979 by the perceptual psychologist James Gibson,[44] who argued that animals are capable of selectively perceiving information in their environment based on its relative importance for their survival. Affordances thus comprise information concerning the possibilities or enticements in the environment. Ten years later, the designer Donald Norman adopted and popularised the concept,[45] using it to refer to those aspects of an object's design that define the possibilities of its use.[46] Norman was primarily interested in studying how users perceive a particular technical design, but, in doing so, he lost sight of a central aspect of Gibson's theory, namely the assumption that the natural environment exists

[43] Ian Hutchby, 'Technologies, Text and Affordances' (2001) *Sociology*, 35 (2), pp. 441–456; Ian Hutchby, 'Affordances and the Analysis of Technologically Mediated Interaction: A Response to Brian Rappert' (2003) *Sociology*, 37 (3), pp. 581–589; Julian Hopkins, 'The Concept of Affordances in Digital Media', in Heidrun Friese, et al. (eds.), *Handbuch Soziale Praktiken und Digitale Alltagswelten*, Wiesbaden: Springer, 2016, pp. 1–8.

[44] James J. Gibson, *The Ecological Approach to Visual Perception*, New York: Psychology Press, 2015 (1979).

[45] Leah A. Lievrouw, 'The Materiality of Mediated Knowledge and Expression', in Tarleton Gillespie, et al. (eds.), *Media Technologies: Essays on Communication, Materiality, and Society*, Cambridge, MA: The MIT Press, 2014, pp. 21–51, at 48.

[46] Donald A. Norman, *The Psychology of Everyday Things*, New York: Basic Books, 1988, at 9.

independently of the representations of it within a biological system.[47] On the philosophical level, Gibson's perspective is more convincing than Norman's, corresponding to what John R. Searle calls 'external realism'. External realism supposes that the natural environment 'exists independently of our representations of it'.[48] This is different from social reality, which we construct by mutually agreeing on its validity. It is, therefore, essential to distinguish between those features of the world which are '*intrinsic* to nature' and those 'that exist *relative to the intentionality of observers, users, etc.*'.[49] For Searle, external realism is a precondition for conceptual relativism: 'The ontological subjectivity of the socially constructed reality requires an ontologically objective reality out of which it is constructed.'[50]

A handful of law-and-technology scholars have advocated for a broad understanding of affordance. Mireille Hildebrandt, for example, has abandoned her original, technology-centred conception of affordance, in favour of a broader one. In her book *Smart Technologies and the End(s) of Law,* she used the term 'affordance' in the technology-centred way, arguing, in Gibson's sense, that what a technology affords is more important than what an agent perceives.[51] In response to criticism that her book lacked a comprehensive theory of affordances, she later expanded the term to include social phenomena, such as 'affordances of the law'.[52] A broad interpretation of the term is also found in the works of Julie E. Cohen, who understands fundamental rights to be affordances.[53] Elsewhere, I have argued that expanding the scope of the term 'affordance' has eliminated its potential to help us think

[47] Thomas Natsoulas, '"To See Things Is To Perceive What They Afford": James J. Gibson's Concept of Affordance' (2004) *The Journal of Mind and Behavior,* 25 (4), pp. 323–347, at 340.

[48] John R. Searle, *The Construction of Social Reality,* London: Penguin, 1995, at 150.

[49] Ibid., at 9 (emphasis in the original).

[50] Ibid., at 191.

[51] Mireille Hildebrandt, *Smart Technologies and the End(s) of Law: Novel Entanglements of Law and Technology,* Cheltenham, UK, and Northampton, MA: Edward Elgar, 2015, at 169–172.

[52] Mireille Hildebrandt, 'Law as an Affordance: The Devil Is in the Vanishing Point(s)' (2017) *Critical Analysis of Law,* 4 (1), pp. 116–128.

[53] Julie E. Cohen, 'Affording Fundamental Rights: A Provocation Inspired by Mireille Hildebrandt' (2017) *Critical Analysis of Law,* 4 (1), pp. 78–90.

critically about the relationship between technology and society. To claim that not only a material object can have affordances but also a discourse or a social system is to water down the concept.[54]

In order to preserve the concept's critical edge, this book uses a narrow, technology-centred understanding of 'affordance'. In what follows, the term describes the opportunities and constraints of a technology that are co-produced via a dialogue between material and social decisions. The idea of co-production, which was discussed in our review of the Latour-inspired STS scholarship, forms the starting point for conceptualising the notion of technical affordance.

5.2.2 HOW DO AFFORDANCES ENTER INTO TECHNOLOGY?

The first question to ask is how affordances enter into a technology. The answer lies in Feenberg's philosophy of technology and Bryan Pfaffenberger's 'technological drama', both of which distinguish multi-layered interactions between the material and the social.

Drawing on Heidegger and Herbert Marcuse, Feenberg postulates a philosophy of design and the uptake of a technological artefact or system that distinguishes between a causal and a cultural layer of construction. While the causal layer refers to the laws of nature, the cultural layer concerns the meaning that an artefact acquires within the lifeworld of which it forms a part.[55] An additional distinction between objective and subjective design conditions turns the analysis scheme into a matrix structure. Informed by Heidegger's phenomenology, the former conditions concern how the object is revealed, while the latter ones relate to how a subject constitutes itself.[56] By combining the different elements in the matrix, Feenberg elevates the theory of the co-production of technological artefacts to a high level of complexity.

[54] Christoph B. Graber, 'Artificial Intelligence, Affordances and Fundamental Rights', in Mireille Hildebrandt and Kieron O'Hara (eds.), *Life and the Law in the Era of Data-Driven Agency*, Cheltenham: Edward Elgar, 2020, pp. 194–213, at 197.

[55] Andrew Feenberg, *Technosystem: The Social Life of Reason*, Cambridge, MA: Harvard University Press, 2017, at 153–154.

[56] Ibid., at 155–156.

> [T]he technical subject exercises a certain freedom or initiative, guided by anticipation of the future, in the discovery of the potentials of its materials. The scope for initiative varies but it is an inevitable aspect of the technical relation. At a minimum, the initiative is defined by a range of activities enabled by the design of the object. But it may go beyond the normal range and inspire new designs. This is the basis of both design work and creative appropriation of technologies by users.[57]

While Feenberg develops his philosophy at a high level of abstraction, Pfaffenberger, a sociologist of technology, explains his understanding of the co-production of artefacts in a more accessible way, using the heuristics of a three-act drama. Act 1, 'regularisation', centres on (independent or corporate) technology designers, the 'design constituency',[58] who shape the material design of a technological artefact and promote their own view, within social discourse, about how this technology should be interpreted. To illustrate Pfaffenberger's point, consider the famous example of a knife, and whether it is a good or bad tool. Suppose that the design constituency is convinced that a newly designed knife is a good tool, because it is very useful for chopping up vegetables. For this reason, it will also defend its interpretation against the alternative interpretation that the new knife is a bad tool, because it can kill.[59]

The interpretative malleability of an artefact indicates that its affordances are shaped through a discursive process. While the discursive aspects of this act are essential, the non-discursive (material) aspects must not be forgotten either. In designing an artefact, the materiality of the technology is important, because it allows values to be embedded in what is produced.[60] The introduction of hashtags on Twitter illustrates how close the interrelation between the discursive and the material aspects often is.

[57] Ibid., at 157.

[58] Bryan Pfaffenberger, 'Technological Dramas' (1992) *Science, Technology & Human Values*, 17 (3), pp. 282–312, at 283.

[59] Katinka Waelbers, *Doing Good with Technologies: Taking Responsibility for the Social Role of Emerging Technologies*, Dordrecht: Springer, 2011, at 18.

[60] For a similar view see Helen Nissenbaum, 'From Preemption to Circumvention: If Technology Regulates, Why Do We Need Regulation (and Vice Versa)?' (2011) *Berkeley Technology Law Journal*, 26 (3), pp. 1367–1386, at 1378.

Chris Messina, a former Google designer, invented the hashtag, as it is used on social media platforms, although he never patented it.[61] In a tweet on 23 August 2007, Messina asked the Twitter community, '[H]ow do you feel about using #(pound) for groups. As in #barcamp [msg]?'[62] The hashtag symbol had been used before – for example to refer to channels in the online chat room Internet Relay Chat[63] – but Messina is credited with persuading Twitter Inc. to adopt the hashtag for the purpose of indexing micro-blogging and group conversations.[64] Although the hashtag's meaning and value were determined by Twitter Inc., this was done based on what Twitter users thought was important. Messina described the hashtag as useful, because it represented 'a solid convention for coordinating ad-hoc groupings and giving people a way to organize their communications in a way that the tool (Twitter) does not currently afford'.[65] After Twitter Inc. initially rejected the idea, he reassured the Twitter community about how useful the hashtag would be for structuring Twitter conversations without having to follow a specific user. That reinterpretation of the technology's affordances later convinced the company to integrate hashtags into the platform's architecture.[66]

In Act 2, 'adjustment', those segments of society impacted by the newly introduced technological artefact (the 'impact constituency')[67]

[61] Jim Edwards, 'The Inventor of the Twitter Hashtag Explains Why He Didn't Patent It', *Business Insider*, 21 November 2013, www.businessinsider.com/chris-messina-talks-about-inventing-the-hashtag-on-twitter-2013-11?r=US&IR=T.

[62] Alex Leavitt, 'From #FollowFriday to YOLO: Exploring the Cultural Salience of Twitter Memes', in Katrin Weller, et al. (eds.), *Twitter and Society*, New York: Peter Lang, 2014, pp. 137–154, at 137.

[63] On Internet Relay Chat, see Wallace Wang, *Steal This File Sharing Book: What They Won't Tell You About File Sharing*, San Francisco: No Starch Press, 2004, chapter 4.

[64] Alexander Halavais, 'Structure on Twitter: Social and Technical', in Katrin Weller, et al. (eds.), *Twitter and Society*, New York: Peter Lang, 2014, pp. 29–41, at 36.

[65] Chris Messina, 'Twitter Hashtags for Emergency Coordination and Disaster Relief', *Factoryjoe*, 22 October 2007, https://factoryjoe.com/2007/10/22/twitter-hashtags-for-emergency-coordination-and-disaster-relief/.

[66] Axel Bruns and Jean Burgess, 'Twitter Hashtags from Ad Hoc to Calculated Publics', in Nathan Rambukkana (ed.), *Hashtag Publics: The Power and Politics of Discursive Networks*, New York: Peter Lang, 2015, pp. 13–27, at 16.

[67] Pfaffenberger, 'Technological Dramas', at 296.

take centre stage. Although the design constituency strives to cloak the artefact in a mythos (e.g., 'the knife is good') and define away any alternative interpretations, ambiguities will always remain. These, in turn, can be exploited by the impact constituency to create a 'counter-mythos' of the technology's ontology and purpose. The design, uptake and subsequent reinterpretation of the Facebook 'like' button illustrate this phenomenon.

In 2007, Leah Pearlman, a designer at Facebook, observed that people only rarely commented on their friends' updates and thought that everybody would benefit from more interaction. Pearlman suspected that 'if people did not have anything new or clever to say they would not say anything at all'.[68] Someone who had nothing witty to say about a friend's post, but still felt positively about it, would instead leave a single-word response, like 'awesome'.[69] However, dozens or hundreds of responses of this kind would simply clutter up the person's Facebook page. To avoid this outcome, Pearlman and her colleague Justin Rosenstein designed an 'awesome' button to be displayed next to every post.[70] A click would be all that would be needed to express support for others. The designers thus aimed to arouse the dormant positivity in every Facebook user. They envisioned pressing a button as the path of least resistance for people who were otherwise hesitant to engage in more interaction.[71] The idea went down well with Facebook's management and, after a name change from 'awesome' to 'like', a small blue-and-white thumbs-up icon was officially activated on 9 February 2009.[72]

[68] Leah Pearlman, 'Do You Like Me? Do I?', *TEDx Talk*, 13 October 2016, www.youtube .com/watch?v=5nwSjRA3kQA.

[69] Clive Thompson, *Coders: The Making of a New Tribe and the Remaking of the World*, New York: Penguin Press, 2019, at 143.

[70] Justin Rosenstein, 'No Dislike Button on Facebook', *Stanford University eCorner*, 8 May 2013, https://ecorner.stanford.edu/in-brief/no-dislike-button-on-facebook/.

[71] Victor Luckerson, 'The Rise of the Like Economy', *The Ringer*, 15 February 2017, www .theringer.com/2017/2/15/16038024/how-the-like-button-took-over-the-internet-ebe778be2459.

[72] Jason Kincaid, 'Facebook Activates "Like" Button', *TechCrunch*, 9 February 2009, https:// techcrunch.com/2009/02/09/facebook-activates-like-button-friendfeed-tires-of-sincere-flattery/.

It soon became evident that Pearlman and Rosenstein's public-interest-oriented interpretation of the 'like' button was not the only possible one. In a discursive process within the Facebook design constituency, the analytics department and the business managers attempted to establish a competing interpretation of the newly designed artefact's affordances as 'valid'.[73] The analytics department perceived the like button as a means for collecting detailed information about user behaviour, which would help tailor content more precisely to a user's profile. The business managers also adopted this interpretation of the artefact's affordances, because the personalisation of content offered the advertising industry the possibility to sell individualised ads. We now know that the business-oriented interpretation of the plugin eventually won out and that the like button has since 'made Facebook billions'.[74] As the plugin rapidly became a huge success, Facebook published 'copy and paste' software so that any website could attach a like button to any post. Moreover, every time a user visited a website with a like button, his or her personal data were transferred to Facebook, even if the visitor was not a Facebook user and had not even clicked on the button.[75]

Pearlman and Rosenstein were unable to resign themselves to the fact that, in place of their public-interest-oriented interpretation of the like button, an understanding had prevailed in the design constituency that permitted Facebook to maximise advertising revenues. As a result, they left the social network and became vocal critics in its impact constituency of what they denounced as a further step towards the economisation of the internet.[76] They took on the role of leaders of a discourse oriented towards creating a 'countermythos' for the like button, invigorating alternative interpretations of its affordances. Pearlman and Rosenstein

[73] See Thompson, *Coders*, at 144.

[74] Andy Kessler, 'The Button That Made Facebook Billions', *The Wall Street Journal*, 2 February 2012, www.wsj.com/articles/SB10001424052970204652904577196992203069570.

[75] Christoph B. Graber, 'How the Law Learns in the Digital Society' (2021) *Law, Technology and Humans*, 3 (2), pp. 12–27, at 22.

[76] Paul Lewis, '"Our Minds can be Hijacked": The Tech Insiders Who Fear a Smartphone Dystopia', *The Guardian*, 6 October 2017, www.theguardian.com/technology/2017/oct/05/smartphone-addiction-silicon-valley-dystopia.

warned the internet community against the adverse side effects of their invention, raising awareness of the dangers resulting from the collection of personal user data on a massive scale and the addictive potential of the like button.

This example illustrates how an impact constituency may be able to discursively re-interpret the affordances of a specific technological artefact. Through their critique, which was endorsed by internet activists, Pearlman and Rosenstein prevented the 'normalisation' of a particular interpretation of the like button and maintained the possibility of socio-political correction. According to Pfaffenberger, 'normalisation' or 'designification' refers to a situation in which specific social and technological dynamics lead to the termination of the dialogue between the design constituency and the impact constituency, with the result that a specific 'mythos' about the artefact comes to seem unalterable.[77]

Act 3, 'reconstitution', involves a material (i.e. non-discursive) redesign of the technology by the impact constituency. An example of this would be the invention of ad-blocking technology as a response to the use of behaviour-tracking cookies for advertising purposes.

Ad-blocking technology was created as a 'counterartefact'[78] to reconstitute the functionality of behaviour-tracking cookies on the *technical* level. According to Nissenbaum, the advertising industry's lobbying contributed to the introduction of the so-called third-party cookie by decision RFC 2965 of the Internet Engineering Task Force in 1997.[79] This cookie turned out to be particularly invasive of people's privacy, as it allows websites to continue to follow users even when they visit other websites. Ad-blocking technology can be seen as a technical answer to third-party cookies. While Adblock Plus, a creation of Eyeo, is the most widely used ad-blocker, many other companies produce similar software. The meaning and value of the counterartefact do not, however, come from such companies, but from those who are negatively affected by the

[77] Pfaffenberger, 'Technological Dramas', at 308. Feenberg uses the term 'closure' in this context (Feenberg, *Technosystem*, at 101).

[78] Pfaffenberger, 'Technological Dramas', at 304.

[79] Nissenbaum, 'From Preemption to Circumvention', at 1382.

original technology – in the case of ad-blocking, the myriad of users who feel annoyed by intrusive online advertisements.[80]

These three acts are ideal types of possible action patterns and do not necessarily represent a concrete sequence of events: the second or third act of a given drama could transform itself into a first act of a new technological drama. The case of ad-blocking once again provides evidence for the correctness of this thesis. Since ad-blocking deprives online publishers of revenue, several companies, including Axel Springer, Spiegel Online and Süddeutsche Zeitung, sued Eyeo in the German courts.[81] In what can be seen as a (new) act of technological adjustment, Eyeo proposed a compromise that would allow web publishers who were willing to pay Eyeo 6 per cent of their revenue to integrate a tag on their sites that would display selected advertising.[82] The technology thus shifted from blocking all ads to selecting ads that, for whatever reason, were not considered harmful. Eyeo, for its part, set about explaining this move through the creation of a counter-myth about its software and used to write on its website:

> [W]e have learned that most users wouldn't mind seeing better, more informative ads. In fact, the majority of people we've talked to are keenly aware that advertising plays a pivotal role in keeping content online free. Trouble is, most Internet ads are still low on quality and high on annoyance, and the two sides – users and advertisers – rarely come together. That's where we come in. We find ourselves uniquely positioned to broker a compromise that makes the Internet better for all parties. We aim to make the entire ecosystem more sustainable by encouraging true innovation and non-intrusive ad standards, on the one end, and a better user experience on the other.[83]

[80] Graber, 'Artificial Intelligence, Affordances and Fundamental Rights', at 199–201.

[81] See, e.g., German Federal Court of Justice (Bundesgerichtshof), *Werbeblocker [ad-blocker] II*, I ZR 154/16, 19 April 2018.

[82] '"Adblock-Plus"-Macher reichen Medienhäusern die Hand', *Neue Zürcher Zeitung*, 14 September 2016.

[83] Eyeo, 'Our Mission', https://eyeo.com/, state of the site as of October 2019, quoted in Graber, 'Artificial Intelligence, Affordances and Fundamental Rights', at 200.

The trade-off between information and inconvenience lay at the heart of the counter-myth proposed by Eyeo. However, as a commercial enterprise, Eyeo could not hide the fact that introducing whitelists was essential to guaranteeing the survival of its business model. Not surprisingly, several sites were unwilling to pay a fee and thus rejected the proposed myth. While some of these websites developed software that blocks users who block their ads, others asked their visitors to voluntarily accept ads as a contribution to high-quality news reporting.[84]

Pfaffenberger notes that 'the drama can drop out of the technology'.[85] The recursively interwoven dynamic can be brought to an end by unforeseen technological or social factors. Nissenbaum warns that this is dangerous, because people would then be 'inclined to accept that technology is neutral' and 'forget that there are values or politics involved in technology at all'.[86]

In sum, the metaphor of the technological drama illustrates how affordances find their way into a specific artefact as a reciprocal interaction between different constituencies involving discursive (social) and non-discursive (material) elements. Concretising the structural coupling of the sphere of meaning and the machine that occurs in the case of the internet shows us the nature of the interface between autopoiesis theory and STS.

5.3 CONCEPTUALISING NORMATIVITY IN THE DIGITAL SOCIETY

So far, the analysis has shown how legal sociology can be linked to STS through the concept of affordance co-production. As far as the methodology of legal sociology is concerned, it was emphasised that an internal perspective, which focuses on the specific logic and systematics of legal doctrine, must be distinguished from a sociological perspective, which observes the law from an external vantage point. This reflects an

[84] 'Block Shock: Internet Users Are Increasingly Blocking Ads, Including on Their Mobiles', *The Economist*, 6 June 2015.

[85] Pfaffenberger, 'Technological Dramas', at 308.

[86] Nissenbaum, 'From Preemption to Circumvention', at 1379.

important practice in legal sociology that goes back to Weber and Hart's distinction (discussed in Chapter 4) between external and internal aspects of the law. In sociological terms, the law is an autopoietic system: it uses existing legal communications to produce new legal communications. Like all other spheres of society that have become differentiated through modernisation, the law has become specialised so as to fulfil a particular function, namely stabilising and generalising normative expectations.[87]

If we understand the design and uptake of a digital artefact as a process of co-production of technical affordances, this enables us to formulate theories of the bottom-up emergence of normative expectations in relation to a novel technology. Ideas about the growth of law beyond the state also make it possible to establish a link to freedom of expression. Once again, the distinction between a sociological and a legal perspective is crucial. In Chapter 6, we will look for evidence in existing fundamental rights practice and regulation that supports the *legal* institutionalisation of technological conditions as a separate dimension of the right to free speech. We will begin by adopting a *sociological* perspective that treats fundamental rights as social institutions. According to Luhmann, an institution is a 'complex of factual behavioral expectations, which are actualised in the context of a social role, and which can always count on social consensus'.[88] Fundamental rights, as social institutions, represent a generalisation of normative expectations and lead to a broadening of the factual consensus.[89] When it comes to the technological preconditions of the right to free speech, it is therefore necessary to reflect on how normative expectations about technologies emerge. Before doing so, however, we need to clarify how the notion of normativity relates to theories of the emergence of law.

For legal practitioners, the first thing that comes to mind when considering the emergence of new legal norms is the legislature's activity. However, legal sociologists see things differently. Since its origins in

[87] Luhmann, *Law as a Social System*, at 147–150.

[88] Niklas Luhmann, *Grundrechte als Institution: Ein Beitrag zur politischen Soziologie*, Berlin: Duncker & Humblot, 1965, at 12–13 (translation by the author).

[89] Helmut Willke, *Stand und Kritik der neueren Grundrechtstheorie: Schritte zu einer normativen Systemtheorie*, Berlin: Duncker & Humblot, 1975, at 147.

the works of Ehrlich, Durkheim and Weber, legal sociology has postulated *legal pluralism*, defending the possibility of the growth of law from non-state sources. In his major work *Fundamental Principles of the Sociology of Law*, Ehrlich argued that the law which emerges directly from society should be considered the substantial source of law: 'At the present as well as at any other time, the center of gravity of legal development lies not in legislation, nor in juristic science, nor in judicial decision, but in society itself.'[90]

The law which grows directly from society, a form of law that he calls *living law*, is assumed to be even more important than statutory law and case law. Although *judge-made law* and *state law* have come to play a more critical role during modernisation, living law continues to represent the fundamental form of law. Emphasising the non-contractual origins of the private contract, Durkheim, too, stressed the social foundation of norms.[91] His argument was underpinned by references to binding behavioural expectations, which can impose obligations on parties even in the absence of a formal agreement.[92] Weber is also convinced that the state as a source of law is the exception rather than the rule.[93] He argues that norms often originate 'aboriginally'. This is a development that starts with an individual's subjective attitudes towards others, then progresses to habituation, an awareness of others' behaviour and, finally, *contrafactually confirmed expectations*.[94] For Weber, contrafactually confirmed expectations represent the essential elements of a legitimate order. The question of whether a legitimate order is custom ('convention' is the term Weber uses) or law depends on the modalities of enforcing such expectations. While the breach of a convention is sanctioned by disapproval within the social group concerned, breaking the law is externally sanctioned through physical or psychological coercion by the state or another legitimate power.[95]

90 Ehrlich, *Fundamental Principles of the Sociology of Law*, at lix.

91 Emile Durkheim, *The Division of Labor in Society*, translated by W. D. Halls, New York: Free Press, 1997 (1893), at 165.

92 Ibid., at 170.

93 Max Weber, *Economy and Society: An Outline of Interpretive Sociology*, translated by Günther Roth, Berkeley: University of California Press, 1978 (1922), at 753.

94 Ibid., at 754.

95 Ibid., at 34.

Luhmann developed his positivist concept of law at the end of the 1960s, in a critical engagement with the classics of legal sociology. Following Weber, albeit with an overall turn in his sociology from action to behaviour, he defines norms as 'counterfactually stabilised behavioural expectations'.[96] In doing so, Luhmann explicitly distances himself from the legal sociology of Theodor Geiger, for whom the unconditional validity of a norm no longer plays a role. According to Geiger, norms are only gradually binding. People either act in conformity with the norm or are subject to sanctions.[97] This means, Luhmann writes, that violations of a norm become conceptually unthinkable 'because the norm includes the alternative of sanctioned behaviour, whilst the deviation that is not subject to sanctions is, in contrast, considered to be a reduction in the degree of norm commitment.' [98] Luhmann criticises Geiger for conceptualising law without the possible antipode of unlaw. In doing so, Geiger overlooks the symbol of *the ought*,[99] which, for Luhmann, is the key to understanding normativity. As he sees it, the question of the normative ought's function should be posed in a more radical way than has so far been the case.[100]

Luhmann's search for an answer is guided by Hart's epochal 1961 work, *The Concept of Law*. Here, Hart deals with the nature of the ought on a more profound level than any legal theorist before him. In the process, he criticises John Austin, who arguably contended that a 'person's beliefs, fears, and motives' are irrelevant to the question of the ought and that all that matters is 'the *chance* or *likelihood* that the person having the obligation will suffer a punishment or "evil" at the hands of others in the event of disobedience'.[101] Hart correctly foresaw that the apparent scientific rigour of Austin's thesis explains its formative effect

[96] Niklas Luhmann, 'Normen in soziologischer Perspektive' (1969) *Soziale Welt*, 20 (1), pp. 28–48, at 37.

[97] Theodor Geiger, *Vorstudien zu einer Soziologie des Rechts*, 4th edn, reviewed and edited by Manfred Rehbinder, Berlin: Duncker & Humblot, 1987 (1947), at 63–67 and 205–209.

[98] Niklas Luhmann, *A Sociological Theory of Law*, translated by Elizabeth King-Utz and Martin Albrow, 2nd edn, Abingdon: Routledge, 2014 (1972), at 33, note 32.

[99] Ibid, at 33.

[100] Luhmann, 'Normen in soziologischer Perspektive', at 29.

[101] H. L. A. Hart, *The Concept of Law*, Oxford: Clarendon Press, 1961, at 81 (emphasis in the original).

on later generations of legal theorists, which continues to this day: 'To many later theorists this has appeared as a revelation, bringing down to earth an elusive notion and restating it in the same clear, hard, empirical terms as are used in science.'[102] Hart objects sharply to the predictive interpretation of obligation.

> If it were true that the statement that a person had an obligation meant that *he* was likely to suffer in the event of disobedience, it would be a contradiction to say that he had an obligation, e.g. to report for military service but that, owing to the fact that he had escaped from the jurisdiction, or had successfully bribed the police or the court, there was not the slightest chance of his being caught or made to suffer. In fact, there is no contradiction in saying this, and such statements are often made and understood.[103]

Like Hart, Luhmann stresses that the ought cannot be captured as a statistical regularity.[104] Instead, he argues, it is expressed mainly in the *expectation of counterfactual validity*, a thought that is best interpreted within the framework of systems theory.

From the perspective of systems theory, expectations represent the structures of a communication system,[105] with modern society having developed a range of cognitive and normative expectations.[106] While cognitive expectations are adapted if they are disappointed, normative expectations are generally upheld even if violations occur in individual cases.[107] As we have seen, law is the social system that stabilises and generalises normative expectations.[108] Because commonly shared values are precarious in a hypercomplex society, stabilising and generalising normative expectations is demanding. Positive law represents the evolutionary solution to this challenge,[109] allowing for the flexible adaptation of legal norms to social change, while simultaneously providing mechanisms to guarantee legal certainty. However, only a tiny subset of these

[102] Ibid., at 81. [103] Ibid., at 82 (emphasis in the original).

[104] Luhmann, *A Sociological Theory of Law*, at 33, note 33.

[105] Alfons Bora, 'Medialität des Wissens', in Gunnar F. Schuppert, et al. (eds.), *Herrschaft und Wissen*, Baden-Baden: Nomos, 2022, pp. 295–324, at 300.

[106] Luhmann, 'Normen in soziologischer Perspektive', at 36. [107] Ibid., at 35–37.

[108] Luhmann, *Law as a Social System*, at 147–148. [109] Ibid., at 261.

expectations are institutionalised in the form of positive law. Moreover, in everyday life, expectations continue to emerge from the midst of society.'[110]

In Chapter 4, I criticised Ladeur and Vesting's thesis about the gradual disappearance of normative expectations in contemporary society, which they ascribe to the enormous pressure to adapt faced by the 'relational subject'. In my view, they overlook the importance of the ought, as well as the possibility that social learning can lead to the emergence of new norms from the bottom up, and not only through legislative and judicial norm production. At the beginning of the twentieth century, Weber wrote that normative patterns continue to grow directly from social life, 'even in economically or socially complex and advanced societies'.[111] While Weber's observations focused on a relatively homogenous society, today's society is hypercomplex, heterogeneous and highly fragmented. For Luhmann, coping with complexity and contingency in the communicative processes is one of modern society's central problems. The distinction between the two types of expectation is a solution that society has developed to deal with this challenge. Although the law is primarily concerned with stabilising normative expectations, cognitive adaptations of such structures are possible. It is to be expected that 'in a cognitive context, normative expectations can also be changed through learning'.[112] According to Luhmann, this raises the question of the reflexivity of expectations, a question that must be clarified at the level of the observation of observations. At this level of reflection, the expecting subject must learn to expect not only the behaviour but also the expectations of others, including those directed at him- or herself.[113] When dealing with natural objects, it is sufficient to anticipate their behaviour, because science provides the expecting subject with the knowledge needed to reduce complexity. When it comes to human beings, learning is incomparably more demanding, because the expecting subject is in a situation of double contingency: both ego and alter are engaged in formulating

[110] Luhmann, 'Normen in soziologischer Perspektive', at 47–48.
[111] Weber, *Economy and Society*, at 753. [112] Luhmann, *Law as a Social System*, at 108.
[113] Luhmann, 'Normen in soziologischer Perspektive', at 32.

expectations. Accordingly, adaptation among humans depends on learned expectations about expectations.[114]

5.4 EXPECTATION FORMATION IN RELATION TO DIGITAL ARTEFACTS

How should we conceive of the formation and adjustment of behavioural expectations in relation to technology? When it comes to newly designed and introduced digital technologies, the user's ability to form or adjust expectations depends on whether he or she is faced with a 'trivial machine' or a 'non-trivial machine'. According to Heinz von Foerster's definition, a trivial machine always follows the same transformation function when converting input into output without changing its internal state in the process, meaning that its output can be predicted.[115] In contrast, a non-trivial machine can also change its internal state,[116] meaning that the output cannot be predicted from the input. The operations of a non-trivial machine are impenetrable.[117] The distinction between trivial and non-trivial machines is relevant, because it is impossible to discuss the evolution of behavioural expectations vis-à-vis a given digital technology without considering the extent to which that technology has reached a state of behavioural self-reference.

Technologies that incorporate artificial intelligence or machine-learning algorithms ('smart' technologies) are generally considered to behave like non-trivial machines. Communication between a user and the smart technology is characterised by a high degree of unpredictability. As this appears to resemble communication between humans, some scholars have suggested conceptualising the communication between a user and an algorithm in terms of a communication between ego and alter. Anna Beckers and Gunther Teubner, for example, have claimed that *personification* is the most successful strategy for coping with

[114] Ibid.

[115] Heinz von Foerster, *Wissen und Gewissen. Versuch einer Brücke*, Frankfurt: Suhrkamp, 1993, at 245–247.

[116] Ibid., at 247–252.

[117] Dirk Baecker, 'Technik im Datenraum', in Dirk Baecker, et al. (eds.), *Post-digitales Management*, Wiesbaden: Springer VS, 2023, pp. 243–256, at 244.

uncertainty in such situations, because personification transforms the relationship between a human and an algorithm 'from a subject-object relation into an Ego-Alter relation'.[118] Conversely, Dirk Baecker argues that attempts to 'anthropomorphise' technologies are of little sociological use and that it would be wrong to see technology as a social partner.[119] He invites us to question the thesis of the impenetrability of digital technology. According to Baecker, today's machines are still trivial. Although they are composed of a multitude of complicated interconnections, including database computations, inputs from sensors and platforms and many other components, they remain analytically and synthetically determinate.[120] He claims that 'it is not the technology but the society that develops it, lets it happen and uses it that is non-trivial'.[121] Baecker thus agrees with Luhmann, who defined technology as *functioning simplification*.[122] It fulfils this simplification function for various systems simultaneously, but in different ways. What is complex is the variety of possible perspectives from which a given data-processing technology can be observed.[123]

I agree with Baecker that smart technologies are *not* impenetrable and that it just takes time to 'get to the bottom of a complicated mechanism'.[124] However, his thesis requires further differentiation with regard to the user who employs this technology. Although, in practice, users tend to have different degrees of technological literacy, a typification in terms of experts and lay users makes sense from a conceptual point of view. Lay users are engaged in a synchronous and recursive relationship with their computer, which is updated with every click. They cannot understand how it functions or analyse its operations. They only see what appears on the computer screen; the underlying operations of the device remain hidden. What is visible on the computer screen is generally also the reference point of debates in legal practice and politics

[118] Anna Beckers and Gunther Teubner, *Three Liability Regimes for Artificial Intelligence: Algorithmic Actants, Hybrids, Crowds*, Oxford: Hart, 2021, at 26.

[119] Baecker, 'Technik im Datenraum', at 246 and 252. [120] Ibid., at 245–246.

[121] Ibid., at 253 (translation by the author).

[122] Luhmann, *Theory of Society*, vol. 1, at 317 (emphasis in the original).

[123] Baecker, 'Technik im Datenraum', at 247.

[124] Ibid., at 246 (translation by the author).

when specific features of digital technologies are discussed. However, sociologists of technology insist that the 'foreground' of the screen must be distinguished from the 'background' of the computer[125] – sometimes the term 'front end' is also used to refer to what users see and 'back end' to how a mechanism works.[126] Since the inner workings of a digital technology are mostly invisible, it is often said that they are hidden behind the walls of a 'black box'.[127] Taina Bucher describes the black box as 'an object whose inner functioning cannot be known – at least not by observation, since the blackness of the box obscures vision'.[128] She warns against falling for the suggestive power of this popular image: '[T]he widespread notion of algorithms as black boxes constitutes something of a red herring – that is, a piece of information that distracts from other (perhaps, more pressing) questions and issues to be addressed.'[129]

Indeed, the metaphor is often used for political purposes. According to Michel Callon and Latour, 'black boxes never remain fully closed or properly fastened [...] but macro-actors can do *as if* they were closed and dark'.[130] The black-box metaphor often suggests that something is unknown or that one cannot know it. Bucher speaks of the strategic use of unknowns: 'By mobilising unknowns strategically, organisations and individuals can insist that detection or prior knowledge was impossible.'[131] In a political-legal context, the black-box metaphor can be employed by tech companies to deny accountability from the outset or to reject liability after harm has been inflicted. Therefore, the myth of the black box should not be embraced lightly. It is not only policymakers

[125] Baecker, 'Digitalisierung als Kalkül', at 25, uses the distinction between 'surface' and 'subface'.

[126] Couldry, et al., 'Real Social Analytics', at 124.

[127] Frank Pasquale, *The Black Box Society: The Secret Algorithms That Control Money and Information*, Cambridge, MA: Harvard University Press, 2015.

[128] Taina Bucher, *If...Then: Algorithmic Power and Politics*, Oxford: Oxford University Press, 2018, at 43.

[129] Ibid., at 44.

[130] Michel Callon and Bruno Latour, 'Unscrewing the Big Leviathan: How Actors Macro-Structure Reality and How Sociologists Help Them to Do So', in Karin Knorr Cetina and Aaron Cicourel (eds.), *Advances in Social Theory and Methodology: Toward an Integration of Micro- and Macro-Sociologies*, London: Routledge, 1981, pp. 277–303, at 285 (emphasis in the original).

[131] Bucher, *If...Then: Algorithmic Power and Politics*, at 56.

and legal advisers, but also ordinary citizens, who should be critical of this image. In our day-to-day life, certain things seem impenetrable at first glance, but a closer look often reveals 'leaks, cracks, and ruptures that allow us to see into them'.[132]

According to Bucher, such a critical attitude should also be taken towards AI and machine-learning applications: 'While it might indeed be difficult to explain what patterns in the data are being caught by the model of a machine learning algorithm [. . .], the general principles and operational logics of these systems are very well-known.'[133] Experts can play an important role here. By means of speculative experimentation or 'reverse engineering' algorithms,[134] they can shed light on seemingly opaque technologies.[135] The aim should not be to fathom the precise functioning of a device, but rather to disseminate knowledge about its operational logic, so that policymakers can take up the thread and put the issue, if necessary, on their regulatory agenda. Experts and semi-professional activists also play a crucial role in detecting the adverse side effects of a smart technology. Within the technological drama, they can raise public awareness about the technology's social risks and mobilise civil society brokers and a broader public to build and invigorate alternative interpretations. As we saw in the case of the Facebook like button, such campaigns can ultimately lead to the development of normative expectations about the artefact's affordances.

Expert knowledge, disseminated through suitable channels, can also provide strategic guidance for lay users who are learning about digital technologies. A phenomenological approach is recommended for understanding how users develop and adapt expectations about the behaviour of digital mechanisms.[136] Guided by such an approach, Couldry and his co-authors have explored in a case study how social actors (both institutional and individual) perceive their relationship with all the automated processes that measure their interactions on social networks, despite not knowing much about how they work.[137] Their case

[132] Ibid., at 60. [133] Ibid., at 57.

[134] Gerardo Canfora, et al., 'Achievements and Challenges in Software Reverse Engineering' (2011) *Communication of the ACM*, 54 (4), pp. 142–151.

[135] Bucher, *If. . . Then*, at 60. [136] Ibid., at 61–63.

[137] Couldry, et al., 'Real Social Analytics' (2016), at 119–120.

study concludes that social actors attempt to maintain some reflexive control over such measurement processes, even though they run through the 'back end' of the digital world. In such attempts, the authors see central moments of social contestation in social networks.[138] Bucher compares those social actors to Alfred Schütz's 'well-informed citizens'[139] who try to develop rationally based opinions in a world of fundamental uncertainty.[140] In such moments of 'resistance and accommodation',[141] behavioural expectations about digital technologies are shaped, reflected, consolidated or adapted.

Legislation and judicial adjudication play a fundamental role in deciding which normative expectations will be stabilised and generalised. At an early stage in the uptake of a technology, normative expectations are mostly 'unsettled'.[142] It is often the courts that first address the social impact of a novel technology. Without appropriate norms, they usually try to interpret existing legal provisions broadly to find suitable solutions. However, at this stage, they lack sufficient information about the socio-political effects of the technology. Legislation mainly occurs at a more advanced settlement stage, when the political actors involved decide to draft a general and abstract framework to regulate the new technology. Of course, legislation in the area of complex digital systems is mostly experimental, as the examples of the General Data Protection Regulation, the Digital Services Act and the AI Act in the European Union show.[143]

[138] Ibid., at 134.

[139] Alfred Schütz, 'The Well-Informed Citizen: An Essay on the Social Distribution of Knowledge' (1946) *Social Research*, 13 (4), pp. 463–478.

[140] Bucher, *If...Then*, at 63.

[141] Andrew Pickering, 'The Mangle of Practice: Agency and Emergence in the Sociology of Science' (1993) *American Journal of Sociology*, 99 (3), pp. 559–589, at 567.

[142] Jonathan Zittrain, *The Future of the Internet and How to Stop It*, New Haven: Yale University Press, 2008, at 122.

[143] For details, see Chapter 7.

CHAPTER 6

The Digital Means of Free Speech

Normative Evidence

The previous chapters examined the effects of technology-driven social change on normative structures. Adopting a *sociological* perspective, we asked how normative orders adjust to the changed circumstances. In contrast, the present chapter reconstructs the technology-specific *normative-prescriptive* contours of freedom of expression as a fundamental right in the internet age. The focus will be placed on the technological conditions for free expression online, with a review of the latest developments in legal practice and regulation. A major issue is the trustworthiness of internet technology as a requirement for privacy protection, considering how relevant privacy is for effective freedom of expression on the internet. Other areas where the close link between technology and free speech is vital include the regulation of open internet access/net neutrality, the allocation of domain names and the governance of technical standards.

6.1 INTRODUCTION

The ability to freely form and express opinions is an essential element of human dignity and a necessary component of a democratic political system, making freedom of expression one of the most important fundamental rights. It is guaranteed by the International Bill of Rights[1] and

[1] The International Bill of Human Rights comprises the Universal Declaration of Human Rights, the International Covenant on Economic, Social and Cultural Rights and the International Covenant on Civil and Political Rights, along with its two Optional Protocols. See Office of the United Nations High Commissioner for Human Rights, www.ohchr.org/en/what-are-human-rights/international-bill-human-rights.

several regional human rights conventions, in addition to being a cornerstone of the constitution of every democratic state. Every state signatory of one or more of those international instruments has duties to respect, protect and fulfil this right vis-à-vis its citizens.

However, the digital age has fundamentally changed the meaning, volume and reach of free expression. It has also altered how opinions are expressed. The creation of the internet has established a platform that democratises free speech and allows anyone to express his or her thoughts. Digitisation and global connectivity have given individuals access to an immense wealth of information, as well as the ability to copy and distribute content worldwide at a click of a mouse. The fact that individuals are empowered to communicate with many addressees directly represents a radical break with the age of mass media, in which large media corporations acted as crucial intermediaries and information providers.

With the transition from mass-media-centred communication to decentralised networks, the technological conditions for freedom of expression have become a major constitutional issue. Under the conditions imposed by the internet, telecommunication companies, platform operators and equipment manufacturers have become the new intermediaries of free communication. While the power of states is limited to their respective territories, many of these companies operate globally. The asymmetry between global communications markets and national political structures makes effective enforcement of the right to freedom of expression on the internet more challenging. The following analysis brings together evidence about normative structures concerning the nexus of law and technology that emerge in legal practice and the regulation of freedom of expression. Questions touching on the implementation of fundamental rights will be addressed in Chapter 7.

6.2 TECHNOLOGY, PRIVACY AND FREE SPEECH

Most national constitutions in Europe guarantee the right to privacy as a fundamental right. It therefore comes as a surprise to many that privacy was first protected as a human right at the international level before being institutionalised at the national level,[2] a development that proponents of transnationalism evoke as a confirmation of their theory. The protection of privacy is closely linked to the protection of human dignity. The core areas of privacy protection are a person's private and family life, home or house and correspondence (Article 8 of the European Convention on Human Rights (ECHR)). In the internet age, privacy has become increasingly linked to the protection of personal data. The Charter of Fundamental Rights of the European Union (CFREU), which pertains to the primary law of the EU, explicitly guarantees the right to the protection of personal data (Article 8 CFREU). The EU's General Data Protection Regulation (GDPR), part of the EU's secondary law, is seen as the world's strictest and most effective data protection act.

Privacy law is a vast subject. The discussion in this book will be limited to normative evidence regarding privacy expectations in the interrelation with technology and free speech. The technologies and commercial dynamics of the virtual world have led to an unprecedented loss of privacy over the past decades,[3] a development that has also changed how the law deals with the relationship between privacy and freedom of expression. While court practice has long been based on the premise that there exist only competing interests to be weighed against each other, nowadays there is a growing awareness that guaranteeing the right to privacy is a prerequisite for freedom of expression.[4] As a result of the traditional liberal conception of rights in Western countries, as well as for procedural reasons (court access is reserved exclusively for individuals), both the courts and legal doctrine understand the right to privacy primarily as an individual right. Under the influence of the transformation of information and communication technologies since the 1970s, however, first sociologists (such as Robert Merton) and then philosophers (such as Helen Nissenbaum) began to argue for the recognition of

[2] Oliver Diggelmann and Maria Nicole Cleis, 'How the Right to Privacy Became a Human Right' (2014) *Human Rights Law Review*, 14 (3), pp. 441–458.

[3] Timothy Garton Ash, *Free Speech: Ten Principles for a Connected World*, New Haven and London: Yale University Press, 2016, at 286.

[4] Ibid., at 285.

the social value of privacy.[5] In data protection, the legal system has recently followed suit, seeking to protect the social dimension of privacy through regulation. The European Union's GDPR, which came into force in 2018, can be seen as a milestone as it provides an objective framework for the protection of user data.

As detailed in Chapters 4 and 5, the reality of the internet requires us to understand the development of normative structures as a process of co-production in which technological and social factors are both equally involved. Users who encounter a new technology often develop an internal model of its affordances,[6] which is then refined or corrected through the actual use of the technological artefact and connected to privacy expectations. These expectations only partially coincide with the established legal norms, since they are also linked to individual privacy expectations, which strongly depend on 'the context in which the user is interacting (e.g., media sharing sites, social networks, apps)'.[7] As we acquire more experience with how the new artefact or system works and our understanding of its implications improves,[8] normative expectations of privacy are revised, adapted or developed anew. Although the technologies of the twenty-first century have changed the parameters, empirical studies nonetheless conclude that 'the normative underpinnings of the value of privacy are still largely shared among members of society'.[9]

A vital aspect of the right to privacy and, by extension, free speech is the trustworthiness of the technological infrastructure. Only when people can trust the technology that they use to connect with others will

[5] For a discussion, see Priscilla M. Regan, 'Privacy and the Common Good: Revisited', in Beate Roessler and Dorota Mokrosinska (eds.), *Social Dimensions of Privacy: Interdisciplinary Perspectives*, Cambridge: Cambridge University Press, 2015, pp. 50–70, at 53–55.

[6] See also Nicholas Proferes, 'The Development of Privacy Norms', in Bart P. Knijnenburg, et al. (eds.), *Modern Socio-Technical Perspectives on Privacy*, Cham: Springer International Publishing, 2022, pp. 79–90, at 84–86.

[7] Theodore Patkos, et al., 'Privacy-by-Norms: Privacy Expectations in Online Interactions', *2015 IEEE International Conference on Self-Adaptive and Self-Organizing Systems Workshops (SASOW 2015)* (Cambridge, MA, 21 to 25 September 2015), pp. 1–6, at 2.

[8] See Ashwini Rao and Juergen Pfeffer, 'Types of Privacy Expectations' (2020) *Frontiers in Big Data*, 3, pp. 1–14, at 9.

[9] Regan, 'Privacy and the Common Good', at 58–59 and 66.

they be able to effectively enjoy their freedom of expression and information.[10] Trust in information and communication technology develops when users can expect equal protection for: 1) the integrity of the data and 2) the integrity of the network. The notion of integrity is defined broadly here as the absence of a violation of the wholeness of the data exchanged in a computer system.

6.2.1 DATA INTEGRITY

In searching for normative evidence for data integrity protection, our first point of reference is the case law of the European Court of Justice (ECJ). 'Fashion ID', a critical decision from 2019, involved Fashion ID, a fashion retailer, which had embedded the Facebook like button on its website. Whenever a user visited the Fashion ID website, the social plugin transmitted protected personal data – including the user's IP address, information on the desired content and the browser's technical data – to Facebook's European headquarters in Ireland.[11] The data transmission occurred 'regardless of whether or not the visitor is a member of the social network Facebook, has clicked on the Facebook "Like" button or is aware of such an operation'.[12] The ECJ ruled that Fashion ID and Facebook are 'data controllers' and, as such, must comply with EU data protection law. According to the Court, such data processing is only legal if the data subject (the user) gives consent before the data is collected. Consent given to Facebook alone would not be enough.[13] The ECJ failed to detail that the interference with the integrity of user data is caused by a technology known as a 'third-party cookie'.[14] HTTP cookies are small

[10] UN Human Rights Council (HRC), 'Report of the Special Rapporteur on the Promotion and Protection of the Right to Freedom of Opinion and Expression, Frank La Rue', 17th session, UN Doc A/HRC/17/27 (2011) (hereafter: HRC Report), at para 53; Council of the European Union, 'EU Human Rights Guidelines on Freedom of Expression Online and Offline', Foreign Affairs Council Meeting, 12 May 2014, at 18. See also Julie E. Cohen, *Configuring the Networked Self: Law, Code and the Play of Everyday Practice*, New Haven: Yale University Press, 2012, at 110–115.

[11] Judgment of 29 July 2019, *Fashion ID v. Verbraucherzentrale NRW*, C-40/17, ECLI:EU:C:2019:629, at para 85.

[12] Ibid., at para 75.

[13] Ibid., at para 102.

[14] Compare the discussion in Chapter 5 on Adblock Plus, which I characterised as a technical response to the third-party cookie.

blocks of data that a website can place on a visitor's computer to authenticate or track users. While authentication cookies can benefit the user, for example, by saving her from having to log in each time she visits the site, tracking or 'third-party' cookies mainly serve the advertising industry.[15] They tell the website that implanted the cookie which other websites the user visits while surfing the internet, thus enabling them to compile user profiles, a prerequisite for personalising advertising. Backed by the advertising industry, the third-party cookie was designed in the 1990s to work without user consent.[16] The decision to put a Trojan horse at the centre of network traffic was a massive infringement on the integrity of user data across the internet. Against this backdrop, the ECJ's decision in Fashion ID represents only a modest victory for online privacy. We will return to this issue below, when we discuss how the advertising industry established the third-party cookie as a technical standard.

Normative evidence for protecting the integrity of user data can also be found in the GDPR. The Regulation mentions the principle of integrity and confidentiality in data protection in Article 5(1)(f). This principle requires that personal data be 'processed in a manner that ensures appropriate security of the personal data, including protection against unauthorised or unlawful processing and against accidental loss, destruction or damage, using appropriate technical or organisational measures'. Although security concerns and privacy interests differ, there are many points of overlap, mainly because effective data protection depends on IT security. The pseudonymisation and encryption of personal data are mentioned in Article 32 GDPR as technical measures that shall be taken to protect processing security, but there does not yet exist any ECJ case law on the normative significance of encryption measures for the protection of data integrity. That said, the link between the use of encryption technology and the ability to protect the integrity of the data

[15] See Joseph Turow, 'Media Buying: The New Power of Advertising', in Matthew McAllister and Emily West (eds.), *The Routledge Companion to Advertising and Promotional Culture*, Abingdon: Routledge, 2013, pp. 99–111, at 100–101.

[16] Helen Nissenbaum, 'From Preemption to Circumvention: If Technology Regulates, Why Do We Need Regulation (and Vice Versa)?' (2011) *Berkeley Technology Law Journal*, 26 (3), pp. 1367–1386, at 1381.

exchanged in the communication flow is obvious: encryption makes it impossible for intrusive governments or data-hungry corporations to identify the parties involved in a communication by analysing the content of the communication.

Especially in political environments where censorship is prevalent or where there may be social or political repercussions for expressing certain views, anonymity can promote freedom of expression. The Special Rapporteur of the United Nations on freedom of opinion and expression considers anonymity on the internet to be covered by Article 19 of the International Covenant on Civil and Political Rights (ICCPR).[17] In his 2011 report, he called upon States 'to ensure that individuals can express themselves anonymously online and to refrain from adopting real-name registration systems'.[18] Moreover, there are rulings by the German Federal Court of Justice (Bundesgerichtshof, BGH) and the Constitutional Court of South Korea (CCSK) on the obligation to use 'real names' – the opposite of encryption.

In 2022, the BGH declared that Facebook's requirement that users give their real name violates a data-protection-motivated provision in the German Telemedia Act. The facts of the case occurred before the GDPR came into force, so the EU data protection rules that applied prior to that date informed the interpretation of the German law in question. Concretely, the BGH ruled that the plaintiff had a right to demand that Facebook allow him to change his profile name to a pseudonym and give him access to the functions of his user account under the chosen profile name.[19] According to the Court, the obligation to use one's real name, as laid down in Facebook's terms of use, violates Paragraph 13(6) (first sentence) of the Telemedia Act, which explicitly entitles users to the anonymous and pseudo-anonymous use of telemedia.[20] This Paragraph is a data protection rule, reflecting the idea that 'anonymous use is immanent to the Internet'.[21] Highlighting the link between anonymity and the right to informational self-determination, the BGH writes:

[17] HRC Report, at para 23. [18] Ibid., at para 84.

[19] BGH, *Klarnamenpflicht [real-name requirement], Facebook*, III ZR 3/21, 27 January 2022, at para 13.

[20] Ibid., at para 18. [21] Ibid., at paras 61 and 63.

> In order to protect the users' right to informational self-determination, it is therefore necessary that the user is not forced to act under a real name in the network. The possibility of using a pseudonym as a profile name is an effective method of self-protection [...]. The use of a pseudonym reduces the probability of identification by third parties [...]. The data subject retains better control over the extent to which the data he or she publishes on the network and the [...] automated processing of this data and its cross-platform linkage with other data is at least made more difficult.[22]

A 2012 ruling of the CCSK ought to be mentioned here, as it established a direct link between the requirement to use a real name, privacy and freedom of expression. The CCSK declared that the mandatory use of real names, which was required by Articles 44 and 45 of the Korean Act on Promotion of Information and Communications Network Utilisation and Data Protection, violated the constitutional right to free speech.[23] The Court reasoned that the public benefits of the legislation with regard to the fight against hate speech and misinformation were insufficient to justify restrictions on the freedom of expression. Instead of achieving its goal, the requirement that internet users give their real names discouraged them from freely expressing themselves, out of fear of punishment by the authorities. Given the importance of privacy for free speech, the CCSK concluded that the statutory requirement mandating the disclosure of users' real names violated the freedom of expression and 'the self-determination of personal information of the users'.[24]

6.2.2 NETWORK INTEGRITY

Normative evidence for the integrity of networks can be found in a famous decision of the German Federal Constitutional Court (Bundesverfassungsgericht, BVerfG) from 2008. In this case, the

[22] Ibid., at para 50 (translation by the author; internal references omitted).

[23] For a summary of the decision, see Whon-il Park and Graham Greenleaf, 'Korea Rolls Back "Real Name" and ID Number Surveillance', *University of New South Wales Research Paper*, 2012-57, October 2012, Sydney: University of New South Wales, https://papers.ssrn.com/sol3/papers.cfm?abstract_id=2187232.

[24] Ibid., at 2–3.

BVerfG recognised a new fundamental right, namely the right to the confidentiality and integrity of information technology (IT) systems.[25] This new right, also known as the 'IT-Grundrecht' (fundamental right protecting the integrity of IT systems), is designed to protect users' trust in the integrity of the IT system they use for information and communication purposes. An 'information technology system' is defined here as software and hardware working together in a system of networked computers, a definition based on the state of discussion in the information technology literature at the time of the ruling.[26] However, the Court indicated that this term and the associated implications for the protection of fundamental rights are to be understood flexibly, in line with technological development.[27] The Court further clarified that the technology must provide detailed insight into a person's personality.[28] The development of complex information technology systems, which allow for a wide range of uses, all of which entail the creation, processing and storage of data, creates new dangers for the personality of users:

> Above all, the system's network connection gives third parties the technical ability to access it, including for the purposes of spying on or manipulating data stored in the system. Individuals will not always be able to detect such third-party access; in any case, they have only limited powers to prevent it. Information technology systems have now evolved to such complexity that taking effective social or technical measures of self-protection presents a considerable challenge and may not be feasible at least for the average user.[29]

The Court ruled that the newly adopted fundamental right prevented the government from using spying or surveillance software to infiltrate IT systems, absent exceptional circumstances. Infiltration is to be understood as a covert intrusion into an information system that makes it possible to monitor the use of the target system, view stored media

[25] BVerfGE 120, 274, 27 February 2008. [26] Ibid., at para 4.

[27] Wolfgang Hoffmann-Riem, 'Der grundrechtliche Schutz der Vertraulichkeit und Integrität eigengenutzter informationstechnischer Systeme' (2008) *JuristenZeitung*, 63 (21), pp. 1009–1022, at 1012.

[28] BVerfGE 120, 274, at para 137. [29] Ibid., at para 180 (translation by the Court).

and control the target system remotely – that is spying on a system as a whole.[30]

The new right is derived from the fundamental right to the protection of personality (Article 2(1) of the German Constitution (Grundgesetz der Bundesrepublik Deutschland, GG)) in conjunction with the protection of human dignity in Article 1(1) GG. It thus has the same constitutional basis as the fundamental right to informational self-determination, which, in 1983, the BVerfG also derived from the fundamental right to the protection of personality in conjunction with the protection of human dignity.[31] While the right to informational self-determination protects individuals against the unlimited collection, storage, use and disclosure of their personal data, the IT-Grundrecht specifically aims to protect the trust of individuals in the confidentiality and integrity of information technology systems in the face of the risk that state authorities secretly infiltrate these systems.[32] Wolfgang Hoffmann-Riem, a former justice of the BVerfG and rapporteur for the case, describes what is unique about the new fundamental right as follows:

> Protection (only) against the collection and further use of personal data does not go far enough if it does not also include protection against access to one's own information technology system, which is used for communicative development, the undisturbed functioning of which is regularly relied upon, and the infiltration or even manipulation of which poses risks to the protection of personality which the protection of the collected data itself cannot adequately avert.[33]

In recognising a new aspect of the fundamental right to personality, the BVerfG took into account the new risks that have become apparent due to technological development. The purpose of the fundamental right is to defend the integrity of a user's own IT system against attacks by the state involving the infiltration of that system. Network integrity protects not only the autonomy of individuals but also certain trans-individual

[30] Ibid., at paras 5 and 122. [31] BVerfGE 65, 1, 15 December 1983.

[32] BVerfGE 120, 274, at para 166.

[33] Hoffmann-Riem, 'Der grundrechtliche Schutz der Vertraulichkeit und Integrität eigengenutzter informationstechnischer Systeme', at 1016 (translation by the author).

(objective) aspects of free communication on the internet.[34] However, goals that go beyond the defensive function of the fundamental right or do not solely protect against state activities must be achieved through legislation.[35] It is in this spirit that the Swiss Parliament has responded to the initiative to create a new fundamental right to digital integrity (see discussion in Chapter 1), having decided that the effective protection of this objective must be achieved through the creation of a statute that is binding not only on the state but also on private actors.

6.3 PROTECTING THE OPEN INTERNET

Timothy Garton Ash summarises the link between freedom of expression and the concept of 'net neutrality' as follows: 'If you are to discriminate between different kinds of mail, you have to know what is in the different envelopes or boxes.'[36] As the quote suggests, net neutrality is associated with prohibiting discrimination between different types of content in online data distribution. However, net neutrality is an oxymoron, insofar as it suggests that we see the technology that runs the internet as something neutral. In Chapters 4 and 5, we learned that technological neutrality is a tricky concept. Technology is not neutral: it has affordances that are shaped by processes of production and uptake, involving many actors and interactions related to both material and immaterial things.

On a normative level, the term 'net neutrality' is closely associated with debates that, starting from civil society circles, call for the open infrastructure of the internet be legally protected. As discussed in Chapter 3, these debates began around 1999 when academics in the United States and Europe warned of the risks of discriminatory broadband treatment by the major telecommunications providers.[37] Over

[34] Vagias Karavas, 'Das Computer-Grundrecht: Persönlichkeitsschutz unter information stechnischen Bedingungen' (2010) *WestEnd: neue Zeitschrift für Sozialforschung*, 7 (2), pp. 95–105.

[35] Hoffmann-Riem, 'Der grundrechtliche Schutz der Vertraulichkeit und Integrität eigengenutzter informationstechnischer Systeme', at 1013–1014 and 1019.

[36] Garton Ash, *Free Speech*, at 358.

[37] Christopher T. Marsden, *Network Neutrality: From Policy to Law to Regulation*, Manchester: Manchester University Press, 2016, at 29.

time, the scope of protection of the alleged norm sharpened. A milestone in this regard was the US Federal Communications Commission's (FCC) 'Open Internet Order' of 26 February 2015, requiring fixed and wireless internet access providers to respect the principle of internet openness and abstain from blocking, throttling or paid-prioritisation practices.[38] However, this decision was reversed with a change of leadership at the FCC, initiated by the Trump administration. The attempts made since then to protect the principle have been thwarted by political and legal obstacles. The EU has thus come to set the pace in the development of normative standards for regulating the open internet. The EU's new Open Internet Regulation (OIR) has been a binding instrument directly applicable in all Member States since 28 November 2015.[39]

Under the OIR, internet service providers are prohibited from blocking or slowing internet traffic. Exceptions are limited to network congestion management, provided that similar traffic categories are treated equally. The rules provide for the right of end-users 'to access and distribute information and content, use and provide applications and services, and use terminal equipment of their choice' (Article 3(1) OIR). The European Court of Justice ensures that these rules are effectively enforced in the EU member-states. In the *Telenor v. Hungary* decision of 15 September 2020, the ECJ delivered the first interpretation of the OIR.[40] At issue was the interpretation of Article 3 OIR, the central provision on open access to the internet in Europe, against the background of so-called zero-rating practices. More specifically, the problem concerned one of Telenor's tariff options by means of which a subscriber in Hungary benefits from a 'zero tariff' for using certain services and applications, whereas the use of 'non-zero tariff' services and applications is blocked or slowed down. The Court did not prohibit zero-rating

[38] FCC, 'Protecting and Promoting the Open Internet', GN Docket No. 14–28, Report and Order on Remand, Declaratory Ruling, and Order, 30 FCC Rcd 5601 (2015), at 7–8.

[39] Regulation (EU) 2015/2120 of the European Parliament and of the Council of 25 November 2015 laying down measures concerning open internet access (Open Internet Regulation), OJ L 310/1, 26 November 2015.

[40] Judgment (GC) of 15 September 2020, *Telenor v. Hungary*, Joined Cases C-807/18 and C-39/19, ECLI:EU:C:2020:708.

outright, stating that Article 3(2), when read in conjunction with Article 3(1), does not exclude agreements between a provider and a particular end-user.[41] However, if zero-rating agreements are 'liable to limit the exercise of end-users' rights [...] on a significant part of the market', they must comply with Article 3(3).[42] Therefore, traffic management measures that result in some services being prioritised while all others are blocked or slowed down (as in the case at hand) are impermissible, because they are based on 'commercial considerations', which are prohibited by Article 3(3).[43]

Zero-rating practices were also at issue in subsequent proceedings bearing on the open internet. In the *Vodafone v. Germany* decision of 2 September 2021, the Court defined zero-rating more generally as a commercial practice,

> whereby an internet access provider applies a 'zero tariff', or a tariff that is more advantageous, to all or part of the data traffic associated with an application or category of specific applications, offered by partners of that access provider. Those data are therefore not counted towards the data volume purchased as part of the basic package. Such an option, offered in the context of limited packages, thus allows internet access providers to increase the attractiveness of their offer.[44]

By incentivising the use of specific applications and services in a non-transparent manner, this practice significantly constrains subscribers in the exercise of their rights as end-users of internet access services in the sense of Article 3(1) OIR. The Court concluded that Vodafone's zero-rating practices violated net neutrality and were thus unlawful under the OIR. As a result of the ECJ ruling in *Vodafone v. Germany* (and two more rulings of 2 September 2021, including C-5/20 *VzBV v. Vodafone* [tethering] and C-34/20 *Telekom Deutschland v. Germany* [throttling]), the Body of

[41] Ibid., at para 42. [42] Ibid., at para 46.

[43] Andrew D. Murray, 'Regulation 2015/2120/EU Laying Down Measure concerning Open Internet Access', in Arno R. Lodder and Andrew D. Murray (eds.), *EU Regulation of E-Commerce: A Commentary*, 2nd edn, Cheltenham: Edward Elgar, 2022, pp. 281–307, at para 8.38.

[44] Judgment of 2 September 2021, *Vodafone v. Germany*, C-854/19, ECLI:EU:C:2021:675, at para 15.

European Regulators for Electronic Communications (BEREC), the EU's telecom regulator, revised its open internet guidelines on 9 June 2022.[45] As the regulator now considers 'any differentiated pricing practices which are not application-agnostic to be inadmissible' for internet access offers, the new guidelines leave virtually no room for zero-rating.[46]

Normative evidence for the link between open internet access/net neutrality and freedom of expression can be found in the European Court of Human Rights (ECtHR) case law on Article 10 of the ECHR.[47]

Article 10 ECHR guarantees freedom of expression and information as a fundamental right. According to the case law of the ECtHR, Article 10 ECHR covers not only the form and content of information but also the technical means used to transmit this information. The Court's conviction that the technical means of communication are essential for the effective enjoyment of freedom of expression first became visible in *Autronic AG v. Switzerland*, a case from 1990 involving satellite technology. In the decision, the ECtHR held that 'Article 10 applied not only to the content of information but also to the means of transmission or reception since any restriction imposed on the means necessarily interferes with the right to receive and impart information'.[48] It has been argued in the literature that the *Autronic*-based case law of the ECtHR suggests the Court's (implicit) recognition of a 'free-standing transmission right' as part of Article 10 ECHR.[49]

The ECtHR's more recent case law reflects the fact that, with the establishment of the internet as the primary distribution medium, the technical means of transmission and reception have become a critical condition of free speech.[50] This case law has also guided the ECJ, most

45 For all references, see BEREC, 'BEREC Guidelines on the Implementation of the Open Internet Regulation', BoR (22) 81, 9 June 2022, at para 1, note 3.

46 Ibid., at para 40b.

47 Parts of this section are an updated version of Christoph B. Graber, 'Net Neutrality: A Fundamental Right in the Digital Constitution?' (2023) *Indiana Journal of Global Legal Studies*, 30 (2), pp. 197–226.

48 *Autronic AG v. Switzerland* App. no. 12726/87 (ECtHR, 22 May 1990), at para 47.

49 Lorna Woods, 'Article 11', in Steve Peers, et al. (eds.), *The EU Charter of Fundamental Rights: A Commentary*, Oxford: Hart, 2021, pp. 333–369, at 363.

50 See *Yıldırım v. Turkey* App. no. 3111/10 (ECtHR, 18 December 2012), at para 50 (with internal reference to *Autronic AG v. Switzerland*).

recently when, with reference to the legality of upload filters, it specified that although Article 10 ECHR does not prohibit prior restraints on a means of dissemination per se, 'such restraints pose such a risk to compliance with that fundamental right that a particularly tight legal framework is required'.[51]

Arguably, net neutrality is an important aspect of the novel 'right to transmit', which is protected under Article 10 ECHR.[52] Although the ECtHR has not explicitly addressed issues of net neutrality or open internet access in the context of Article 10, it may do so in the future. This is because the Court understands the ECHR as a 'living instrument, which must be interpreted in the light of present-day conditions'.[53] The judge-made law emerging from such a dynamic interpretation of the Convention is constantly required to prove its legitimacy. Already in *Tyrer v. United Kingdom,* the first enunciation of this principle, the Court indicated the sources to which it could refer to legitimise an evolutive interpretation of individual Convention provisions.[54] The sources of inspiration mentioned in *Tyrer* include the commonly accepted standards of the Member States of the Council of Europe,[55] with the recommendations of the Committee of Ministers on important issues of social or technological development providing important indications of these normative standards. Indeed, the ECtHR has been using such recommendations in several judgments 'for the purpose of interpretation of the Convention'.[56]

With regard to an evolutive interpretation of Article 10 ECHR in the context of the internet, the Court will, at present, most probably seek

[51] Judgment (GC) of 26 April 2022, *Poland v. European Union,* C-401/19 2022, ECLI:EU: C:2022:297, at para 68.

[52] Jasper P. Sluijs, 'From Competition to Freedom of Expression: Introducing Article 10 ECHR in the European Network Neutrality Debate' (2012) *Human Rights Law Review,* 12 (3), pp. 509–554, at 541–542; Woods, 'Article 11', at 336–364.

[53] *Vo v. France* App. no. 53924/00 (ECtHR (GC), 8 July 2004), at para 82.

[54] *Tyrer v. United Kingdom* App. no. 5856/72 (ECtHR, 25 April 1978), at paras 33–34.

[55] Ibid., at paras 15–16; see Christos Rozakis, 'The European Judge as a Comparatist' (2005) *Tulane Law Review,* 80 (1), pp. 257–279, at 261–262.

[56] *Demir and Baykara v. Turkey* App. no. 34503/97 (ECtHR (GC), 12 November 2008), at para 74. See also *Öneryildiz v. Turkey* App. no. 48939/99 (ECtHR (GC), 30 November 2004), at para 59; Rozakis, 'The European Judge as a Comparatist', at 274.

guidance from Committee of Ministers Recommendation CM/Rec (2016)1 on net neutrality.[57] The main target of this recommendation is cases of interference with internet traffic that 'result in blocking, discrimination or prioritization of specific types of content, applications or services'.[58] For the Committee of Ministers, such practices raise concerns about the freedom of expression, the right to private life and personal data protection. Drawing a direct link between Article 10 ECHR and net neutrality, the Committee continues to emphasise that

> [t]he principle of network neutrality underpins non-discriminatory treatment of Internet traffic and the users' right to receive and impart information and to use services of their choice. It reinforces the full exercise and enjoyment of the right to freedom of expression because Article 10 of the Convention applies not only to the content of information but also to the means of its dissemination.[59]

The Committee of Ministers is obviously cross-referencing the ECtHR's reasoning in *Autronic*, but since the ECtHR has not yet established a direct link with net neutrality or open internet access in its case law on Article 10 ECHR, the scope of the 'right to transmit' is unclear. Would this novel right only be invoked for the benefit of end-users? What if an internet access provider were to use Article 10 ECHR as the basis for a complaint against a government measure regulating net neutrality, such as the EU's OIR?

The Charter of Fundamental Rights of the European Union provides for a right in Article 11 that corresponds with Article 10 ECHR.[60] While the CFREU is part of the primary law, the EU enacted detailed rules on net neutrality in the OIR discussed above, which is part of secondary legislation. In its interpretation of the OIR, the ECJ has not established a direct link between net neutrality/open internet access and the fundamental rights guaranteed in Article 10 ECHR or Article 11 CFREU.

[57] Council of Europe Committee of Ministers, 'Recommendation CM/Rec(2016)1 of the Committee of Ministers to member States on protecting and promoting the right to freedom of expression and the right to private life with regard to network neutrality', adopted by the Committee of Ministers on 13 January 2016 at the 1,244th meeting of the Ministers' Deputies.

[58] Ibid., at para 2. [59] Ibid., at para 4. [60] Woods, 'Article 11', at 333.

6.4 NAMING, ADDRESSING AND ROUTING FREE SPEECH

Jonathan Zittrain has described the internet's architecture as a layered structure comparable to an hourglass.[61] At the bottom, we find the physical layer (cables, airwaves, etc.), with the layer of applications above it, while, at the top, we find the social layer of behaviours enabled by the internet, with the content layer underneath it. At the centre of the hourglass, at the point of contact between the lower and upper layers, is the protocol layer, which ensures that connections are established between communication partners and that data flows. As a result of this architecture, the allocation of numerical internet addresses has rightly been termed the 'master key' to the entire global internet.[62] The Internet Corporation for Assigned Names and Numbers (ICANN) has been administering internet domain names and Internet Protocol (IP) addresses, as well as coordinating the root hierarchy,[63] since the late 1990s.[64] Without IP addresses, the flow of information on the internet would not be possible. To understand why this is the case, it is necessary to recall that information online is divided into data packets and that each packet is sent individually. The packet's route is not predetermined, but depends on the network load. The packets are only reassembled at their destination. The prerequisite for data packets to reach their destination is that each packet must be provided with a numerical address (i.e. the IP address), and every computer connected to the internet must likewise have an IP address. Because numeric addresses are not very user-friendly for internet traffic, IP addresses are assigned domain names – that is, names in alphabetical form, such as www.wikipedia.org. These domain names are used as addresses in place of the IP numbers when users surf the internet or send emails. However, the alphabetical domain names must be translated into numerical IP

[61] Jonathan Zittrain, *The Future of the Internet and How to Stop It*, New Haven: Yale University Press, 2008, at 67–68.

[62] Garton Ash, *Free Speech*, at 354.

[63] See note 75 and surrounding text.

[64] Milton L. Mueller and Farzaneh Badiei, 'Inventing Internet Governance: The Historical Trajectory of the Phenomenon and the Field', in Laura DeNardis, et al. (eds.), *Researching Internet Governance: Methods, Frameworks, Futures, Information Policy*, Cambridge, MA: The MIT Press, 2020, pp. 59–83, at 63–65.

addresses in order for the data packets to reach their destination.[65] The translation of domain names into IP numbers (and vice versa) is accomplished by a system of root servers.[66] In carrying out its naming, addressing and rooting functions (the so-called IANA functions[67]), ICANN ensures that the network of networks is held together and that global connectivity is guaranteed.[68] Thus, it is fair to say that ICANN guarantees critical technical preconditions of the freedom of expression and information on the internet.

ICANN's initial legal foundation was a contract with the US National Telecommunications and Information Administration (NTIA).[69] Since 1998, this contract has provided the US government with leverage to exercise oversight over ICANN's management of the Domain Name System (DNS).[70] However, the US government's control over ICANN has long been criticised on the international level. After Edward Snowden revealed the extent of US surveillance of internet traffic, the United States decided to cede control, fearing that otherwise numerous governments would challenge ICANN's authority in internet governance.[71] As control over ICANN shifted to the 'Global Internet Community' in 2016,[72] the initial public-private legal structure was transformed into a multi-stakeholder structure, involving governments,

65 Milton L. Mueller, *Ruling the Root: Internet Governance and the Taming of Cyberspace*, Cambridge, MA: The MIT Press, 2002, at 6.

66 Jochen von Bernstorff, 'The Structural Limitations of Network Governance: ICANN as a Case in Point', in Christian Joerges, et al. (eds.), *Transnational Governance and Constitutionalism*, Oxford and Portland: Hart, 2004, pp. 257–285, at 265.

67 See, e.g., US National Telecommunications and Information Administration, 'IANA Functions', www.ntia.gov/category/iana-functions.

68 A. Michael Froomkin, 'Wrong Turn in Cyberspace: Using ICANN to Route Around the APA and the Constitution' (2000) *Duke Law Journal*, 50 (1), pp. 17–186, at 42.

69 Ibid., at 70–71.

70 David G. Post and Danielle Kehl, 'Controlling Internet Infrastructure: Part 1: The "IANA Transition," and Why It Matters for the Future of the Internet', Washington, DC: Open Technology Institute, April 2015, at 17.

71 Mueller and Badiei, 'Inventing Internet Governance', at 73.

72 ICANN, 'Stewardship of IANA Functions Transitions to Global Internet Community as Contract with U.S. Government Ends', 1 October 2016, www.icann.org/en/announcements/details/stewardship-of-iana-functions-transitions-to-global-internet-community-as-contract-with-us-government-ends-1-10-2016-en.

industry, technical experts and civil society.[73] As of October 2016, neither the United States nor any other government or international organisation has control over the internet, but rather a private non-profit corporation representing the community of internet stakeholders.[74] This development is extraordinary if we consider that the functions ICANN performs are of critical importance to all nations and organisations, and indeed to all of the planet's inhabitants.

ICANN's power to govern the DNS stems from its de facto control over the DNS root.[75] As this power could be used to regulate and enforce content controls on the internet,[76] a limitation is needed. Since the 2016 transition removed government control, ICANN's Bylaws are the only instrument that limits ICANN's power.[77] Because these Bylaws define and limit the scope of ICANN's activity, they function analogously to a state constitution,[78] even though ICANN is legally a private corporation. Section 1.1(a) of the Bylaws limits ICANN's power significantly by defining its mission narrowly as 'to ensure the stable and secure operation of the internet's unique identifier system'. In order to fulfil its mission, ICANN 'coordinates the allocation and assignment of names in the root zone' of the DNS (Section 1.1(a)(i)). The root zone (sometimes referred to as 'root' or 'legacy root') is the name for the top of the DNS hierarchy,[79] consisting of a file containing 'the list of machines that have the master lists of registrations in each [top-level domain]'.[80] This list is thus the authoritative record of all top-level domains (TLDs),[81]

[73] Niels ten Oever, 'Productive Contestation, Civil Society, and Global Governance: Human Rights as a Boundary Object in ICANN' (2019) *Policy & Internet*, 11 (1), pp. 37–60, at 38.

[74] See Rolf H. Weber, *Internet Governance at the Point of No Return*, Zurich: EIZ Publishing, 2021, at 55.

[75] Mueller, *Ruling the Root*, at 47–56.

[76] Froomkin, 'Wrong Turn in Cyberspace', at 47–48.

[77] ICANN, 'Bylaws for Internet Corporation for Assigned Names and Numbers: A California Nonprofit Public-Benefit Corporation – ICANN', as amended 9 January 2025, www.icann.org/resources/pages/governance/bylaws-en.

[78] For the distinction between formal and functional perspectives on the concept of 'constitution', see Chapter 2.

[79] Mueller, *Ruling the Root*, at 47–48. [80] Froomkin, 'Wrong Turn in Cyberspace', at 42.

[81] Kenneth Merrill, 'Domains of Control: Governance of and by the Domain Name System', in Francesca Musiani, et al. (eds.), *The Turn to Infrastructure in Internet Governance*, New York: Palgrave Macmillan, 2016, pp. 89–106, at 94.

including both generic and country-code TLDs. Generic TLDs (gTLDs) include suffixes such as '.com', '.org' and '.net', while country-code TLDs (ccTLDs) provide country-specific address spaces with two-letter endings like '.us', '.uk' and '.ch'.[82]

According to Section 1.1 (a) (i) of the Bylaws, ICANN coordinates 'the development and implementation of policies concerning the registration of second-level domain names' in gTLDs. It does so through accredited registries and registrars, which must sign contracts with ICANN as a condition to access the root. While registries administer top-level domain names, registrars sell domain names. Those contracts (registry agreements and registrar accreditation agreements) provide ICANN with the leverage needed to compel registries and registrars (and thus, by extension, hundreds of millions of users) to respect the specific commitments and values set out in the Bylaws (Section 1.2). As a general commitment, Section 1.2(a) requires ICANN to operate for the benefit of 'the Internet community as a whole'; the values listed in Section 1.2(b) include, inter alia, 'internationally recognised human rights'. The Bylaws contain provisions designed to ensure that ICANN conducts its activities within the narrowly defined scope of its authority and does not directly or indirectly infringe on values held dear by the multi-stakeholder community. To this end, Section 1.1 (b) states that ICANN shall not act outside the bounds of its mission. The most crucial provision for the protection of freedom of expression and information is Section 1.1 (c), which states that 'ICANN shall not regulate (i.e., impose rules and restrictions on) services that use the Internet's unique identifiers or the content that such services carry or provide, outside the express scope of Section 1.1 (a)'.

The question then arises as to how to resolve conflicts that would result from complaints that ICANN or its contractors have acted outside the scope of the Bylaws. The idea of using ICANN's Uniform Dispute

[82] ICANN is responsible for delegating a trustee for each ccTLD, who will then administer and control the ccTLD. However, according to Section 4.2 (d) (i) of the Bylaws, ICANN is not competent to review disputes relating to ccTLD delegations and re-delegations. This is because governments consider ccTLDs to fall under their sovereignty. See Peter K. Yu, 'The Origins of ccTLD Policymaking' (2004) *Cardozo Journal of International and Comparative Law*, 12 (2), pp. 387–408, at 402.

Resolution Policy (UDPR)[83] for this purpose has been ruled out. Due to the UDPR's success at effectively and efficiently resolving conflicts between domain names and trademarks, demands were made in the run-up to the 2016 stewardship transition that ICANN use its contractual leverage over the DNS to combat illegal content, including child pornography, copyright infringement and so on.[84] This proposal rightly failed to gain acceptance, as commenters warned that content regulation of this sort goes beyond ICANN's mission as set out in Section 1.1(c) of the Bylaws.[85] The narrow formulation of ICANN's mission can be seen as the result of the lesson learned from the so-called .xxx incident.[86] This controversy arose in 2005, when the US government vetoed ICANN's plans to create a new top-level domain for adult content. ICANN, which at the time was still operating under a contract with a branch of the US government, had carefully reviewed an application by ICM Registry, a US-based domain name registry, to introduce .xxx as a 'red light district' on the internet. The idea behind the proposal was to designate a space for adult content on the internet. The clear designation was intended to make it easier both for those seeking and for those fighting such content to identify it.[87] The US government's veto was seen as an attack on the fundamental right to freedom of expression, as it was assumed that a specific type of opinion would be expressed under the top-level domain.[88] The execution of the .xxx gTLD registry agreement was approved by the ICANN Board only in March 2011 after concerns had dissipated within the Government Advisory Committee (GAC – for

[83] A. Michael Froomkin, 'ICANN's "Uniform Dispute Resolution Policy": Causes and (Partial) Cures' (2002) *Brooklyn Law Review*, 67 (3), pp. 605–718.

[84] For a discussion, see David G. Post and Danielle Kehl, 'Controlling Internet Infrastructure: Part I', at 22–23.

[85] David G. Post and Danielle Kehl, 'Controlling Internet Infrastructure: The "IANA Transition" and ICANN Accountability, Part II', Washington, DC: Open Technology Institute, September 2015, at 5.

[86] See Jonathan Weinberg, 'Governments, Privatization, and "Privatization": ICANN and the GAC' (2011) *Michigan Telecommunications and Technology Law Review*, 18, pp. 189–218, at 203.

[87] Milton L. Mueller, *Networks and States: The Global Politics of Internet Governance*, Cambridge, MA: The MIT Press, 2010, at 71.

[88] Ibid., at 202.

ICANN's organisational structure, see below).[89] This example shows how dangerous it is for freedom of expression when states are given a veto over the development of gTLDs. Against this background, it is understandable that – in the context of the IANA transition in 2016 – limiting state influence to an advisory role within the GAC was a priority.

That said, how should conflicts between states, corporations, standards experts and other stakeholders over important technical, economic, legal, political and cultural issues be resolved within ICANN?[90] How can ICANN pursue a network policy independent of state influence without running the risk of encouraging excessive commercialisation or violating mandatory provisions of public international law in certain cases? ICANN's answer in the 2016 IANA transition was that conflicts should be resolved by the community of ICANN stakeholders itself (Article 4 of the Bylaws).

This seemingly straightforward solution is, however, complicated to implement. ICANN's organisational structure comprises supporting organisations, advisory committees and the ICANN Board of Directors. Decisions are taken exclusively by the ICANN Board, which has 16 voting members. In keeping with ICANN's multi-stakeholder approach, the Board comprises representatives from academia, industry and civil society from around the world.[91] Decisions on policy for the technical management of the internet are prepared by the supporting organizations. The advisory committees have an advisory role on specific issues. As provided by Section 12.2(a)(ii), national governments are represented in the GAC. Accordingly, the power of national governments within ICANN is limited to exercising advisory functions. Section 12.2(a)(x) sets out how the Board is to deal with the advice of the GAC: If the Board determines it cannot follow the GAC's advice, it must work with the GAC to understand the reasoning underlying their advice and to try to find a mutually acceptable solution. If the advice of the GAC is reached by consensus, the Board can

[89] Jacqueline Lipton and Mary Wong, 'Trademarks and Freedom of Expression in ICANN's New gTLD Process' (2012) *Monash University Law Review*, 38 (1), pp. 188–227, at 195.

[90] For a discussion of challenges for multi-stakeholderism in internet governance, see Rolf H. Weber, 'A Legal Lens into Internet Governance', in Laura DeNardis, et al. (eds.), *Researching Internet Governance: Methods, Frameworks, Futures*, Cambridge, MA: The MIT Press, 2020, pp. 105–121, at 113–114.

[91] See ICANN, 'Board Members', www.icann.org/en/board/directors.

only overrule the GAC's advice if at least 60 per cent of its members support the decision. If the Board insists, it will have to state the reasons why the GAC's advice was not followed and, according to Section 12.2(a)(xi), 'such statement will be without prejudice to the rights or obligations of Governmental Advisory Committee members with regard to public policy issues falling within their responsibilities'.

In the context of the ongoing further expansion of the generic top-level domains, it is becoming apparent that this sophisticated architecture is not immune to a variety of less transparent influences. Milton Mueller has drawn attention to the risk that registries might be tempted to reject applications for certain new TLDs to pre-empt anticipated opposition from governments, intellectual property rights holders and other stakeholders represented in the ICANN organisation.[92] Overall, the 2016 IANA transition shifted ICANN's governance from US government oversight to a global multi-stakeholder structure, limiting direct government influence and giving more power to ICANN's community of stakeholders, including industry representatives, civil society and technical experts. While this has reduced the dominance of the US government and weakened the influence of governments in general, it has increased the risk that the decision-making process could be disproportionately influenced by major commercial entities with significant financial and technical resources. Large corporations, which are often better positioned to participate in ICANN's complex processes, could use their influence to shape policy in ways that prioritise profit over the public interest, potentially sidelining smaller stakeholders, underrepresented groups and principles such as equal access and freedom of expression.

6.5 THE GOVERNANCE OF INTERNET TECHNICAL STANDARDS

The Internet Architecture Board (IAB) and the Internet Engineering Task Force (IETF) are the most important organisations when it comes to the governance of technical standards related to the internet.

[92] Milton L. Mueller, 'The Big Question Facing ICANN's Contractual Governance Regime', *Internet Governance Project*, 15 June 2023, www.internetgovernance.org/2023/06/15/the-big-question-facing-icanns-contractual-governance-regime/.

Founded in 1979, the IAB is primarily responsible for administering, reviewing and validating all internet architecture decisions.[93] Its responsibilities also include coordinating the work of other network organisations and selecting/appointing the Request for Comments (RFC) Editor.[94] RFCs are documents written by individual or collective members of one of the network organisations describing behaviours, research, innovations, or methods related to the internet's technical working conditions. It is essential to understand that RFCs do not only concern technical standards, but that they are also documents with considerable normative significance, above all because they often deal with fundamental values or procedures of internet regulation.[95] By way of illustration, I would like to mention RFC 1591, which established the top-level structure of internet domain names four years before ICANN's founding.[96] The RFC Editor oversees the administration of the RFC series. While in the early days of the internet, the task was fulfilled by a single person, since 2007, several people have undertaken the work required by the RFC process as a collective.[97] The RFCs are hosted on the RFC editor's website.[98] More than 9,500 RFCs have been written and archived so far,[99] collectively representing a publicly accessible series of documents that allow us to reconstruct the history of the discourse concerning the development of technical standards for the internet.[100] The effects of the RFCs go far beyond mere description, since they are the 'official source of technical standards' for internet management.[101]

[93] Internet Architecture Board, 'Role of the IAB', www.iab.org/about/iab-overview/.

[94] Brian E. Carpenter (ed.), 'Charter of the Internet Architecture Board (IAB)', RFC 2850 (2000), www.rfc-editor.org/rfc/rfc2850.

[95] Sandra Braman, 'Laying the Path: Governance in Early Internet Design' (2013) *info*, 15 (6), pp. 63–83.

[96] Jon Postel, 'Domain Name System Structure and Delegation', RFC 1591 (1994), www.rfc-editor.org/rfc/rfc1591.

[97] Leslie Daigle, 'The RFC Series and RFC Editor', RFC 4844 (2007), www.rfc-editor.org/rfc/rfc4844.

[98] Braman, 'Laying the Path', at 65.

[99] RFC Index, www.rfc-editor.org/rfc-index.html.

[100] Barry M. Leiner, et al., *Brief History of the Internet*, Reston: The Internet Society, 1997, at 12.

[101] Braman, 'Laying the Path', at 65.

A large part of the RFC documents have been produced under the supervision of the IETF, which is one of the working groups operating under the umbrella of the IAB. The IETF aims to address technical issues and, in a process of self-regulation, to develop technical standards that shape the internet's architecture. Professionals active in the IETF's standard-setting task include software engineers, equipment manufacturers, network operators and service providers.[102] As stated in RFC 3935, the IETF's mission is: '[T]o produce high quality, relevant technical and engineering documents that influence the way people design, use, and manage the Internet in such a way as to make the Internet work better. These documents include protocol standards, best current practices, and informational documents of various kinds.'[103]

Protocol standards are technical determinations that allow the parties involved in an online communication process to connect.[104] From its inception, the IETF sought to clearly distinguish itself from ordinary standardisation bodies, which mainly produce documents. As one participant at an IETF meeting of the late 1990s put it: 'In IETF we produce running code that has documents that describe it.'[105] This statement echoes IETF's main slogan, invented in 1992 by Dave Clark, one of the pioneers of the internet: 'We reject presidents, kings and voting, we believe in rough consensus and running code.'[106] RFCs that successfully attracted group consensus became the organisational practice of the internet, something akin to its 'law'.[107]

The IETF is not incorporated and there is no IETF membership. As stated in RFC 1391, 'the closest thing there is to being an IETF

[102] Niels ten Oever, '"This Is Not How We Imagined It": Technological Affordances, Economic Drivers, and the Internet Architecture Imaginary' (2021) *New Media & Society*, 23 (2), pp. 344–362, at 345.

[103] Harald Alvestrand, 'A Mission Statement for the IETF', RFC 3935 (2004), www.rfc-editor.org/rfc/rfc3935.

[104] Ten Oever, '"This Is Not How We Imagined It"', at 346.

[105] See quotation in Sabine Helmers, et al., 'Internet... The Final Frontier: An Ethnographic Account: Exploring the Cultural Space of the Net from the Inside', *WZB Discussion Paper*, No. FS II 00-101, Berlin: Wissenschaftszentrum Berlin für Sozialforschung (WZB), 2000, at 46, https://nbn-resolving.org/urn:nbn:de:0168-ssoar-125524.

[106] See quotation in Helmers, et al., 'Internet... The Final Frontier', at 46.

[107] Mueller, *Ruling the Root*, at 94.

member is being on the IETF mailing lists'.[108] Although anyone can register and participate in meetings,[109] many IETF attendees are employed by transnational tech companies.[110] The proximity to the industry is remarkable considering that, besides specifying internet standards, RFCs also often define values, rules and procedures for the co-production of technical standards.[111] The three architectural principles guiding the work of those involved in drafting RFCs are interconnectedness (any endpoint can reach any other endpoint), innovation without prior permission and openness of technology, economy, society and governance.[112] Those who helped build what we know today as the internet sought to create 'a common carrier network', where all hosts were equally free to adopt new protocols.[113] This vision of the internet as a public good is also reflected in the IETF standardisation process. From the outset, it was potentially at odds with the commercial interests that guided many players. Economic motivations became increasingly dominant after the US government relinquished direct control over the internet in the early 1990s.[114] The privatisation of the internet architecture sparked a battle for data-flow control between network operators, equipment manufacturers and content providers. The result was a 'reconfiguration of the technical affordances of the internet

[108] Gary S. Malkin, 'The Tao of IETF. A Guide for New Attendees of the Internet Engineering Task Force', RFC 1391 (1993), www.rfc-editor.org/rfc/rfc1391.

[109] Mueller, *Ruling the Root*, at 91.

[110] Ten Oever, '"This Is Not How We Imagined It"', at 346.

[111] Braman, 'Laying the Path', at 65–67; Sandra Braman, 'The Interpenetration of Technical and Legal Decision-Making for the Internet' (2010) *Information, Communication & Society*, 13 (3), pp. 309–324.

[112] Internet Society, 'Internet Invariants: What Really Matters', 3 February 2012, www.internetsociety.org/internet-invariants-what-really-matters/. On openness, see specifically Internet Society, 'The Value of Openness for a Sustainable Internet', 24 October 2013, www.internetsociety.org/resources/doc/2013/the-value-of-openness-for-a-sustainable-internet/. See also ten Oever, '"This Is Not How We Imagined It"', at 346.

[113] D. W. Davies, et al., 'A Digital Communication Network for Computers Giving Rapid Response at Remote Terminals', in John A. Gosden and Brian Randell (eds.), *Proceedings of the First ACM Symposium on Operating System Principles (SOSP'67)* (Gatlinburg, 1 to 4 October 1967), New York: Association for Computing Machinery, 1967, pp. 2.1–2.17, at 2.3.

[114] Ten Oever, '"This Is Not How We Imagined It"', at 349.

architecture', undermining the 'equality of hosts and the ability to deploy new protocols between hosts'.[115] This was where the downside of the IETF's self-regulatory approach became apparent. Initially, privatisation was justified by the idea of competition,[116] but competition soon yielded to the sheer power of transnational corporations.

How is this standardisation process relevant to free speech? We have noted the importance of adequate privacy protection as a prerequisite for freedom of expression. As we have seen, the legal institutionalisation of privacy converges on protecting expectations about the integrity of personal data, on the one hand, and the integrity of network technology, on the other. Something similar applies in the context of standardisation. On the basis of an analysis of RTFs from 1969 to 1979, Sandra Braman shows that privacy was 'the most frequently discussed policy issue' in those 'framing years'.[117] The technology experts discussing privacy were interested in privacy as a design problem, and two issues that are still critical to free expression today can be distilled from that discussion: network integrity and data integrity.

Protecting network integrity was considered particularly important in these discussions on privacy. As early as 1971, network designers discussed the issue of protecting trust in the network, emphasising that users of protected file systems should be able to trust that servers have correctly identified remote users.[118] The concept of privacy was also utilised to justify claims to protect the integrity of the server process, which was seen as a prerequisite for establishing a trustworthy connection between networked computers.[119] In these cases, the designers involved in the discussion applied the concept of privacy to a non-human entity, focusing their thinking on 'a set of logistical problems intertwined with security issues'.[120]

Although the word had yet to be taken up in the *Oxford English Dictionary*, data integrity has been a topic of interest since 1971 and was

[115] Ibid., at 357.

[116] Barbara van Schewick, *Internet Architecture and Innovation*, Cambridge, MA: The MIT Press, 2010, at 215–216.

[117] Sandra Braman, 'Privacy by Design: Networked Computing, 1969–1979' (2011) *New Media & Society*, 14 (5), pp. 798–814, at 799.

[118] Ibid., at 801–802. [119] Ibid., at 802. [120] Ibid., at 811.

discussed in thirty RFCs up to 1979, as Braman shows.[121] Protecting privacy at both the host and user levels was essential to ensuring data integrity. At the host level, user identification was an issue: to ensure the integrity of the data exchanged in a computer system, it was necessary to keep unauthorised users out.[122] At the user level, the focus was on data access issues and the prevention of data manipulation, including what is today known as metadata. Other topics included the maintenance of secrecy as well as specific matters guaranteed by the US Constitution, such as respect for anonymous speech and the secrecy of authorship.[123] Various techniques for protecting data integrity were also discussed, such as logging in, connection identity and encryption.

After the Snowden revelations of 2013, encryption became crucial for protecting data integrity against governments. Several RFCs assessed the US government's systematic snooping on users as a threat to the standardisation process,[124] prompting the IETF to recommend that more DNS traffic be encrypted. As the IETF meeting in July 2023 showed, the recommendation has been heeded. While, in 2013, the web was primarily unencrypted, ten years later, more than 80 per cent of all web pages used HTTPS and most email traffic was encrypted.[125] Looking back on the steps taken in the ten years since 2013, RFC 9464 noted that the IETF community had gotten several things right, but had overlooked the issue of countering data tracking by corporate actors for advertising purposes.[126]

The history of the approval of the so-called third-party cookie (mentioned in Section 2.1.) illustrates the failure of the IETF (and related working groups) to achieve their privacy goals in the face of opposition from the private advertising industry. The HTTP cookie was reportedly

[121] Braman, 'Laying the Path', at 66. [122] Braman, 'Privacy by Design', at 803.

[123] Ibid., at 804.

[124] See, e.g., Stephen Farrell and Hannes Tschofenig, 'Pervasive Monitoring Is an Attack', RFC 7258 (2014), www.rfc-editor.org/rfc/rfc7258.

[125] See Stephen Farrell, et al., 'Reflections on Ten Years Past the Snowden Revelations', *Presentation at IETF 117* (San Francisco, 22 to 28 July 2023), https://datatracker.ietf.org/meeting/117/materials/slides-117-hrpc-reflections-on-ten-years-past-the-snowden-revelations-01.

[126] See Stephen Farrell, et al., 'Reflections on Ten Years Past the Snowden Revelations', RFC 9446 (2023), www.rfc-editor.org/rfc/rfc9446.

invented in the first half of the 1990s by two software designers employed at Netscape, a browser company,[127] with the aim of assisting market analysts in identifying multiple visits to the same webpage by the same user.[128] They designed the cookie to be placed on the users' computer without their consent.[129] RFC 2109 of 1997 introduced the HTTP cookie as a standard, intended 'to restrict cookies to one, or a closely related set of hosts'.[130] At the same time, the advertising industry was working on technologies that would extend the reach of the cookie and allow users' behaviour to be tracked on any website. In 2000, advertising industry lobbying succeeded in replacing RFC 2109 with RFC 2965,[131] leading to the introduction of the third-party cookie as a new standard.[132]

6.6 CONCLUDING REMARKS

Evidence about the relationship between free speech and technology is found in case law and regulation, including self-regulatory structures. The most substantial evidence of normative structures can be found in the case law of courts, especially the ECtHR on Article 10 ECHR and the ECJ on select provisions of the GDPR and the OIR. Evidence of the emergence of normative structures in relation to the technological requirements of freedom of expression can also be found in the self-regulatory efforts of ICANN and the informal processes of technical standardisation of the IAB and IETF. The fact that these organisations are subject to considerable commercial influence also poses a risk to the effective implementation of freedom of expression.

127 Turow, 'Media Buying', at 100.

128 Lynette I. Millett, et al., 'Cookies and Web Browser Design: Toward Realizing Informed Consent Online', in Michel Beaudouin-Lafon and Robert J. K. Jacob (eds.), *Proceedings of the ACM CHI 2001 Human Factors in Computing Systems Conference* (Seattle, 31 March to 5 April 2001), pp. 46–52, at 46.

129 Turow, 'Media Buying', at 101.

130 David Kristol and Lou Montulli, 'HTTP State Management Mechanism', RFC 2109 (1997), www.rfc-editor.org/rfc/rfc2109, at para 7.2.

131 David Kristol and Lou Montulli, 'HTTP State Management Mechanism', RFC 2965 (2000), www.rfc-editor.org/rfc/rfc2965.

132 Nissenbaum, 'From Preemption to Circumvention', at 1382.

On the whole, the picture confirms some of the assumptions underlying the transnationalisation thesis. Particularly noteworthy is the fact that privacy was acknowledged as a global human right before it was acknowledged in national constitutions. It should also be emphasised that ICANN is a private company that performs tasks that are essential for the internet to function for all people, states and businesses worldwide. Moreover, states are active in the GAC: they have advisory functions and do not have the right to veto the decisions of the ICANN Board. Finally, the IAB and its working groups, mainly the IETF, are informal, non-governmental processes that produce technological standards which significantly impact online connectivity and privacy for users around the world.

CHAPTER 7

Fundamental Rights, Constitutional Stability and Social Change

Chapter 5 laid out the sociological foundations for a conception of normativity that can meet the demands of a rapidly changing digital ecosphere. Then, in Chapter 6, normative evidence was collected from case law and regulations concerning the technology-related prerequisites for the fundamental right to freedom of expression. Building on this analysis, the present chapter aims to examine how this fundamental right can be adapted to address the new questions raised by the realities of the internet.

In identifying the technology-related factors that complement free speech online, Chapter 6 already indicated the direction in which the doctrine of freedom of expression ought to develop in the future. However, the issue of fundamental rights in the private sphere has not yet been tackled. This issue is raised by the activity of private actors (including telecoms companies, equipment manufacturers and platform operators) who provide hardware and software, thus conferring on them the capacity to directly or indirectly interfere with the freedom of expression in various ways. The goal of this chapter is therefore to clarify how the fundamental rights doctrine has responded, on a general level, to the challenge of private actors infringing on fundamental rights. Does the nexus between technology and freedom of expression require further steps to be taken? As far as methodology is concerned, the sociological reflection on fundamental rights as institutions of society will serve as a benchmark for evaluating future developments of constitutional legal doctrine. A preliminary analysis will focus on the mechanisms that are generally available to legal systems to adapt constitutional norms without jeopardising legal certainty and the stability of a normative order.

7.1 NEGOTIATING STABILITY AND CHANGE IN CONSTITUTIONAL ORDERS

The analysis conducted in Chapter 6 revealed that technology-related free-speech norms are emerging from constitutional or administrative case law (concerning freedom of expression, privacy or the open internet), as well as from formal and informal processes of regulation (data protection, the open internet, etc.) and self-regulation (ICANN, IAB, IETF, etc.). These developments are gradually changing the *value* of freedom of expression[1] and tend to give rise to a tension between the written constitutional text and the demands of social change to adapt it to new realities. How can this pressure be negotiated in light of the widespread view among jurists that constitutional amendments (and hence amendments to fundamental rights) can only be implemented through the formalised procedures established for that purpose? The goal of this section is to clarify the concept of constitutional change. What means, other than formal revision, are available to change the meaning of a constitutional provision? How can 'informal' changes to constitutional norms be assessed from the perspective of necessary legitimacy? These questions are discussed below with a focus on Swiss constitutional law. As explained in the introduction to this book, the Swiss system of constitutional adjudication is particularly interesting due to its long, uninterrupted development and its pioneering role, at the international level, through the Federal Supreme Court's practice of recognising unwritten fundamental rights, which dates back to the late 1950s. Although constitutional adjudication in Switzerland has its peculiarities,[2] this does not preclude the transferability of the findings *mutatis mutandis* to other legal systems.

Legal systems in democratic countries have come up with different solutions to deal with the tension between social change and

[1] For a distinction between free speech values and free speech rights, see Jack M. Balkin, 'Digital Speech and Democratic Culture: A Theory of Freedom of Expression for the Information Society' (2004) *New York University Law Review*, 79 (1), pp. 1–55, at 49–51.

[2] For a comprehensive analysis, see Giovanni Biaggini, 'Constitutional Adjudication in Switzerland', in Armin von Bogdandy, et al. (eds.), *The Max Planck Handbooks in European Public Law*, Oxford: Oxford University Press, 2020, pp. 779–840.

constitutional stability. Generally speaking, ordinary law is easier to change than constitutional law.[3] That constitutional change should be difficult, but not impossible, is something most countries would agree on,[4] and certain countries even require a supermajority in parliament in order to do so. Article V of the US Constitution, for example, prescribes a two-stage process, distinguishing between proposal and ratification, with a supermajority being required for each stage.[5] Some countries, like Switzerland, also require that constitutional changes be ratified through a referendum: Article 140(1)(a) of the Swiss Federal Constitution (Bundesverfassung der Schweizerischen Eidgenossenschaft, BV) requires that both a majority of the citizens who vote in the referendum and a majority of the cantons approve the change. In a number of countries, specific provisions are immune from being amended under any circumstances. Article 79(3) of the German Constitution (Grundgesetz für die Bundesrepublik Deutschland, GG), the so-called eternity guarantee, establishes that key provisions in the relationship between the federation and the 'Länder' (sub-federal territorial entities) and certain fundamental principles in Articles 1 (human dignity) and 20 (including the rule of law, democracy and social state) cannot be amended.[6] The German Federal Constitutional Court can also strike down amendments to the GG if they are determined to contradict the eternity guarantee.[7] Article 89 of the French Constitution similarly declares that the republican form of government cannot be altered by a constitutional amendment. The tension between social change and constitutional immutability similarly arises at the level of international human rights law, especially in the context of the European Convention

[3] John Ferejohn, 'The Politics of Imperfection: The Amendment of Constitutions' (1997) *Law & Social Inquiry*, 22 (2), pp. 501–530, at 503.

[4] Jon Elster, *Ulysses Unbound: Studies in Rationality, Precommitment, and Constraints*, Cambridge: Cambridge University Press, 2000, at 94.

[5] Laurence H. Tribe, *American Constitutional Law*, 3rd edn, New York: Foundation Press, 2000, at 95.

[6] German Federal Constitutional Court (Bundesverfassungsgericht, BVerfG), 2 BvE 2/08, 30 June 2009, at para 216. (For an English translation, see www.bverfg.de/e/es20090630_2bve000208en.html.)

[7] Ulrich K. Preuss, 'The Implications of "Eternity Clauses": The German Experience' (2011) *Israel Law Review*, 44 (3), pp. 429–448, at 442.

on Human Rights (ECHR). As mentioned in Chapter 6, this is because the European Court of Human Rights (ECtHR) understands the ECHR as a 'living instrument that must be interpreted in the light of today's conditions'.[8] The 'living instrument doctrine'[9] has come under considerable criticism in recent years,[10] to the extent that the case law developed in the process of adapting the ECHR to a changing social reality departs from the text that was agreed by the parties when they ratified the Convention and thus violates state sovereignty. While at the national level, courts can be constrained by legislators enacting corrective statutes, there is no such possibility at the international level.

Constitutional entrenchment promotes legal certainty and predictability.[11] It serves as a shield that the powerless and disadvantaged use to protect themselves against the dominant groups in society, who have more significant resources with which to promote their interpretation of the constitution.[12] At the same time, constitutional orders must be flexible enough to cope with growth in complexity and social change. Beyond the procedures set out in the constitutional documents, constitutions can be amended in unspecified ways, primarily through judicial interpretation.[13] Change often occurs gradually through evolutionary interpretation,[14] leading to almost imperceptible shifts in jurisprudence. Evolutionary interpretation takes place in a grey area that is not explicitly regulated in the formal constitution, and, as such, it is often confronted

[8] *Vo v. France* App. no. 53924/00 (ECtHR (GC) 8 July 2004), at para 82.

[9] George Letsas, 'The ECHR as a Living Instrument: Its Meaning and Legitimacy', in Andreas Føllesdal, et al. (eds.), *Constituting Europe: The European Court of Human Rights in a National, European and Global Context*, Cambridge: Cambridge University Press, 2013, pp. 106–141.

[10] See the various contributions in Patricia Popelier, et al. (eds.), *Criticism of the European Court of Human Rights*, Cambridge: Intersentia, 2017.

[11] Michael D. Gilbert, 'Entrenchment, Incrementalism, and Constitutional Collapse' (2017) *Virginia Law Review*, 103 (4), pp. 631–671, at 632.

[12] Preuss, 'The Implications of "Eternity Clauses"', at 446.

[13] Ferejohn, 'The Politics of Imperfection', at 522.

[14] On evolutive interpretation from a comparative perspective, see Kanstantsin Dzehtsiarou and Conor O'Mahony, 'Evolutive Interpretation of Rights Provisions: A Comparison of the European Court of Human Rights and the U.S. Supreme Court' (2013) *Columbia Human Rights Law Review*, 44 (2), pp. 309–365.

with accusations of judicial activism.[15] However, constitutional change by way of 'creative' interpretation of the wording of a right is not a new phenomenon. In the United States, for example, the Supreme Court recognised the right to privacy in *Griswold v. Connecticut* in 1965.[16] The Court constructed the right to privacy from 'penumbras' of privacy interests protected in various amendments,[17] arguing that the new right is 'implicit in, or rather [...] a precondition for, rights grouped under the First Amendment'.[18] Another example of an extended interpretation of an existing guarantee is the IT-Grundrecht, which the German Federal Constitutional Court derived from the right to protection of personality, which is explicitly provided for in the German Constitution (see Chapter 6). The Swiss Federal Supreme Court (Schweizerisches Bundesgericht, Bger) has gone a step further in that, since 1959, it has incorporated *unwritten* fundamental rights into the constitution.[19] In its jurisprudence relating to the BV of 1874, the Court recognised several new fundamental rights, despite the absence of a direct reference in the formal constitutional document. These unwritten fundamental rights included such essential freedoms as the right to own property, the right to personal liberty, the freedom of assembly and, most notably for our purposes, the freedom of expression. These rights were all formally incorporated into the revised constitutional document during the total revision of the BV in 1999. The power of the Court to recognise unwritten fundamental rights, if necessary, still exists under the new BV of 1999.[20]

[15] Marko Bošnjak and Kacper Zajac, 'Judicial Activism and Judge-Made Law at the ECtHR' (2023) *Human Rights Law Review*, 23 (3), pp. 1–15.

[16] *Griswold v. Connecticut* 381 US 479 (1965).

[17] See Bruce Fein, '*Griswold v. Connecticut*: Wayward Decision-Making in the Supreme Court' (1989) *Ohio Northern University Law Review*, 16 (3), pp. 551–560, at 553.

[18] Chris Thornhill, *A Sociology of Transnational Constitutions: The Social Foundations of the Post-National Legal Structure*, Cambridge: Cambridge University Press, 2016, at 391.

[19] René A. Rhinow, et al., *Schweizerisches Verfassungsrecht*, 3rd edn, Basel: Helbing & Lichtenhahn, 2016, at 185.

[20] Regina Kiener, et al., *Grundrechte*, 4th edn, Bern: Stämpfli, 2024, at 13 and 21; Giovanni Biaggini, 'Grundrechtsinnovation im Bundesstaat – ein Streifzug durch 175 Jahre Verfassungsgeschichte', in Frédéric Bernard, et al. (eds.), *Le droit au service de l'humanité: Mélanges en l'honneur de Michel Hottelier*, Zurich: Schulthess, 2023, pp. 33–50, at 44.

How can the recognition of unwritten fundamental rights by a country's highest court be justified in a constitutional state? Zaccaria Giacometti (1893–1970), a renowned constitutionalist, was the first person to address this question in the Swiss context. In 1955, he elaborated the theoretical framework necessary for the BGer to recognise fundamental rights not explicitly mentioned in the text of the BV. Giacometti believed that the essence and axiomatic principle of fundamental rights is that they provide a comprehensive guarantee of individual freedom and human dignity within the framework of the state.[21] According to Giacometti, the given catalogue of fundamental rights contained in the written constitution can only include those articulations of human freedom that were known to be at risk when it was drafted. As time passes and social conditions change, 'every new aspect of individual freedom that receives clear form as a consequence of new interferences with human dignity or individual personality must also be guaranteed by the catalogue of human rights'.[22] Since the possibility of state interference in individual freedom seems unlimited, the enumeration of fundamental rights in a formal constitutional document can never be exhaustive.

It is important to note that Giacometti's understanding of fundamental rights is positivist, rather than metaphysical or political.[23] It ties in with the provision in Article 2 BV 1848 (and later Article 2 BV 1874), according to which the purpose of the Confederation is to protect the independence and freedom of the citizens. The protection of freedom is also recognised as a purpose of the Confederation in Article 2(1) of BV 1999.[24]

Nonetheless, constitutional changes brought about by the judiciary are not unproblematic, insofar as they interfere with the separation and

[21] Zaccaria Giacometti, 'Die Freiheitsrechtskataloge als Kodifikation der Freiheit: Festrede des Rektors Zaccaria Giacometti, gehalten an der 122. Stiftungsfeier der Universität Zürich am 29. April 1955', in *Jahresbericht der Universität Zürich 1954/1955*, pp. 3–24, at 18.

[22] Ibid., at 17 (translation by the author).

[23] Ibid., at 8.

[24] Giovanni Biaggini, 'Über Aufgaben und Grenzen der Verfassungsgerichtsbarkeit im ökologischen Verfassungsstaat', in Claudia Seitz, et al. (eds.), *Rechtsschutz in Theorie und Praxis: Festschrift für Stephan Breitenmoser*, Basel: Helbing & Lichtenhahn, 2022, pp. 545–559, at 552.

division of powers, which is itself one of the cornerstones of the rule of law. The BGer has been aware of this problem since it began identifying unwritten fundamental rights. Only with great reluctance, when a pressing social need exists and certain self-imposed formal conditions are met, has it recognised new fundamental rights. In these cases, the Court has examined whether the new guarantee is a prerequisite for exercising other freedoms, whether it appears to be an indispensable component of the liberal and democratic order of the Confederation and whether it corresponds to something that is already a widespread constitutional reality in the cantons.[25] According to Giovanni Biaggini, the criterion that the new right already be a widespread reality in cantonal constitutions reflects the idea that new unwritten rights grow from the bottom up rather than being decreed top-down by the Court.[26] The commitment to a broad basic consensus is intended to ensure that changes in fundamental rights do not occur in leaps and bounds, but rather step by step, in accordance with the convictions shared in the cantons.

When the BGer recognised the freedom of expression in 1961, it expressed particular appreciation for the fact that this freedom was a necessary precondition for the freedom of the press, which was already explicitly provided for in the written constitution.[27] The Court's reasoning shows the influence of Giacometti's theory. If the Constitution comprehensively protects individual freedom, it logically follows that an (unwritten) right that is necessary for exercising an explicitly guaranteed right should also be recognised. This criterion allows for a certain degree of flexibility without violating the constitutional principle of the division of power. The reasoning according to which a newly created right is a prerequisite for the effective exercise of rights already formalised in the Constitution was also invoked by the US

[25] BGE 121 I 367, at 370. See Regina Kiener, 'Grundrechte in der Bundesverfassung', in Oliver Diggelmann, et al. (eds.), *Verfassungsrecht der Schweiz*, vol. 2, 2nd edn, Zurich: Schulthess, 2020, pp. 1193–1221, at 1205.

[26] Biaggini, 'Grundrechtsinnovation im Bundesstaat', at 40–41.

[27] BGE 87 I 114, at 117 – confirmed in BGE 91 I 480, at 485. See Peter Saladin, *Grundrechte im Wandel*, 3rd edn, Bern: Stämpfli, 1982 (1970), at 75, and Kiener, 'Grundrechte in der Bundesverfassung', at 1195.

Supreme Court in *Griswold v. Connecticut*.[28] In my view, this reasoning could be generalised beyond Swiss and US practice and, *mutatis mutandis*, guide the ECtHR when considering whether Article 10 ECHR should be enriched with a 'right to transmit',[29] given that the technological infrastructure of the internet is a precondition for the freedom of expression.

7.2 HOW FREE SPEECH DOCTRINE RESPONDS TO INTERFERENCE FROM PRIVATE ACTORS

Giacometti took it for granted that the prospective invader of a constitutionally guaranteed freedom would be the state.[30] Even today, legal practitioners think first and foremost of state interference when they imagine potential threats to freedom of expression. Such an understanding of fundamental rights is rooted in liberal political philosophy, which construes the state as a social contract between citizens who cede a monopoly on power to the state while, at the same time, retaining fundamental individual rights with which the state must not interfere. Public law procedures reinforce the state–society dichotomy found in liberal political philosophy by providing exclusively for individual actions against the state to enforce fundamental rights in the courts. In Switzerland, procedural law, as a rule, holds that only individuals have the right to challenge a violation of constitutional rights before the Federal Supreme Court[31] and that only State acts can be challenged.[32] The state-centrism of fundamental rights doctrine continues at the international level, where Article 34 ECHR states that the ECtHR will receive applications directed against one of the Contracting States.

[28] See note 16 and accompanying text. [29] See discussion in Chapter 6.

[30] On Giacommetti's state-centred conception of fundamental rights, see Andreas Kley, 'Der wissenschaftliche Streit um die Drittwirkung der Grundrechte 1987–1989', in Jean-Baptiste Zufferey, et al. (eds.), *L'homme et son droit: Mélanges en l'honneur de Marco Borghi à l'occasion de son 65e anniversaire*, Zurich: Schulthess, 2011, pp. 227–240, at 229–230.

[31] Biaggini notes that the conception of constitutional jurisdiction in Switzerland is individualistic. Giovanni Biaggini, 'Über Aufgaben und Grenzen der Verfassungsgerichtsbarkeit im ökologischen Verfassungsstaat', at 547.

[32] See Articles 113–119 of the Federal Act on the Federal Supreme Court (Bundesgesetz über das Bundesgericht) of 17 June 2005, SR 173.119.

A state-centred view of fundamental rights will necessarily find it difficult to conceptualise the actions of private companies on the internet as a fundamental rights issue. As the previous chapters in this book have shown, interference with the freedom of expression on the internet stems not only from states but in many cases from private parties. Through their control of critical features of the technical infrastructure, telecom companies, platform operators and equipment manufacturers can directly interfere with free expression, as well as indirectly shape its conditions of possibility. This new reality raises the question of whether the conventional understanding of fundamental rights is still adequate.

The doctrine of fundamental rights in Switzerland has evolved considerably in recent years[33] under the (direct or indirect) influence of international law,[34] a development that can be seen as a confirmation of the transnationalisation thesis discussed in Chapter 3.[35] Until the 1970s, the *negative dimension* of fundamental rights remained in the foreground: the rights of individuals were to be protected from interference by the state. While the concept of fundamental rights refers to the legal positions guaranteed by national constitutional law, human rights protect the elementary rights of every human being as enshrined in international law.[36] In substance, most fundamental rights *are* human rights. Under international law, human rights are understood as obligations of states arising from treaties with other states or customary international law. The obligations of states include a duty to respect (negative duty), as well as a duty to protect and a duty to fulfil (positive duties).[37] Under the ECHR, positive obligations have been recognised since 1979,[38] with the effect of gradually

[33] For a detailed reconstruction, see Andreas Kley, *Geschichte des öffentlichen Rechts der Schweiz*, Zurich: Dike, 2011, at 304–322. See also Biaggini, 'Grundrechtsinnovation im Bundesstaat', pp. 33–50.

[34] Kiener, 'Grundrechte in der Bundesverfassung', at 1195–1196.

[35] Thornhill argues that there has been a fusion of international human rights law with national constitutional law. Chris Thornhill, 'Transnational Constitutional Law', in Peer Zumbansen (ed.), *The Oxford Handbook of Transnational Law*, New York: Oxford University Press, 2021, pp. 134–156, at 143.

[36] Kiener, et al., *Grundrechte*, at 12.

[37] Walter Kälin and Jörg Künzli, *The Law of International Human Rights Protection*, 2nd edn, Oxford: Oxford University Press, 2019, at 87–112.

[38] See *Airey v. Ireland* App. no. 6289/73 (ECtHR, 9 October 1979).

extending the protection of the Convention to private relationships.[39] The implementation of international human rights law at the domestic level and its reception in legal doctrine has led to the view being promoted, in Switzerland and many other democratic countries,[40] that fundamental rights have a *positive* dimension in addition to a defensive one.

In *Verein Tierfabriken Schweiz (VgT) v. Switzerland*, the ECtHR stated that Article 10 ECHR confers on Switzerland positive obligations to protect freedom of expression.[41] The Court reiterated 'the importance of freedom of expression as one of the preconditions for a functioning democracy. Genuine, "effective" exercise of this freedom does not depend merely on the State's duty not to interfere, but may require positive measures'.[42] The Court then continued:

> In determining whether or not a positive obligation exists, regard must be had to the fair balance that has to be struck between the general interest of the community and the interests of the individual, the search for which balance is inherent throughout the Convention. The scope of this obligation will inevitably vary, having regard to the diversity of situations obtaining in Contracting States and the choices which must be made in terms of priorities and resources. However, this obligation must not be interpreted in such a way as to impose an impossible or disproportionate burden on the authorities.[43]

The Court's reasoning reveals that the concept of positive obligations is based on fundamental principles that must be implemented gradually and, in practice, with a sense of balance. The ECtHR thus takes account of Member States, such as Switzerland, which, due to their federalism, have reservations about the idea of positive obligations that would be directly enforceable in court.[44]

39 Bošnjak and Zajac, 'Judicial Activism and Judge-Made Law at the ECtHR', at 7.

40 With the notable exception of the US Supreme Court. See Bošnjak and Zajac, 'Judicial Activism and Judge-Made Law at the ECtHR', at 7.

41 *Verein gegen Tierfabriken Schweiz (VgT) v. Switzerland (no.2)* App. no. 32772/02 (ECtHR (GC), 30 June 2009), at paras 78–82.

42 Ibid., at para 80 (internal references omitted).

43 Ibid., at para 81 (internal references omitted).

44 Biaggini, 'Grundrechtsinnovation im Bundesstaat', at 47.

Positive and negative duties can have an effect at the *individual-legal level* and the *objective-legal level*. Under Article 46 of the ECHR, the ECtHR may recommend that a State found to have breached the Convention undertake individual or general measures to fulfil its obligations under the Convention, with general measures being indicated in cases where the situation that has been found to violate the ECHR was caused by a general practice or structural problems.[45] In Switzerland, an individual's ability to form and hold opinions, as well as to express them, is covered at the individual-legal level of freedom of expression (Article 16 of the Swiss Constitution). At the objective-legal level, the focus is on the transindividual (hence 'objective') dimension of freedom of expression. At this level, decisions are taken to ensure a diverse range of journalistic offerings as a prerequisite for citizens to freely form opinions. Based on a competence in Article 93(2) of the BV, the Confederation has implemented this objective primarily in the Radio and Television Act.[46] Legislative measures to protect an open internet infrastructure and other technical requirements for freedom of expression are also assigned to the objective-legal level. For reasons related to the separation of powers, the Federal Supreme Court cannot act as a substitute legislator.[47] Since the highest Swiss court has little expertise in assessing future developments and lacks the competence to set the political course, concretising the objective-legal dimension of fundamental rights is understood as a programmatic mandate to the legislator.[48]

How has the ECtHR specified the objective-legal dimension of free expression online? The Court considers the internet one of the most important means for individuals to exercise their freedom to express and

[45] ECtHR, 'Guide on Article 46 of the European Convention on Human Rights', 31 August 2024, at 10–11, https://ks.echr.coe.int/documents/d/echr-ks/guide_art_46_eng.

[46] Christoph B. Graber, 'Personalisierung im Internet, Autonomie der Politik und Service public' (2017) *sic! Zeitschrift für Immaterialgüter-, Informations- und Wettbewerbsrecht*, 5, pp. 257–270, at 264.

[47] Biaggini, 'Über Aufgaben und Grenzen der Verfassungsgerichtsbarkeit im ökologischen Verfassungsstaat', at 554.

[48] Kiener, 'Grundrechte in der Bundesverfassung', at 1211–1212; Markus Schefer, 'Kommunikationsgrundrechte', in Oliver Diggelmann, et al. (eds.), *Verfassungsrecht der Schweiz*, vol. 2, 2nd edn, Zurich: Schulthess, 2020, pp. 1413–1451, at 1424.

receive information, as guaranteed by Article 10 ECHR. On the internet, 'one finds essential tools for the participation in activities and debates related to questions of politics or public interest'.[49] Although the ECtHR speaks of 'tools', this is a reference not only to social networks, search engines and the like but also to the technological conditions necessary to access them. The Court has pronounced itself in several rulings on state interference with the internet's technical infrastructure. In *Cengiz v. Turkey* (2015), the ECtHR found that the Turkish authorities' imposition of a blanket blocking order on access to YouTube violated the rights of the applicants under Article 10 ECHR. Although the measure did not directly target the applicants, the blocking order affected their rights under Article 10 ECHR since YouTube was an essential means for them to exercise their right to receive and impart information or ideas.[50] For similar reasons, the ECtHR had already decided in *Yıldırım v. Turkey* that a general block on the Google search engine violated Article 10 ECHR.[51] In both cases, the applicable Turkish Law No. 5651 did not allow the judicial authorities to impose a blanket order blocking access to the websites concerned. In the case of *Cengiz v. Turkey*, Law No. 5651 was amended while the case was pending, and it now allows the imposition of a blocking order on an entire website under certain conditions. As the case had to be decided on the facts given at the time of the application, the Court did not decide whether such a broad blocking order would be compatible with Article 10 ECHR. The ECtHR did note, *obiter*, that any blocking order must be strictly delimited and that efficient judicial review mechanisms must be provided.[52] More recently, the ECtHR ruled in *Kablis v. Russia* that the Russian authorities violated Article 10 ECHR when they blocked a user's account on VKontakte, a Russian social networking service, as a prior restraint.[53] These judgments all concern access to the internet as a distribution medium. Although the Court was called to rule on individual complaints in each case, it has recognised – at

[49] *Yıldırım v. Turkey* App. no. 3111/10 (ECtHR, 18 December 2012), at para 54.

[50] *Cengiz and Others v. Turkey* App. nos 48226/10 and 14027/11 (ECtHR, 1 December 2015).

[51] *Yıldırım v. Turkey*.

[52] *Cengiz and Others v. Turkey*, at paras 62 and 74.

[53] *Kablis v. Russia* App. nos 48310/16 and 59663/17 (ECtHR, 30 April 2019).

least indirectly – the *objective* importance of the internet as a communication technology.

This body of case law is noteworthy. Although the doctrine of duties indirectly implicates private actors who interfere with freedom of expression,[54] there is no mechanism under Article 10 ECHR that would enable private actors to be taken directly to court. Is the protection it provides sufficient if we consider the goal of effectively protecting freedom of expression from private interference in the technological infrastructure? Should the scope of fundamental rights be extended to include horizontal effects between private parties?

7.3 FUNDAMENTAL RIGHTS AS SOCIAL INSTITUTIONS

Advocates of the position that fundamental rights have a horizontal effect argue for the inclusion of private actors within the scope of fundamental rights.[55] Assessing such claims requires us to think deeply about fundamental rights. What does it mean for a constitutional order when fundamental rights are interpreted more broadly? In order to better understand fundamental rights and their legal and social significance, it is necessary to take a step back, look at the matter from a certain distance and shift our point of view from law to sociology. From a sociological perspective, it is the question of the *function* of fundamental rights that comes to the fore. Sociology aims to impartially observe social facts as objective data, without being influenced by personal beliefs, attitudes or values.[56] This methodology contrasts with that of law, which is a normative discipline operating within the framework of a societal

[54] For the most recent case law on a state's positive obligation to protect freedom of expression in the face of interference by private persons, see *Boronyák v. Hungary* App. no. 4110/20 (ECtHR, 20 June 2024), at para 33, with reference to *Halet v. Luxembourg* App. no. 21884/18 (ECtHR (GC), 14 February 2023).

[55] See, e.g., Eleni Frantziou, 'The Horizontal Effect of the Charter of Fundamental Rights of the EU: Rediscovering the Reasons for Horizontality' (2015) *European Law Journal*, 21 (5), pp. 657–679; Florian Rödl, 'Fundamental Rights, Private Law, and Societal Constitution: On the Logic of the So-Called Horizontal Effect' (2013) *Indiana Journal of Global Legal Studies*, 20 (2), pp. 1015–1034.

[56] Christoph B. Graber, 'Legal Sociology', in Marc Thommen (ed.), *Introduction to Swiss Law*, 2nd edn, Zurich: sui generis, 2022, pp. 91–112, at 93.

perception of how things ought to be. Law and legal doctrine are preoccupied with the form of the law, with legal doctrine being interested in the systematic relationship between various abstract principles that can be used to reach logical decisions in concrete cases. The added value of a sociological observation of the law lies in broadening the perspective from 'law in books' to 'law in action',[57] exploring the social context of legal communication and asking questions such as: Why does a rule exist or what is a rule's effect? From a sociological perspective, fundamental rights appear as institutions of society.

As a foundation for my sociological analysis of fundamental rights, I refer to Niklas Luhmann's theory of autopoietic social systems, as introduced in Chapter 5. Indeed, fundamental rights were a key topic in Luhmann's sociology of law. In 1965, Luhmann published *Grundrechte als Institution* (*Fundamental Rights as an Institution*).[58] Although the book has not (yet) been translated into English, it has significantly impacted the debate about fundamental rights in German-speaking academia and beyond. The title reveals that Luhmann understands fundamental rights as *institutions of society*. Let us recall Luhmann's definition of an 'institution' as a 'complex of factual behavioural expectations, which are actualised in the context of a social role, and which can always count on social consensus'.[59] As this definition suggests, there is a link between fundamental rights as social institutions and normative expectations. For the generalisation of normative expectations, the law relies on the de facto social consensus embodied in fundamental rights. It is also worth recalling the remarks made in Chapter 2, where we pointed to the constitutive and limitative functions of the constitution, which can be distinguished from a sociological perspective. Fundamental rights, we argued, have a crucial *limitative function*, helping *to protect the functional differentiation of society from self-destructive tendencies.*

To better understand this point, it is necessary to pause for a moment. In line with the theories of Georg Simmel, Emile Durkheim, Max Weber

57 Roscoe Pound, 'Law in Books and Law in Action' (1910) *American Law Review*, 44 (1), pp. 12–36.

58 Niklas Luhmann, *Grundrechte als Institution: Ein Beitrag zur politischen Soziologie*, Berlin: Duncker & Humblot, 1965.

59 Ibid., at 12–13 (translation by the author).

and other classical sociologists,[60] Luhmann recognises functional differentiation as a distinctive feature of modern society.[61] Functional differentiation is distinct from pre-modern forms of differentiation, which are structured into segments (archaic societies), divided between centre and periphery (ancient cities and empires) or hierarchically stratified (aristocratic societies).[62] In the process of modernisation, particular spheres, which Luhmann calls 'systems', have emerged in society over the centuries. The most critical sub-systems of society are law, politics, economics, science, the mass media, art, education and religion. Social sub-systems renew their structures by operating a binary code, constantly distinguishing themselves (system) from everything else (environment).[63] In the case of the legal system, for example, the juxtaposition of the (binary) values of 'legal' and 'illegal' is constitutive. Systems are operatively closed, which implies that, in order to reproduce, they exclusively monitor their own operations, excluding every other consideration. The various sub-systems differ from each other in virtue of the specific functions that they fulfil within society. For example, the function of the legal system is to stabilise and generalise normative expectations, while the function of the political system is to provide the capacity that is required to arrive at collectively binding decisions.[64]

The treatment of functional differentiation as the primary feature of modernity lends a normative quality to this type of social structure. Although Luhmann never tires of emphasising that his theory is purely observational and descriptive, it is here that the normative core of the

[60] Georg Simmel, one of the founders of sociology in Germany, published his major contribution to the theory of social and functional differentiation in 1890, three years before Durkheim's *Division of Labour in Society*. See Georg Simmel, 'Über sociale Differenzierung', in Heinz-Jürgen Dahme (ed.), *Georg Simmel, Gesamtausgabe in 24 Bänden, Band 2: Aufsätze 1887-1890. Über sociale Differenzierung (1890). Die Probleme der Geschichtsphilosophie (1892)*, Frankfurt: Suhrkamp, 1989, pp. 109–295; Emile Durkheim, *The Division of Labor in Society*, translated by W. D. Halls, New York: Free Press, 1997 (1893).

[61] Niklas Luhmann, *Theory of Society*, translated by Rhodes Barret, vol. 2, Stanford: Stanford University Press, 2013 (1997), at 87.

[62] Claudio Baraldi, et al., *Unlocking Luhmann*, Bielefeld: Bielefeld University Press, 2021, at 65–67.

[63] Luhmann, *Theory of Society*, vol. 2, at 91.

[64] Graber, 'Legal Sociology', at 98.

theory of autopoiesis lies hidden.[65] In *Grundrechte als Institution*, the normative connection between fundamental rights and functional differentiation is only hinted at. Luhmann recognises that fundamental rights are more than mere norms protecting individual interests since '[t]heir division into individual fundamental rights also reflects the social differentiation into several relatively autonomous spheres of social meaning formation'.[66] However, he did not go so far as to highlight the normative dimension of the connection between fundamental rights and functional differentiation – this was done by legal scholars who unlocked this critical potential of Luhmann's theory for jurisprudential purposes.[67]

Historically speaking, the progressive differentiation of society into the above-mentioned functional systems has been promoted by symbolically generalised communication media, such as money, power, truth or law. Luhmann also refers to symbolically generalised media as 'success media'.[68] This designation makes sense if we recall that successful communication is generally highly unlikely. Since communicative offers often risk rejection, the use of success media increases the chances of successful communication.[69] As Gunther Teubner puts it:

> Inconvenient or bothersome communicative offers become successful as soon as a specialized communication medium furthers drastically the chances for their acceptance: the seduction of money for handing over goods and services, power threats for obedience to commands, theoretical

[65] Christoph B. Graber, 'Freedom and Affordances of the Net' (2018) *Washington University Jurisprudence Review*, 10, pp. 221–256, at 245.

[66] Luhmann, *Grundrechte als Institution: Ein Beitrag zur politischen Soziologie*, at 79 (translation by the author).

[67] Christoph B. Graber and Gunther Teubner, 'Art and Money: Constitutional Rights in the Private Sphere' (1998) *Oxford Journal of Legal Studies*, 18 (1), pp. 61–73, at 65. See also Gunther Teubner, 'The Anonymous Matrix: Human Rights Violations by "Private" Transnational Actors' (2006) *Modern Law Review*, 69 (3), pp. 327–346, at 338; Christoph B. Graber, 'Internet Creativity, Communicative Freedom and a Constitutional Rights Theory Response to "Code is Law"', in Sean Pager and Adam Candeup (eds.), *Transnational Culture in the Internet Age*, Cheltenham: Edward Elgar, 2012, pp. 135–164, at 156–157.

[68] See Chapter 5.

[69] Luhmann, *Theory of Society*, vol. 1, at 122.

> or empirical proof for implausible assertions, the pressure of credits and exams for accepting learning offers, and normative persuasion for legal judgments.[70]

The stronger the communication medium of a system, the faster it will grow.[71] Luhmann observes that success media may incite excessive growth developments in all function systems,[72] which raises the sociological question of how much 'monetization, juridification, scientification, politicization' is produced in this way.[73] In his theory of communicative action, Jürgen Habermas criticises the growth tendencies of the political system and the economic system, which he sees as threatening the *colonisation of the lifeworld*. The concept 'lifeworld' refers to the whole set of cultural values, social norms and socialisation patterns that often go unquestioned by the actors involved.[74] According to Habermas, the colonisation of the lifeworld in advanced capitalist societies

> sets in when the destruction of traditional forms of life can no longer be offset by more effectively fulfilling the functions of society as a whole. The functional ties of money and power media become noticeable only to the degree that elements of a private way of life and a cultural-political form of life get split off from the symbolic structures of the lifeworld through the monetary redefinition of goals, relations and services, life-spaces and life-times, and through the bureaucratization of decisions, duties and rights, responsibilities and dependencies.[75]

On the methodological level, the distinction between system and lifeworld allows him to critique real developments from a normative perspective. Whereas, for Habermas, it is the lifeworld that is at stake, for systems

[70] Gunther Teubner, 'The Constitution of Non-monetary Surplus Values' (2021) *Social & Legal Studies*, 30 (4), pp. 501–521, at 504.

[71] Ibid., at 509.

[72] Niklas Luhmann, *Law as a Social System*, translated by Klaus Alex Ziegert, Oxford and New York: Oxford University Press, 2004 (1993), at 272.

[73] Luhmann, *Theory of Society*, vol. 2, at 95.

[74] See Gerard H. Fairtlough, 'Habermas' Concept of "Lifeworld"' (1991) *Systems Practice*, 4 (6), pp. 547–563.

[75] Jürgen Habermas, *The Theory of Communicative Action: Lifeworld and System: A Critique of Functionalist Reason*, translated by Thomas MacCarthy, vol. 2, Cambridge: Polity Press, 2007 (1981), at 322.

theory, it is rather functional differentiation that is threatened by the growth tendencies of politics, economics and other expansive systems.

As one response to such threats, fundamental rights have emerged as counterinstitutions of modern society. Their primary function is to ensure that an overly successful communication medium does not endanger social differentiation.[76] In their limiting effect, they embody what Armin Nassehi calls 'stop rule'. Nassehi believes that modern society lacks such a stop rule, 'because modern functional systems are coded systems'.[77] Binary coding, Nassehi argues, lies at the root of the unbroken increase in option in modernity, which manifests itself in growth tendencies in a range of social sub-systems.[78] While Teubner recognises that binary coding is a necessary condition for the expansion of systems, he also rightly sees that the leading cause of growth tendencies lies not in binary coding, but in the 'motivational force' of certain communication media, such as money, power, truth and so on.[79]

But then how exactly do fundamental rights unfold their limiting effect vis-à-vis expanding systems? For Teubner, the answer lies in the theory of societal constitutionalism (as introduced in Chapter 2).[80] Teubner's version of societal constitutionalism roughly distinguishes three steps, starting with the emergence of normative expectations from a reflexive process within a social system (phase 1),[81] followed by a *juridification* of those newly generated normative expectations in a structural coupling with the law (phase 2) and, finally, their constitutionalisation within a reflexive process of the law (phase 3).[82]

[76] Christoph B. Graber, 'Bottom-Up Constitutionalism: The Case of Net Neutrality' (2016) *Transnational Legal Theory*, 7 (4), pp. 524–552; Christoph B. Graber, 'Net Neutrality: A Fundamental Right in the Digital Constitution?' (2023) *Indiana Journal of Global Legal Studies*, 30 (2), pp. 197–226, at 217–218.

[77] Armin Nassehi, *Muster: Theorie der digitalen Gesellschaft*, Munich: C.H. Beck, 2019, at 181 (translation by the author).

[78] Ibid., at 178–185.

[79] Teubner, 'The Constitution of Non-monetary Surplus Values', at 509.

[80] Ibid., at 514.

[81] See Emilios Christodoulidis, 'On the Politics of Societal Constitutionalism' (2013) *Indiana Journal of Global Legal Studies*, 20 (2), pp. 629–663, at 630.

[82] Gunther Teubner, *Constitutional Fragments: Societal Constitutionalism and Globalization*, translated by Gareth Norbury, Oxford: Oxford University Press, 2012, at 88–113.

As discussed in Chapter 2, Teubner employs a very broad concept of 'constitution', in which developments outside the political-legal context are also interpreted as constitutional issues. It is therefore impossible to apply his theory directly to the doctrine of constitutional law. Its value lies rather in the observation and description of empirical processes. Elsewhere, I applied his schema to empirically monitor constitutionalisa tion processes in the context of net neutrality,[83] with the goal of determining whether there exists empirical evidence for the bottom-up emergence of normative expectations about net neutrality (phase 1) and their subsequent juridification (phase 2) and constitutionalisation (phase 3). Unlike Teubner, who ascribes a prescriptive-normative level of meaning to the theory of societal constitutionalism alongside the descriptive one,[84] I see the theory's value above all in its potential to discover constitutional developments in social contexts where they would not otherwise be expected.[85] The main reason for this is that self-consti tutionalisation is not a valid substitute for political legitimacy, which can, as a rule, only be established through formalised democratic processes.[86] On the other hand, it is important to recall that there is a difference between democratic legitimacy and social acceptance.[87] It is not unrealistic to imagine circumstances in which the processes of democratic legitimation are flawed because they lead to the over-representation of particular interests or because they fail to take sufficient account of relevant social values that have not yet been given clear normative contours. In such situations, which are likely to occur under conditions of rapid technological change, the empirical-descriptive analysis of processes of social norm production can serve to reveal such dysfunctions. For benchmarking purposes, I will draw on the descriptive potential of Teubner's theory in the following.

83 Graber, 'Net Neutrality', at 218–222.

84 As explicitly argued in Angelo Jr Golia and Gunther Teubner, 'Societal Constitutionalism: Background, Theory, Debates' (2021) *ICL Journal*, 15 (4), pp. 357–411, at 387–395.

85 Graber, 'Bottom-Up Constitutionalism', at 548–552; Graber, 'Net Neutrality', at 223–225.

86 Christodoulidis, 'On the Politics of Societal Constitutionalism', pp. 629–663.

87 Armin von Bogdandy, et al., *In Whose Name?: A Public Law Theory of International Adjudication*, Oxford: Oxford University Press, 2014, at 155.

An important question to be clarified in phase 1 is which social subsystem will be chosen as the starting point for observing a process of social constitutionalisation. For Teubner, the criterion for selecting the sub-system of reference is the threat posed by the specific success medium of the social system that shows expansive tendencies.[88] On the basis of this criterion, I have chosen the economic system, in order to observe whether there is a society-driven constitutionalisation dynamic in the realm of the internet's technological infrastructure.

This choice is empirically justified. As the debates on net neutrality in the United States, Europe and India have shown (see Chapters 3 and 6), it is the medium of money that drives telecom companies to maximise their business interests. These companies oppose net neutrality out of a desire to preserve their ability to engage in price discrimination, offering faster internet at higher prices to paying customers. The interactions observed between telecommunications companies and civil society representatives in relation to net neutrality reflect what Teubner described as the interplay between the organised professional sphere and the spontaneous sphere of the sub-system. While telecom corporations belong to the organised professional sphere of the economy, civil society organisations populate the spontaneous sphere. The latter argued for strict net-neutrality regulation; the former fought against it. Telecom companies mainly defended their business interests. Civil society representatives argued that equal access to the network should not be sacrificed to economic considerations, as internet openness is a prerequisite for freedom of expression.[89] The reflexive interaction between the two spheres eventually unleashed self-limiting forces within the system, giving rise to normative expectations about net neutrality and internet access. The debates thus followed the pattern of a reflexive process within the sub-system at issue, as propagated by Teubner's theory.[90] The proponents of net neutrality came out on top, especially as they were able to give the initially vague concept a more precise normative contour. On the

[88] Gunther Teubner, 'Societal Constitutionalism: Alternatives to State-Centred Constitutional Theory?', in Christian Joerges, et al. (eds.), *Transnational Governance and Constitutionalism*, Oxford and Portland: Hart, 2004, pp. 3–28, at 19.

[89] Graber, 'Net Neutrality', at 219.

[90] Teubner, *Constitutional Fragments*, at 90–92.

whole, normative expectations emerged that reject opaque discrimination in content distribution for economic reasons.

The second phase involved observing whether a *juridification* of the normative expectations emerging from the first phase could be empirically determined. According to Teubner's theory, a structural coupling between the sub-system and the law occurs at this stage.[91] The legal reformulation of normative expectations that have grown out of society would significantly strengthen the possibility of their counterfactual enforceability. Ultimately, this thesis could only be empirically confirmed for the European Union, which has created an effective and enforceable legal standard with the Open Internet Regulation (OIR) and the related case law of the European Court of Justice (ECJ).[92] A *constitutionalisation* in the sense of the third phase postulated by Teubner could not be assessed empirically, given that neither the ECtHR nor the ECJ have explicitly recognised net neutrality or the right to open internet access as a fundamental right. I will return to this point in the final section of this chapter to assess the broader prospects for the development of a new fundamental right that explicitly protects the technological conditions of freedom of expression.

In conclusion, the theory of societal constitutionalism makes it possible to observe, from a sociological perspective, the emergence of new constitutional norms in contexts where this would not normally be expected. In the realm of net neutrality, this process involves constitutionalising values that see the open internet as a prerequisite for free expression and want to protect it from colonisation by economic forces.

7.4 WHAT CAN FUNDAMENTAL RIGHTS LAW LEARN FROM SOCIOLOGY?

Now that we have juxtaposed the classic fundamental rights doctrine with a sociological perspective on fundamental rights, consideration should be given to the relationship between these two perspectives. It would be a misunderstanding to hold that the socio-legal picture should replace the doctrinal one. It is not that we see *more* from a sociological standpoint;

[91] Teubner, 'Societal Constitutionalism', at 20. [92] For details, see Chapter 6.

what we see is merely different. Sociology provides a macro-perspective on law in society, enabling us to observe potentially asymmetrical relationships between sub-systems that create risks of de-differentiation. In the digital networked environment, the risk of de-differentiation is primarily related to the growth tendencies of the overly successful medium of money – the unique persuasive power of money as a communication medium favours the expansion of the economic system.

The force of economic rationality is evident not only in the case of net neutrality mentioned above, but also, for example, in the addictive design of online services. According to a sub-committee of the European Parliament, 'many digital services, such as online games, social media, streaming services for films, series or music, online marketplaces or web shops and dating apps are designed to keep users on the platform for as long as possible'. These services are designed 'to be as addictive as possible [...] to maximise the time and money [users] spend there'.[93] In this case, time is money, because the more time a user spends on a platform, the more money the platform can make from the advertising it sells.[94]

The expansive force of the economy has also been assessed in personalised advertising, which is the business model of social networks. The formalisation of normative expectations in this area is already well advanced, thanks to the General Data Protection Regulation (GDPR) and corresponding ECJ case law. In *Meta v. Bundeskartellamt*, the ECJ held on 4 July 2023 that the business model of social networks is

> 'based on financing through online advertising, which is tailored to the individual users of the social network according, inter alia, to their consumer behaviour, interests, purchasing power and personal situation. Such advertising is made possible in technical terms by the automated production of detailed profiles in respect of the network users [...].'[95]

[93] European Parliament resolution of 12 December 2023 on addictive design of online services and consumer protection in the EU single market (2023/2043(INI)), at para A.

[94] Tim Wu, *The Attention Merchants: The Epic Scramble to Get Inside Our Heads*, New York: Alfred A. Knopf, 2016.

[95] Judgment (GC) of 4 July 2023, *Meta v. Bundeskartellamt*, C-252/21, ECLI:EU:C:2023:537, at para 27.

The social networks' money-making engine comes with a significant social cost, raising questions about privacy, the colonisation of free speech and the fragmentation of political discourses. With regard to privacy protection, the ECJ ruled that the GDPR requires Meta to obtain users' consent before collecting and processing personal data.[96] Meta must have seen this ruling as an attack on its business model. The ban on collecting and processing user data strikes at its heart, preventing it from exploiting user data to sell personalised advertising. How did Meta react? On 1 November 2023, it introduced a subscription option for European users who do not want their data exploited for personalised ads. The subscription cost between 10 and 13 euro per month until 1 March 2024. Since 1 March 2024, an additional fee of 6 to 8 euro per month has been charged.[97] The economic value of internet services to consumers has so far been unclear. In the future, this will be reflected, at least in part, in the willingness of users to pay the requested amounts.

Meta's move from 'payment by data' to 'payment by money' confirms that ongoing EU regulation of digital architectures in the GDPR and the Digital Services Act (DSA) is forcing social media companies to rethink their business model. Users who are unable or unwilling to pay Meta's fees will either have to pay with their data (as in the past) or stop using Facebook or Instagram. We do not yet know how this measure will impact consumers' use of Meta's services for their communication on social networks. This case illustrates how the ECJ intends to counter the money-driven expansion of the corporate players in the digital environment, but we do not know yet whether the Court's move will succeed. In methodological terms, it shows how the courts take in sociological knowledge about the functioning of the digital economy and its social impacts, incorporating it into the interpretation of legal provisions.

It is not only the implications of money as a success medium that become apparent from a sociological perspective but also the links between digital technology, economic expansion and free speech. The

[96] Ibid., at para 73.

[97] Meta, 'Facebook and Instagram to Offer Subscription for No Ads in Europe', 30 October 2023, https://about.fb.com/news/2023/10/facebook-and-instagram-to-offer-subscription-for-no-ads-in-europe/.

focus is on observing the implications of the internet as a *distribution medium*. As discussed in Chapters 4 and 5, a sociological perspective is necessary if we are to appreciate how technological frameworks provide the conditions for freedom of expression. The sociology and philosophy of technology provide an understanding of digital artefacts and systems as affordances. The conceptualisation of affordances as possibilities or constraints of a technology co-created in a dialogue between technology developers and affected users enables the development of an anti-determinist perspective on technology. It creates the conditions for formulating a socio-political critique of new artefacts or systems. From a socio-political and legal-normative perspective, the insight gained from science and technology studies (STS) is paramount: technology is not impenetrable. Although it is often demanding and time-consuming, civil society experts can identify threats to the public good posed by new technological systems, raise political awareness and contribute to formulating proposals for an appropriate regulatory response.

The critical role of civil society experts in bringing problematic aspects of a complex technology to the surface has also been highlighted, for example, in the debates on net neutrality and open internet in India. Meta's launch of Free Basics in 2015 coincided with the public consultation on net neutrality conducted by the Telecom Regulatory Authority of India (TRAI).[98] A group of civil society activists and semi-professional experts took this as an opportunity to launch the 'Save the Internet' campaign in India, mobilising hundreds of thousands to participate in the consultation process and protest against Meta's project. The campaign drew TRAI's attention to the negative impact of Free Basics on open internet access in India, ultimately leading the regulator to ban the project.[99]

In principle, law has much to learn from the findings of the sociology of technology. However, there exists a methodological difficulty, insofar as this knowledge cannot simply be copied and pasted into law. Because

[98] Anita Gurumurthy and Nandini Chami, 'Internet Governance as "Ideology in Practice" – India's "Free Basics" Controversy' (2016) *Internet Policy Review*, 5 (3), pp. 1–17, at 2; Subhayan Mukerjee, 'Net Neutrality, Facebook, and India's Battle to #SaveTheInternet' (2016) *Communication and the Public*, 1 (3), pp. 356–361.

[99] For a detailed discussion, see Graber, 'Net Neutrality', at 215.

the law is a cognitively open but operatively closed system that produces new legal communication from existing legal communication, directly importing sociological knowledge into the system is impossible. Instead, the law must reformulate STS knowledge in its own language, which requires a review of the doctrinal categories in the affected areas of law.

One essential difference between sociology and law concerns democratic legitimacy. Democratically legitimised institutions produce and enact legal norms according to formally prescribed procedures. From a doctrinal-legal perspective, the specific dynamics of the social institutionalisation of norms can be criticised for their lack of democratic legitimacy. Hence, the sociological view of the value change of a fundamental right is not intended to replace the doctrinal view, but rather to complement it. Instead, the distinction between a sociological and a legal concept of fundamental rights leads to the simultaneous existence of empirical-descriptive and normative-prescriptive semantic levels. For legal scholarship, this means that when interpreting the fundamental right of freedom of expression, a given constitutional norm should be reflected in its real social context. This enables the *social concept* of fundamental rights to 're-enter'[100] the *legal doctrinal concept* of fundamental rights. Consequently, freedom of expression, understood as a social institution, always remains latently present as a difference when the legal doctrinal interpretation of this fundamental right by courts, other law-applying authorities and the legislature is analysed by scholars. In this way, it is possible to provide legal scholarship with the impulse and scope to further develop the doctrine of fundamental rights, which is closer to the reality of society.

In practice, the approach chosen will mostly be procedural.[101] Courts intervene ex post, *after* the infringement of a fundamental right has occurred. Their ability to respond in a general way to the particular challenges of a new technology *pro futuro* is minimal. Even under the

[100] The theory of distinction uses the term to denote the re-entry of the distinction into what it distinguishes. See Niklas Luhmann, *Die Wissenschaft der Gesellschaft*, Frankfurt: Suhrkamp, 1990, pp. 83–84 and 379–380.

[101] For a procedural approach to fundamental rights implementation, see Graber, 'Internet Creativity, Communicative Freedom and a Constitutional Rights Theory Response to "Code is Law"', at 158–163.

common law doctrine of *stare decisis*, precedents may only have authoritative effects on later cases if certain conditions (e.g. similarity or identity of facts) are met.[102] Moreover, judgments relate to individual conflicts, and are thus not formulated in general terms. The legislator is better positioned than the constitutional judge to decide on the complex issues of weighing up, setting priorities and allocating financial resources.[103] Hence, proceduralising a fundamental right often results in a programmatic mandate to the legislature.[104] In the context of the comprehensive regulation of a particular technology, the legislator can take measures to protect objective interests or formulate responses to violations of fundamental rights caused by private actors. A democratically organised legislative process provides the best guarantee that the different social concerns and political and economic interests will find their way into the law. Thus, fundamental rights conflicts in the private sphere are 'verticalised'.[105] Such a development can be seen in the latest EU legislation, such as the GDPR, the OIR, the DSA and the Artificial Intelligence Act. For the lawmaker, it is very difficult to assess the risks posed by the new digital artefacts and systems, as well as to design appropriate measures to address the social costs to which they give rise. Often it takes years before it becomes clear whether the regulatory goal has been adequately defined, the means are appropriate and the legislation as a whole is effective in achieving this goal. There is therefore something experimental about these regulations,[106] although the EU legislator would be

[102] See Stephen R. Perry, 'Judicial Obligation, Precedent and the Common Law' (1987) *Oxford Journal of Legal Studies*, 7 (2), pp. 215–257; Evan H. Caminker, 'Why Must Inferior Courts Obey Superior Court Precedents' (1994) *Stanford Law Review*, 46 (4), pp. 817–874.

[103] Biaggini, 'Über Aufgaben und Grenzen der Verfassungsgerichtsbarkeit im ökologischen Verfassungsstaat', at 554.

[104] On the programmatic dimension of fundamental rights in Swiss constitutional law, see Kiener, 'Grundrechte in der Bundesverfassung', at 1211–1212.

[105] Claire Loven, *Fundamental Rights Violations by Private Actors and the Procedure before the European Court of Human Rights: A Study of Verticalised Cases*, Antwerp: Intersentia, 2022.

[106] For an early characterisation of experimental lawmaking, see Luzius Mader, 'Experimentelle Gesetzgebung', in Dieter Grimm and Werner Maihofer (eds.), *Gesetzgebungstheorie und Rechtspolitik*, Wiesbaden: VS Verlag für Sozialwissenschaften, 1988, pp. 211–221. For more recent discussions, see Sofia Ranchordás, 'The Whys and Woes of Experimental Legislation' (2013) *The Theory and Practice of Legislation*, 1 (3),

careful not to use that term, as regulations, which are the result of a lengthy legislative process, are generally intended to be permanent. The AI Act provides for regulatory sandboxes (chapter 6 of the AI Act) that offer regulatory spaces to test new AI systems under specific conditions. While explicitly experimental regulations are still rare in the EU, the Digital Services Act contains many rules (e.g. on consent, sensitive personal data and ad profiling of minors) whose effect will only become clear in the future.[107] One of the peculiarities of this type of proactive regulation of complex technologies is that such comprehensive laws, once introduced, have a certain inertia, and therefore, high hurdles must be overcome to get rid of them if they have not proved valuable.

7.5 THE PROSPECTS FOR THE DEVELOPMENT OF FREE SPEECH

The preceding analysis has concluded that courts generally have less legitimacy than the legislator and are less well suited to effectively protect the technological preconditions of free speech. However, this does not alter the fact that the transformation of fundamental rights, that is the development of freedom of expression in the context of the particular challenges posed by digital technology, is taking place at the centre of the law (i.e., in the courts).

Drawing on the idea that the social and legal institutionalisation of fundamental rights need to be distinguished, we can articulate the prospects for future adjustments to the doctrine of freedom of expression. How should this fundamental right evolve to protect the technological preconditions of free speech? In order to answer this question, we must return to the analysis in Chapter 6, where we found evidence for the connection between free speech and technology in constitutional

pp. 415–440; Sofia Ranchordás, *Constitutional Sunsets and Experimental Legislation: A Comparative Perspective*, Cheltenham: Edward Elgar, 2014, and Michiel A. Heldeweg, 'Experimental Legislation Concerning Technological & Governance Innovation: An Analytical Approach' (2015) *The Theory and Practice of Legislation*, 3 (2), pp. 169–193.

107 Gunther Teubner and Angelo Jr Golia, 'Societal Constitutionalism in the Digital World' (2023) *Indiana Journal of Global Legal Studies*, 30 (2), pp. 1–23, at 10.

amendment,[108] the case law of courts, governmental regulation, co-regulation and (formal or informal) self-regulation. We can use this evidence as a starting point to ask how the jurisprudence of the ECtHR and ECJ on technology-related preconditions of freedom of expression might develop in the future.

One likely development would be the formal recognition by the ECtHR of a novel 'right to transmit' as part of Article 10 ECHR, which might include a prohibition on unreasonable blocking and throttling of content dissemination. As we have seen, the Committee of Ministers of the Council of Europe has adopted a recommendation on net neutrality, which targets interference with internet traffic that results in the 'blocking, discrimination or prioritization of specific types of content, applications or services'.[109] As this language indicates, the scope of the Recommendation extends to prohibiting zero-rating practices that mislead users by incentivising the use of specific applications and services in a non-transparent manner. Recall that the ECJ strongly restricted zero-rating in its jurisprudence on the OIR and that BEREC banned such practices in its June 2022 Guidelines.[110]

As the legal developments in open internet access show, soft-law instruments provide sources that the courts can draw upon to further develop existing case law on freedom of expression. At the periphery of the legal system, they attempt to absorb vox populi and social pressure that has been building up in various sub-systems of society.[111] When a court references values and principles affirmed in soft-law documents,

[108] It is worth mentioning that the cantons of Geneva and Neuchâtel recognised 'digital integrity' as an independent fundamental right in referendums held in 2023 and 2024, respectively. See Nesa Zimmermann, 'Entre innovations et résistances: La garantie des droits humains dans l'État fédéral suisse' (2023) *Zeitschrift für Schweizerisches Recht*, 142, pp. 151–249, at 197.

[109] Council of Europe Committee of Ministers, 'Recommendation CM/Rec(2016)1 of the Committee of Ministers to member States on protecting and promoting the right to freedom of expression and the right to private life with regard to network neutrality', adopted by the Committee of Ministers on 13 January 2016 at the 1,244th meeting of the Ministers' Deputies.

[110] BEREC, 'BEREC Guidelines on the Implementation of the Open Internet Regulation', BoR (22) 81, 9 June 2022, at para 40b.

[111] Luhmann, *Law as a Social System*, at 291–304.

they move from the periphery of the legal system to the judiciary, that is to the centre of the law.

Just as the Council of Europe Recommendation provides inspiration for the ECtHR, the European Declaration on Digital Rights and Principles for the Digital Decade of 23 January 2023 will likely inform future jurisprudence in the EU.[112] The Declaration resulted from a public consultation and was jointly issued by the European Parliament, the Council and the Commission. With the aim of expressing the convictions shared within the EU on the importance of digital rights, it should 'guide policy makers when reflecting on their vision of the digital transformation'[113] and 'serve as a reference point for businesses and other relevant actors when developing and deploying new technologies'.[114] The Declaration emphasises the essential significance of technology for protecting and promoting fundamental rights, addressing several issues discussed in Chapter 6 under the heading 'Digital Means of Free Speech'. Connectivity is a prominent commitment in the context of open internet access objectives. The EU commits to 'protecting a neutral and open internet where content, services, and applications are not unjustifiably blocked or degraded'.[115] With regard to 'participation in the digital public space', the EU also commits to 'continuing safeguarding fundamental rights online, notably the freedom of expression and information'[116] and to 'supporting the development and best use of digital technologies to stimulate citizen engagement and democratic participation'.[117] In a chapter on safety, security and privacy, the Declaration underscores that 'everyone should have the right to the confidentiality of their communications and the information on their electronic devices, and no one shall be subjected to unlawful online surveillance or interception measures'.[118]

7.6 CONCLUDING REMARKS

Understanding how fundamental rights change requires us to distinguish between a legal and a sociological perspective. From a sociological

[112] European Declaration on Digital Rights and Principles for the Digital Decade 2023/C 23/01, OJ C 23, 23 January 2023.

[113] Ibid., Recital 7. [114] Ibid., Recital 8. [115] Ibid., chapter II, 3(b).

[116] Ibid., chapter IV, 15(a). [117] Ibid., chapter IV, 15(b). [118] Ibid., chapter V, 18.

perspective, fundamental rights appear as social institutions whose primary function is to protect social differentiation from the expansionist tendencies of specific sub-systems. In the context of this book, the focus is primarily on the economic system, which possesses a particularly successful medium in the form of money and is, therefore, growing especially vigorously. There is a danger that the expansion of the economic system will 'colonise' free speech, as corporate interests – beyond policing content – control the technological infrastructure needed to exercise freedom of expression online.

As *institutions of society*, fundamental rights embody a de facto social consensus that the law can use to constitutionalise limitative counter-forces. The theory of societal constitutionalism provides an analytical scheme that can be used to empirically monitor the growth of normative expectations regarding new technologies, their juridification and, ultimately, their constitutionalisation. This perspective can give legal scholarship the impetus necessary to provide democratic legislators with concepts for regulation. However, a normative-prescriptive reconstruction of the theory, as propagated by Teubner and his co-author,[119] would go too far due to a lack of democratic legitimation.

The sociological analysis of changes in fundamental rights contrasts with the understanding of fundamental rights as *institutions of the law*. From this perspective, which is decisive for jurisprudence, the stability of the legal order and the constitutional principle of legal certainty take centre stage. It would therefore be wrong to expect a more accurate account of fundamental rights from sociological analysis. It is not that sociology sees *more*; it merely sees something else. Sociology, like legal science, has its blind spot, as every act of observation involves a distinction that enables it to observe its proper object. The blind spot is the initial distinction that guides the observation, which is to be found at the point where the line of separation is drawn.[120] As a consequence, every observation is blind to its own operation, as it cannot observe itself 'without coming up against the paradox of the unity of the different'.[121] What sociology can contribute to legal science is an empirical

[119] Golia and Teubner, 'Societal Constitutionalism', at 387–395.

[120] Luhmann, *Theory of Society*, vol. 1, at 110 and 258. [121] Ibid., at 326.

observation of the functioning of fundamental rights in the context of society from a law-external perspective. The knowledge gained from the sociological analysis can subsequently be utilised by jurisprudence to contrast the normative-prescriptive dimension with an empirically descriptive one when interpreting fundamental rights. The doubling of perspectives achieved in this way provides fundamental rights doctrine with a horizon that potentially enables its further development. However, because social systems stand in a relationship of second-order observation (observation of observation), it is impossible to copy and paste insights from sociology into law.

The problem that fundamental rights lack binding force vis-à-vis important private actors on the internet can be solved if we remember that these guarantees not only provide subjective rights, which courts enforce in individual cases, but, accessorily, are also objective mandates to the legislator. Legislation and other legally based (self-)regulatory processes can provide a normative framework that ensures that new technologies (and those who control them) develop in a way that is compatible with the values, objectives and rights enshrined in the Constitution.

CHAPTER 8

Conclusion

This book has sought to draw the attention of legal scholars to the technological preconditions of freedom of expression. This issue has been neglected in legal practice due to the prevalence of an instrumental understanding of technology, which sees it as a means to an end, while ignoring the complex interplay between technological materiality and communicative sociality that characterises the reality of digital distribution media. In our search for a more convincing way of conceptualising technology, we found what we were looking for in the works of Andrew Feenberg. Within the philosophical framework of science and technology studies (STS), he has developed a synthetic conception of technology that reconstructs the relationship between the material and the social without falling into the extremes of essentialism or radical constructivism. Feenberg conceives of technology as something that offers manifold flexibility and opportunities for co-determination, both in the design phase and in its adoption by society. Guided by the values of the Enlightenment and the ideals of the Frankfurt School, Feenberg has succeeded in taking a critical stance towards technological development. The integration of this concept of technology into sociological systems theory enables us to build a bridge between STS and legal science. On this basis, normative-prescriptive counter-positions can be substantiated in opposition both to the motto 'move fast and break things',[1] which has been influential in tech circles, *and* to the

[1] This expression was originally coined by Mark Zuckerberg, the founder of Facebook and current chair of Meta.

corresponding fatalistic acceptance of the 'normative force of the factual'[2] that still defines the mindset of many jurists.

If, from a systems-theory perspective, we understand law as a subsystem of society whose function is to stabilise and generalise normative expectations, it is necessary to ask how existing normative structures can change as the result of learning processes and how expectations about newly introduced digital technologies can develop. In our discussion of theories of law-making, we concluded that legal norms can not only be changed or created in legislative processes or court practice, but that civil society dynamics can also play a role here. This applies in particular to expectations about new technologies on the internet. At an early stage in the introduction of a technology, normative expectations are usually diffuse, due to the enormous complexity of these technologies, whose social impact only becomes apparent in the medium to long term. Because smart technologies display a high degree of behavioural self-reference, they often seem impenetrable to the average user, with scholars speaking of technology as a 'black box', whose walls obscure its functionality and effects. The situation is different for technology experts, who possess the knowledge needed to peer inside the box through 'leaks, cracks, and ruptures'.[3] Experts therefore play an important role in informing the public about how new technologies work and the associated opportunities and risks. Their expertise helps civil rights organisations, NGOs, consumer protection groups and similar entities to warn of possible negative effects, call for resistance or formulate concrete demands for government regulation. It is often civil society actors who bring this information to the attention of legislators, although in other cases it is the courts that are the first to deal with the social impact of a

[2] On Georg Jellinek's famous concept, see, e.g., Matthias Klatt, 'Law as Fact and Norm. Georg Jellinek and the Dual Nature of Law', in Nicoletta Bersier Ladavac, et al. (eds.), *The Normative Force of the Factual: Legal Philosophy Between Is and Ought*, Cham: Springer International Publishing, 2019, pp. 45–64, and Christoph Bezemek, 'The "Normative Force of the Factual": A Positivist's Panegyric', in Nicoletta Bersier Ladavac, et al. (eds.), *The Normative Force of the Factual: Legal Philosophy Between Is and Ought*, Cham: Springer International Publishing, 2019, pp. 65–77.

[3] Taina Bucher, *If. . . Then: Algorithmic Power and Politics*, Oxford: Oxford University Press, 2018, at 60.

new technology. In the absence of statutory regulation, the courts are usually restricted to interpreting existing legal provisions in a broad sense as a means of finding (provisional) answers to urgent questions.

In order to stabilise and generalise normative expectations, the law relies on fundamental rights, which, as social institutions, embody a factual consensus that has emerged in society. Gunther Teubner's theory of societal constitutionalism reminds us that fundamental rights fulfil a limitative constitutional function, protecting functional differentiation from self-destructive tendencies. This protection is necessary because 'strong' social sub-systems are likely to show expansionist tendencies that restrict the space that 'weaker' systems need to reproduce their proper communication medium. In the context of the digital technologies required for communication via the internet, the growth compulsion of the economic system takes centre stage. The emergence of norms guaranteeing non-discriminatory access to the technical infrastructure of the internet has provided an empirical test of Teubner's theory, revealing that, first, normative expectations about the open internet emerge bottom-up, as the result of a self-limiting process that takes place within the economic system. It has also provided empirical confirmation of the juridification of these normative expectations, which the theory postulates will occur at the second stage.

While Teubner recognises a normative-prescriptive dimension to the theory of social constitutionalism, I have used the theory strictly in its empirical-descriptive dimension. This is because self-constitutionalisation processes cannot be a substitute for democratically legitimised political regulation.[4] Interpreted as an empirical-descriptive theory, societal constitutionalism makes it possible to perceive processes of constitutional norm production not only in a formalised political-legal context but also outside of it, in transnational forums. The methodological advantage of this approach for legal sociology is that the sociological-descriptive and legal-prescriptive analyses are carried out in parallel. The doubling of perspectives provides a way out of the epistemological dilemma that no observation can see its own blind spot, but only the blind spots of other

[4] Emilios Christodoulidis, 'On the Politics of Societal Constitutionalism' (2013) *Indiana Journal of Global Legal Studies*, 20 (2), pp. 629–663.

observations. It is therefore necessary to distinguish between a legal and a social understanding of fundamental rights. By re-introducing this distinction on the side of the legal understanding of fundamental rights, a horizon of change opens up for legal practice, which it can use to orientate itself, with the result that lived social reality is made available to the legislator or court as a benchmark for the further development of the positive legal order.

The history of the development of fundamental rights doctrine in Switzerland shows the formative influence of international law on the Swiss legal system.[5] From the 1960s onwards, the prevalent conception of human rights at the international level as the duty of states to protect has challenged the purely defensive interpretation of fundamental rights. Since Switzerland's accession to the European Convention on Human Rights (ECHR) in 1974, the protection provided by the Convention has continuously influenced the case law of the Federal Supreme Court. It is certainly true that the European Court of Human Rights' (ECtHR) interpretation of the ECHR as a 'living instrument' has led to a number of judgments in recent years that have been strongly criticised in Switzerland. The clearest reaction has been to what is called the 'climate judgment', a 2024 verdict that condemned Switzerland for violating Article 8 ECHR (right to private and family life) because the State failed to comply with its regulatory obligations to implement effective measures to protect individuals against the effects of climate change.[6] Subsequently, both chambers of Parliament adopted declarations criticising the ECtHR's interpretation of the Convention as a 'living instrument' for exceeding the limits of dynamic treaty interpretation and recalling that, according to the principle of subsidiarity contained in the preamble to the ECHR, it is primarily the task of the contracting parties to guarantee the rights and freedoms enshrined in the Convention.[7]

[5] See Chapter 7, Section 7.2.

[6] *Verein KlimaSeniorinnen Schweiz and Others v. Switzerland* App. no. 53600/20 (ECtHR (GC), 9 April 2024).

[7] Council of States, declaration of 5 June 2024 on the judgment of the ECtHR in *Verein KlimaSeniorinnen Schweiz v. Switzerland* (24.053), www.parlament.ch/de/ratsbetrieb/amtliches-bulletin/amtliches-bulletin-die-verhandlungen?SubjectId=64711. See also

With regard to freedom of expression, the level of protection afforded by court practice in relation to Article 16 of the Swiss Constitution and Article 10 of the ECHR is generally very high. For this reason, the comments of the UN Human Rights Committee on Article 19 of the International Covenant on Civil and Political Rights (freedom of expression) have had relatively little impact on Swiss constitutional law. Far more important are legal developments in the EU that do not directly affect constitutional jurisdiction, but that may have an indirect impact as they are often (explicitly or implicitly) incorporated into Swiss law on a voluntary basis. Examples that are relevant to this study include data protection laws and the regulation of the open internet and net neutrality. In addition to these formal legal developments, the informal norm-building processes of transnational law have a direct or indirect impact on Swiss law, in particular the dynamics of the self-regulatory forums of the Internet Corporation for Assigned Names and Numbers (ICANN), the Internet Architecture Board (IAB) and the Internet Engineering Task Force (IETF), which influence the technical conditions for free communication on the internet.[8] The technical standards emerging there can be postulated as a horizon for the further development of freedom of expression, with a stronger emphasis on technical requirements.

It is not the case that transnational legal developments find their way into Swiss law in an unfiltered form. On the one hand, this can be explained by the democratic and federalist foundations of the Swiss Federal Constitution. On the other hand, it has to do with the self-confidence behind the Swiss understanding of the Federal Constitution, as the country can look back on a history of fundamental rights jurisprudence that is unique in the world. In Switzerland, fundamental rights are enriched not only by formally supplementing the catalogue of fundamental rights through constitutional revisions but also through the incremental development of existing fundamental rights by

National Council, declaration of 12 June 2024 on the judgment of the ECtHR in *Verein KlimaSeniorinnen Schweiz v. Switzerland* (24.054), www.parlament.ch/de/ratsbetrieb/amtliches-bulletin/amtliches-bulletin-die-verhandlungen?SubjectId=64937#votum2.

[8] See Chapter 6.

means of interpretation or the recognition of unwritten fundamental rights by the Federal Supreme Court. While the formalised procedures of constitutional revision ensure democratic legitimacy, this legitimacy is partially lacking in cases involving the judicial development of fundamental rights. The Court therefore seeks to reduce the tension between social change and constitutional stability by compensating for the lack of democratic legitimacy through the imposition of strict conditions on the recognition of unwritten fundamental rights. The Federal Supreme Court recognises new fundamental rights only with great reluctance and only in relation to needs 'which are a prerequisite for the exercise of other freedoms (mentioned in the Constitution) or otherwise appear to be indispensable components of the democratic and constitutional order of the Confederation'.[9] It also always examines 'whether the guarantee in question already corresponds to a widespread constitutional reality in the cantons and is supported by a general consensus'.[10] The reference to the constitutional reality of the cantons reveals that the Federal Supreme Court understands fundamental rights as something that grows from the bottom up. The criterion that there should exist a 'general consensus' also shows that the Court does not seek to place itself above the widely shared convictions of the Swiss people.[11]

This practice represents a remarkable example of a national supreme court exercising restraint in its interpretation of its role as the guardian of the development of fundamental rights, while also compensating for a lack of formal democratic legitimacy by appealing to social acceptance. This approach could inspire judgments in other jurisdictions, especially in cases involving the technical means of free expression, where there is a pronounced tension between change and stability.

As highlighted throughout the book, the power of the courts to effectively protect freedom of expression is limited in the face of global digital networks and powerful private technology companies. It is

[9] BGE 121 I 367, E. 2a, 370 (translation by the author).

[10] Ibid. (translation by the author).

[11] Giovanni Biaggini, 'Grundrechtsinnovation im Bundesstaat – ein Streifzug durch 175 Jahre Verfassungsgeschichte', in Frédéric Bernard, et al. (eds.), *Le droit au service de l'humanité: Mélanges en l'honneur de Michel Hottelier*, Zurich: Schulthess, 2023, pp. 33–50, at 40.

therefore all the more important to recognise not only the individual but also the institutional dimension of fundamental rights as objective value judgements under constitutional law, the implementation of which falls under the state's duty to protect. Given the enormous technical and social complexity of the digital revolution, such tasks can only be accomplished through legislation. However, since it is difficult to assess the risks of a new technology in advance, to design measures to counteract its expected social cost and to monitor whether the regulation as a whole leads to the achievement of its objectives, such attempts often have an experimental character.

Bibliography

Anderson Peter Bøgh, 'WWW as Self-Organizing System' (1998) *Cybernetics & Human Knowing*, 5 (2), pp. 5–41

Arnold René C. G., et al., 'All But Neutral: Citizen Responses to the European Commission's Public Consultation on Network Neutrality', in Luca Belli and Primavera De Filippi (eds.), *Net Neutrality Compendium: Human Rights, Free Competition and the Future of the Internet*, Cham: Springer International Publishing, 2016, pp. 199–210

Baecker Dirk, 'Digitalisierung als Kalkül', in Dirk Baecker, et al. (eds.), *Post-digitales Management*, Wiesbaden: Springer VS, 2023, pp. 23–37

Baecker Dirk, 'Technik im Datenraum', in Dirk Baecker, et al. (eds.), *Post-digitales Management*, Wiesbaden: Springer VS, 2023, pp. 243–256

Balkin Jack M., 'Digital Speech and Democratic Culture: A Theory of Freedom of Expression for the Information Society' (2004) *New York University Law Review*, 79 (1), pp. 1–55

Balla Steven J., et al., 'Responding to Mass, Computer-Generated, and Malattributed Comments' (2022) *Administrative Law Review*, 74 (1), pp. 95–160

Baraldi Claudio, et al., *Unlocking Luhmann*, Bielefeld: Bielefeld University Press, 2021

Baxter Hugh, 'Niklas Luhmann's Theory of Autopoietic Legal Systems' (2013) *Annual Review of Law and Social Science*, 9, pp. 167–184

Beckers Anna and Teubner Gunther, *Three Liability Regimes for Artificial Intelligence: Algorithmic Actants, Hybrids, Crowds*, Oxford: Hart, 2021

Bellamy Richard, 'The Democratic Legitimacy of International Human Rights Conventions: Political Constitutionalism and the European Convention on Human Rights' (2014) *European Journal of International Law*, 25 (4), pp. 1019–1042

Berman Harold J., *Law and Revolution*, Cambridge, MA: Harvard University Press, 1983

Berners-Lee Tim with Fischetti Mark, *Weaving the Web: The Original Design and Ultimate Destiny of the World Wide Web by Its Inventor,* New York: Harper Collins, 1999

Bezemek Christoph, 'The "Normative Force of the Factual": A Positivist's Panegyric', in Nicoletta Bersier Ladavac, et al. (eds.), *The Normative Force of the Factual: Legal Philosophy Between Is and Ought,* Cham: Springer International Publishing, 2019, pp. 65–77

Biaggini Giovanni, 'Constitutional Adjudication in Switzerland', in Armin v. Bogdandy, et al. (eds.), *The Max Planck Handbooks in European Public Law,* Oxford: Oxford University Press, 2020, pp. 779–840

Biaggini Giovanni, 'Über Aufgaben und Grenzen der Verfassungsgerichtsbarkeit im ökologischen Verfassungsstaat', in Claudia Seitz, et al. (eds.), *Rechtsschutz in Theorie und Praxis: Festschrift für Stephan Breitenmoser,* Basel: Helbing & Lichtenhahn, 2022, pp. 545–559

Biaggini Giovanni, 'Grundrechtsinnovation im Bundesstaat – ein Streifzug durch 175 Jahre Verfassungsgeschichte', in Frédéric Bernard, et al. (eds.), *Le droit au service de l'humanité: Mélanges en l'honneur de Michel Hottelier,* Zurich: Schulthess, 2023, pp. 33–50

Biagioli Mario and Buning Marius, 'Technologies of the Law/Law as a Technology' (2019) *History of Science,* 57 (1), pp. 3–17

Bickert Monika, 'Defining the Boundaries of Free Speech on Social Media', in Geoffrey R. Stone and Lee C. Bollinger (eds.), *The Free Speech Century,* Oxford: Oxford University Press, 2018, pp. 254–271

Bijker Wiebe E., *Of Bicycles, Bakelites, and Bulbs: Toward a Theory of Sociotechnical Change,* Cambridge, MA: The MIT Press, 1995

Bijker Wiebe E., 'Technology, Social Construction of', in James D. Wright (ed.), *International Encyclopedia of the Social & Behavioral Sciences,* 2nd edn, Oxford: Elsevier, 2015, pp. 135–140

Bonanno Alessandro and Antonio Robert J., 'Multinational Corporations', in George Ritzer (ed.), *The Wiley-Blackwell Encyclopedia of Globalization,* Chichester: Wiley-Blackwell, 2012, pp. 1–9

Bora Alfons, 'Medialität des Wissens', in Gunnar F. Schuppert, et al. (eds.), *Herrschaft und Wissen,* Baden-Baden: Nomos, 2022, pp. 295–324

Bošnjak Marko and Zajac Kacper, 'Judicial Activism and Judge-Made Law at the ECtHR' (2023) *Human Rights Law Review,* 23 (3), pp. 1–15

Bowker Geoffrey C., et al., 'Toward Information Infrastructure Studies: Ways of Knowing in a Networked Environment', in Jeremy Hunsinger, et al. (eds.), *International Handbook of Internet Research,* Dordrecht: Springer Netherlands, 2010, pp. 97–117

Bowker Geoffrey C., 'The Theory/Data Thing Commentary' (2014) *International Journal of Communication*, 8, pp. 1795–1799

Boyle James, 'Foucault in Cyberspace: Surveillance, Sovereignty, and Hardwired Censors' (1997) *University of Cincinnati Law Review*, 66 (1), pp. 177–205

Braman Sandra, 'The Interpenetration of Technical and Legal Decision-Making for the Internet' (2010) *Information, Communication & Society*, 13 (3), pp. 309–324

Braman Sandra, 'Privacy by Design: Networked Computing, 1969–1979' (2011) *New Media & Society*, 14 (5), pp. 798–814

Braman Sandra, 'Laying the Path: Governance in Early Internet Design' (2013) *info*, 15 (6), pp. 63–83

Bruns Axel and Burgess Jean, 'Twitter Hashtags from Ad Hoc to Calculated Publics', in Nathan Rambukkana (ed.), *Hashtag Publics: The Power and Politics of Discursive Networks*, New York: Peter Lang, 2015, pp. 13–27

Bucher Taina, *If...Then: Algorithmic Power and Politics*, Oxford: Oxford University Press, 2018

Callon Michel and Latour Bruno, 'Unscrewing the Big Leviathan: How Actors Macro-Structure Reality and How Sociologists Help Them to Do So', in Karin Knorr Cetina and Aaron Cicourel (eds.), *Advances in Social Theory and Methodology: Toward an Integration of Micro- and Macro-Sociologies*, London: Routledge, 1981, pp. 277–303

Caminker Evan H., 'Why Must Inferior Courts Obey Superior Court Precedents'? (1994) *Stanford Law Review*, 46 (4), pp. 817–874

Canfora Gerardo, et al., 'Achievements and Challenges in Software Reverse Engineering' (2011) *Communication of the ACM*, 54 (4), pp. 142–151

Carillo Arturo J., 'Having Your Cake and Eating It Too?: Zero-Rating, Net Neutrality, and International Law' (2016) *Stanford Technology Law Review*, 19 (3), pp. 364–429

Cass Deborah Z., *The Constitutionalization of the World Trade Organization*, Oxford and New York: Oxford University Press, 2005

Celeste Edoardo, *Digital Constitutionalism: The Role of Internet Bills of Rights*, London: Routledge, 2022

Celeste Edoardo, 'Internet Bills of Rights: Generalisation and Re-specification Towards a Digital Constitution' (2023) *Indiana Journal of Global Legal Studies*, 30 (2), pp. 25–54

Chander Anupam, 'Facebookistan' (2012) *North Carolina Law Review*, 90 (5), pp. 1808–1844

Christodoulidis Emilios, 'On the Politics of Societal Constitutionalism' (2013) *Indiana Journal of Global Legal Studies*, 20 (2), pp. 629–663

Cloatre Emilie and Pickersgill Martyn, 'Introduction', in Emilie Cloatre and Martyn Pickersgill (eds.), *Knowledge, Technology and Law,* London and New York: Routledge, 2015, pp. 1–14

Cockfield Arthur and Pridmore Jason, 'A Synthetic Theory of Law and Technology' (2007) *Minnesota Journal of Law, Science & Technology,* 8 (2), pp. 475–513

Cohen Julie E., *Configuring the Networked Self: Law, Code and the Play of Everyday Practice,* New Haven: Yale University Press, 2012

Cohen Julie E., 'Affording Fundamental Rights: A Provocation Inspired by Mireille Hildebrandt' (2017) *Critical Analysis of Law,* 4 (1), pp. 78–90

Cole David, 'The Chinese Room Argument', in Edward N. Zalta and Uri Nodelman (eds.), *The Stanford Encyclopedia of Philosophy* (Summer 2023 Edition), https://plato.stanford.edu/archives/sum2023/entries/chinese-room/

Cole Simon A. and Bertenthal Alyse, 'Science, Technology, Society, and Law' (2017) *Annual Review of Law and Social Science,* 13, pp. 351–371

Couldry Nick et al., 'Real Social Analytics: A Contribution Towards a Phenomenology of a Digital World' (2016) *The British Journal of Sociology,* 67 (1), pp. 118–137

Couldry Nick, 'Recovering Critique in an Age of Datafication' (2020) *New Media & Society,* 22 (7), pp. 1135–1151

Cowls Josh et al., 'Constitutional Metaphors: Facebook's "Supreme Court" and the Legitimation of Platform Governance' (2022) *New Media & Society,* 26 (5), pp. 1–25

Cuéllar Mariano-Florentino and Huq Aziz Z., 'Economies of Surveillance' (2020) *Harvard Law Review,* 133 (4), pp. 1280–1336

Davies D. W. et al., 'A Digital Communication Network for Computers Giving Rapid Response at Remote Terminals', in John A. Gosden and Brian Randell (eds.), *Proceedings of the First ACM Symposium on Operating System Principles (SOSP '67)* (Gatlinburg, 1 to 4 October 1967), New York: Association for Computing Machinery, 1967, pp. 2.1–2.17

De Gregorio Giovanni, 'Digital Constitutionalism Across the Atlantic' (2022) *Global Constitutionalism,* 11 (2), pp. 297–324

De la Cadena Marisol et al., 'Anthropology and STS' (2015) *HAU: Journal of Ethnographic Theory,* 5 (1), pp. 437–475

De Wet Erika, 'The International Constitutional Order' (2006) *International and Comparative Law Quarterly,* 55 (1), pp. 51–76

Diggelmann Oliver and Cleis Maria Nicole, 'How the Right to Privacy Became a Human Right' (2014) *Human Rights Law Review,* 14 (3), pp. 441–458

Doherty Neil F. et al., 'A Re-conceptualization of the Interpretive Flexibility of Information Technologies: Redressing the Balance Between the Social and the Technical' (2006) *European Journal of Information Systems*, 15 (6), pp. 569–582

Douek Evelyn, 'Facebook's "Oversight Board": Move Fast with Stable Infrastructure and Humility' (2019) *North Carolina Journal of Law & Technology*, 21 (1), pp. 1–77

Durkheim Emile, *The Division of Labor in Society*, translated by W. D. Halls, New York: Free Press, 1997 (1893)

Dzehtsiarou Kanstantsin and O'Mahony Conor, 'Evolutive Interpretation of Rights Provisions: A Comparison of the European Court of Human Rights and the U.S. Supreme Court' (2013) *Columbia Human Rights Law Review*, 44 (2), pp. 309–365

Edwards Lilian, 'Articles 12–15 ECD: ISP Liability: The Problem of Intermediary Service Provider Liability', in Lilian Edwards (ed.), *The New Legal Framework for E-Commerce in Europe*, Oxford: Hart, 2005, pp. 93–136

Ehrlich Eugen, *Fundamental Principles of the Sociology of Law*, translated by Walter L. Moll, New Brunswick, NJ: Transaction Publishers, 2002 (1913)

Ellul Jacques, *The Technological Society*, translated by John Wilkinson, New York: Knopf, 1964 (1954)

Elster Jon, *Ulysses Unbound: Studies in Rationality, Precommitment, and Constraints*, Cambridge: Cambridge University Press, 2000

Elster Jon, 'Don't Burn Your Bridge Before You Come to It: Some Ambiguities and Complexities of Precommitment' (2003) *Texas Law Review*, 81 (7), pp. 1751–1788

Fairtlough Gerard H., 'Habermas' Concept of "Lifeworld"' (1991) *Systems Practice*, 4 (6), pp. 547–563

Faris Robert et al., 'Score Another One for the Internet?: The Role of the Networked Public Sphere in the U.S. Net Neutrality Policy Debate', *Berkman Center Research Publication*, No. 2015-4, February 2015, Cambridge, MA: The Berkman Center for Internet & Society, https://cyber.harvard.edu/sites/cyber.harvard.edu/files/2015_02_10_Score_Another_One_for_the_Internet_0.pdf

Fassbender Bardo, '"We the Peoples of the United Nations": Constituent Power and Constitutional Form in International Law', in Neil Walker and Martin Loughlin (eds.), *The Paradox of Constitutionalism. Constituent Power and Constitutional Form*, Oxford: Oxford University Press, 2007, pp. 269–290

Fassbender Bardo, *The United Nations Charter as the Constitution of the International Community*, Leiden: Nijhoff, 2009

Fässler Michael, 'Google's Privacy Sandbox Initiative: Old Wine in New Skins', *i-call Working Paper*, No. 01/2023, Zurich: University of Zurich, www.zora.uzh.ch/id/eprint/232978/

Faulkner Alex et al., 'Introduction: Material Worlds: Intersections of Law, Science, Technology, and Society' (2012) *Journal of Law and Society*, 39 (1), pp. 1–19

Feenberg Andrew, *Transforming Technology: A Critical Theory Revisited*, New York: Oxford University Press, 2002

Feenberg Andrew, 'A Critical Theory of Technology', in Ulrike Felt, et al. (eds.), *The Handbook of Science and Technology Studies*, Cambridge, MA, and London: The MIT Press, 2017, pp. 635–663

Feenberg Andrew, *Technosystem: The Social Life of Reason*, Cambridge, MA: Harvard University Press, 2017

Fein Bruce, '*Griswold v. Connecticut*: Wayward Decision-Making in the Supreme Court' (1989) *Ohio Northern University Law Review*, 16 (3), pp. 551–560

Ferejohn John, 'The Politics of Imperfection: The Amendment of Constitutions' (1997) *Law & Social Inquiry*, 22 (2), pp. 501–530

Francioni Francesco, 'An International Bill of Rights: Why It Matters, How Can It Be Used' (1997) *Texas International Law Journal*, 32 (3), pp. 471–482

Frankford David M., 'The Critical Potential of the Common Law Tradition: Theory of Societal Constitutionalism: Foundations of a Non-Marxist Critical Theory' (1994) *Columbia Law Review*, 94 (3), pp. 1076–1124

Frantziou Eleni, 'The Horizontal Effect of the Charter of Fundamental Rights of the EU: Rediscovering the Reasons for Horizontality' (2015) *European Law Journal*, 21 (5), pp. 657–679

Froomkin A. Michael, 'Wrong Turn in Cyberspace: Using ICANN to Route Around the APA and the Constitution' (2000) *Duke Law Journal*, 50 (1), pp. 17–186

Froomkin A. Michael, 'ICANN's "Uniform Dispute Resolution Policy": Causes and (Partial) Cures' (2002) *Brooklyn Law Review*, 67 (3), pp. 605–718

Fuchs Christian, *The Online Advertising Tax as the Foundation of a Public Service Internet*, London: University of Westminster Press, 2018

Garton Ash Timothy, *Free Speech: Ten Principles for a Connected World*, New Haven and London: Yale University Press, 2016

Geiger Christophe and Izyumenko Elena, 'Towards a European "Fair Use" Grounded in Freedom of Expression' (2019) *American University International Law Review*, 35 (1), pp. 1–74

Geiger Theodor, *Vorstudien zu einer Soziologie des Rechts*, 4th edn, reviewed and edited by Manfred Rehbinder, Berlin: Duncker & Humblot, 1987 (1947)

Gerlach Jan, *The Informational Ecosystem of Net Neutrality: A Comparison of Regulatory Discourses in the U.S. and the E.U.*, St Gallen: Dike, 2016

Geyer Stefan, *Die Unterwerfung der Zeichen: Zur 'Konstitution' von Herrschaftsrecht durch das Krönungszeremoniell im späten Mittelalter am Beispiel der Krönung in den Königreichen Aragon und Frankreich*, Zurich: Chronos, 2020

Giacometti Zaccaria, 'Die Freiheitsrechtskataloge als Kodifikation der Freiheit: Festrede des Rektors Zaccaria Giacometti, gehalten an der 122. Stiftungsfeier der Universität Zürich am 29. April 1955', in *Jahresbericht der Universität Zürich 1954/1955*, pp. 3–24

Gibson James J., *The Ecological Approach to Visual Perception*, New York: Psychology Press, 2015 (1979)

Giere Ronald, 'What Everyone Should Know About STS' (2006) *Social Studies of Science*, 36 (3), pp. 489–493

Gilbert Michael D., 'Entrenchment, Incrementalism, and Constitutional Collapse' (2017) *Virginia Law Review*, 103 (4), pp. 631–671

Gillespie Tarleton, *Custodians of the Internet: Platforms, Content Moderation, and the Hidden Decisions That Shape Social Media*, New Haven: Yale University Press, 2018

Golia Angelo Jr and Teubner Gunther, 'Societal Constitutionalism: Background, Theory, Debates' (2021) *ICL Journal*, 15 (4), pp. 357–411

Golia Angelo Jr, 'Beyond Oversight: Advancing Societal Constitutionalism in the Age of Surveillance Capitalism', *Working Paper*, 25 February 2021, Heidelberg: Max Planck Institute for Comparative Public Law and International Law, https://ssrn.com/abstract=3793219

Golia Angelo Jr, 'Critique of Digital Constitutionalism: Deconstruction and Reconstruction from a Societal Perspective' (2023) *Global Constitutionalism*, 13 (3), pp. 1–31

Graber Christoph B. and Teubner Gunther, 'Art and Money: Constitutional Rights in the Private Sphere' (1998) *Oxford Journal of Legal Studies*, 18 (1), pp. 61–73

Graber Christoph B., 'Internet Creativity, Communicative Freedom and a Constitutional Rights Theory Response to "Code is Law"', in Sean Pager and Adam Candeup (eds.), *Transnational Culture in the Internet Age*, Cheltenham: Edward Elgar, 2012, pp. 135–164

Graber Christoph B., 'Bottom-Up Constitutionalism: The Case of Net Neutrality' (2016) *Transnational Legal Theory*, 7 (4), pp. 524–552

Graber Christoph B., 'Personalisierung im Internet, Autonomie der Politik und Service public' (2017) *sic! Zeitschrift für Immaterialgüter-, Informations- und Wettbewerbsrecht*, pp. 257–270

Graber Christoph B., 'Freedom and Affordances of the Net' (2018) *Washington University Jurisprudence Review*, 10 (2), pp. 221–256

Graber Christoph B., 'Artificial Intelligence, Affordances and Fundamental Rights', in Mireille Hildebrandt and Kieron O'Hara (eds.), *Life and the Law in the Era of Data-Driven Agency*, Cheltenham: Edward Elgar, 2020, pp. 194–213

Graber Christoph B., 'How the Law Learns in the Digital Society' (2021) *Law, Technology and Humans*, 3 (2), pp. 12–27

Graber Christoph B., 'Legal Sociology', in Marc Thommen (ed.), *Introduction to Swiss Law*, 2nd edn, Zurich: sui generis, 2022, pp. 91–112

Graber Christoph B., 'Net Neutrality: A Fundamental Right in the Digital Constitution?' (2023) *Indiana Journal of Global Legal Studies*, 30 (2), pp. 197–226

Grimm Dieter, 'The Achievement of Constitutionalism and Its Prospects in a Changed World', in Petra Dobner and Martin Loughlin (eds.), *The Twilight of Constitutionalism?*, Oxford: Oxford University Press, 2010, pp. 3–22

Grimm Dieter, 'Constitution Beyond the Nation State?' (2011) *Zeitschrift für Rechtssoziologie*, 32 (2), pp. 181–188

Grint Keith and Woolgar Steve, *The Machine at Work: Technology, Work and Organization*, Cambridge: Polity, 1997

Gurumurthy Anita and Chami Nandini, 'Internet governance as "ideology in practice": India's "Free Basics" Controversy' (2016) *Internet Policy Review*, 5 (3), pp. 1–17

Habermas Jürgen, *The Theory of Communicative Action: Lifeworld and System: A Critique of Functionalist Reason*, translated by Thomas MacCarthy, vol. 2, Cambridge: Polity Press, 2007 (1981)

Halavais Alexander, 'Structure on Twitter: Social and Technical', in Katrin Weller, et al. (eds.), *Twitter and Society*, New York: Peter Lang, 2014, pp. 29–41

Hart H. L. A., *The Concept of Law*, Oxford: Clarendon Press, 1961

Headland Thomas N., 'Introduction: A Dialogue Between Kenneth Pike and Marvin Harris on Emics and Etics', in Thomas N. Headland, et al. (eds.), *Emics and Etics: The Insider/Outsider Debate*, Newbury Park: SAGE, 1990, pp. 13–27

Heidegger Martin, 'The Question Concerning Technology [1954]', in *The Question Concerning Technology and Other Essays*, translated by William Lovitt, New York: Harper Collins, 2013

Heldeweg Michiel A., 'Experimental Legislation Concerning Technological & Governance Innovation: An Analytical Approach' (2015) *The Theory and Practice of Legislation*, 3 (2), pp. 169–193

Helmers Sabine, et al., 'Internet ... The Final Frontier. An Ethnographic Account: Exploring the Cultural Space of the Net from the Inside', *WZB Discussion Paper*, No. FS II 00-101, Berlin: Wissenschaftszentrum Berlin für Sozialforschung (WZB), 2000

Hildebrandt Mireille, *Smart Technologies and the End(s) of Law: Novel Entanglements of Law and Technology*, Cheltenham, UK, and Northampton, MA: Edward Elgar, 2015

Hildebrandt Mireille, 'Law as an Affordance: The Devil Is in the Vanishing Point (s)' (2017) *Critical Analysis of Law*, 4 (1), pp. 116–128

Hoffmann-Riem Wolfgang, 'Der grundrechtliche Schutz der Vertraulichkeit und Integrität eigengenutzter informationstechnischer Systeme' (2008) *JuristenZeitung*, 63 (21), pp. 1009–1022

Hoffmann Stacie, et al., 'Standardising the Splinternet: How China's Technical Standards Could Fragment the Internet' (2020) *Journal of Cyber Policy*, 5 (2), pp. 239–264

Hopkins Julian, 'The Concept of Affordances in Digital Media', in Heidrun Friese, et al. (eds.), *Handbuch Soziale Praktiken und Digitale Alltagswelten*, Wiesbaden: Springer, 2016, pp. 1–8

Horten Monica, *The Closing of the Net*, Cambridge and Malden: Polity, 2016

Humphrey John P., 'The International Bill of Rights: Scope and Implementation' (1976) *William and Mary Law Review*, 17 (3), pp. 527–542

Hutchby Ian, 'Technologies, Text and Affordances' (2001) *Sociology*, 35 (2), pp. 441–456

Hutchby Ian, 'Affordances and the Analysis of Technologically Mediated Interaction: A Response to Brian Rappert' (2003) *Sociology*, 37 (3), pp. 581–589

Ihde Don, *Technology and the Lifeworld: From Garden to Earth*, Bloomington and Indianapolis: Indiana University Press, 1990

Jasanoff Sheila, *Science at the Bar: Law, Science, and Technology in America*, Cambridge, MA: Harvard University Press, 1995

Jasanoff Sheila, 'Science and Judgment in Environmental Standard Setting' (1998) *Applied Measurement in Education*, 11 (1), pp. 107–120

Jasanoff Sheila, 'Between Risk and Precaution: Reassessing the Future of GM Crops' (2000) *Journal of Risk Research*, 3 (3), pp. 277–282

Jasanoff Sheila, 'The Idiom of Co-Production', in Sheila Jasanoff (ed.), *States of Knowledge: The Co-Production of Science and Social Order*, London: Routledge, 2004, pp. 1–12

Jasanoff Sheila, 'Law's Knowledge: Science for Justice in Legal Settings' (2005) *American Journal of Public Health*, 95, (S1), pp. 49–58

Jasanoff Sheila, 'Just Evidence: The Limits of Science in the Legal Process' (2006) *Journal of Law, Medicine & Ethics*, 34 (2), pp. 328–341

Jasanoff Sheila, 'Making Order: Law and Science in Action', in Edward J. Hackett, et al. (eds.), *The Handbook of Science and Technology Studies*, 3rd edn, Cambridge, MA: The MIT Press, 2008, pp. 761–786

Jessup Philip, *Transnational Law*, New Haven: Yale University Press, 1956

Johns Fleur, 'The Invisibility of the Transnational Corporation: An Analysis of International Law and Legal Theory' (1994) *Melbourne University Law Review*, 19, pp. 893–923

Johnson David R. and Post David, 'Law and Borders: The Rise of Law in Cyberspace' (1996) *Stanford Law Review*, 48 (5), pp. 1367–1402

Kahn Paul W., *The Cultural Study of Law: Reconstructing Legal Scholarship*, Chicago: University of Chicago Press, 1999

Kälin Walter and Künzli Jörg, *The Law of International Human Rights Protection*, 2nd edn, Oxford: Oxford University Press, 2019

Karavas Vagias, 'The Force of Code: Law's Transformation under Information Technological Conditions' (2009) *German Law Journal*, 10 (4), pp. 463–481

Karavas Vagias, 'Das Computer-Grundrecht: Persönlichkeitsschutz unter informationstechnischen Bedingungen' (2010) *WestEnd: neue Zeitschrift für Sozialforschung*, 7 (2), pp. 95–105

Kiener Regina, 'Grundrechte in der Bundesverfassung', in Oliver Diggelmann, et al. (eds.), *Verfassungsrecht der Schweiz*, vol. 2, 2nd edn, Zurich: Schulthess, 2020, pp. 1193–1221

Kiener Regina, et al., *Grundrechte*, 4th edn, Bern: Stämpfli, 2024

Klatt Matthias, 'Law as Fact and Norm. Georg Jellinek and the Dual Nature of Law', in Nicoletta Bersier Ladavac, et al. (eds.), *The Normative Force of the Factual: Legal Philosophy Between Is and Ought*, Cham: Springer International Publishing, 2019, pp. 45–64

Kley Andreas, 'Der wissenschaftliche Streit um die Drittwirkung der Grundrechte 1987–1989', in Jean-Baptiste Zufferey, et al. (eds.), *L'homme et son droit: Mélanges en l'honneur de Marco Borghi à l'occasion de son 65e anniversaire*, Zurich: Schulthess, 2011, pp. 227–240

Kley Andreas, *Geschichte des öffentlichen Rechts der Schweiz*, Zurich: Dike, 2011

Kline Ronald R., 'Technological Determinism', in James D. Wright (ed.), *International Encyclopedia of the Social & Behavioral Sciences*, 2nd edn, Oxford: Elsevier, 2015, pp. 109–112

Klonick Kate, 'The New Governors: The People, Rules, and Processes Governing Online Speech' (2018) *Harvard Law Review*, 131 (6), pp. 1598–1670

Knorr-Cetina Karin, 'Introduction: The Micro-Sociological Challenge of Macro-Sociology: Towards a Reconstruction of Social Theory and Methodology', in Karin Knorr-Cetina and Aaron Cicourel (eds.), *Advances in Social Theory and*

Methodology: Toward an Integration of Micro- and Macro-Sociologies, London: Routledge, 1981, pp. 1–47

Krämer Sybille, *Medium, Messenger, Transmission: An Approach to Media Philosophy*, Amsterdam: Amsterdam University Press, 2015

Ladeur Karl-Heinz, 'Toward a Network-Oriented Law of the Internet!: The Necessity to Find a New Balance Between Risk and Opportunity in Network Communication' (2009) *German Law Journal*, 10 (9), pp. 1201–1214

Ladeur Karl-Heinz, 'Die Netzwerke des Rechts und die Evolution der "Gesellschaft der Netzwerke"', in Michael Bommes and Veronika Tacke (eds.), *Netzwerke in der funktional differenzierten Gesellschaft*, Wiesbaden: VS Verlag, 2011, pp. 143–171

Ladeur Karl-Heinz, 'Warum nach den Medien des Rechts fragen?' (2012) *Ancilla Iuris*, pp. 105–110

Ladeur Karl-Heinz, 'Die Gesellschaft der Netzwerke und ihre Wissensordnung: Big Data, Datenschutz und die "relationale Persönlichkeit"', in Florian Süssenguth (ed.), *Die Gesellschaft der Daten: Über die digitale Transformation der sozialen Ordnung*, Bielefeld: transcript, 2015

Ladeur Karl-Heinz, 'Die Zukunft der Medienverfassung', in Karl-Heinz Ladeur, et al. (eds.), *Die Zukunft der Medienverfassung*, Tübingen: Mohr Siebeck, 2021, pp. 17–89

Latour Bruno, *Science in Action: How to Follow Scientists and Engineers Through Society*, Harvard: Harvard University Press, 1987

Latour Bruno, *We Have Never Been Modern*, translated by Catherine Porter, Cambridge, MA: Harvard University Press, 1993 (1991)

Latour Bruno, *Politics of Nature: How to Bring the Sciences into Democracy*, translated by Catherine Porter, Cambridge, MA: Harvard University Press, 2004 (1999)

Latour Bruno, *The Making of Law: An Ethnography of the Conseil d'État*, translated by Marina Brilman and Alain Pottage, Cambridge: Polity, 2010 (2002)

Law John and Singleton Vicky, 'Performing Technology's Stories: On Social Constructivism, Performance, and Performativity,' (2000) *Technology and Culture*, 41 (4), pp. 765–775

Law John, 'STS as Method', in Ulrike Felt, et al. (eds.), *The Handbook of Science and Technology Studies*, Cambridge, MA, and London: The MIT Press, 2017, pp. 31–57

Leavitt Alex, 'From #FollowFriday to YOLO: Exploring the Cultural Salience of Twitter Memes', in Katrin Weller, et al. (eds.), *Twitter and Society*, New York: Peter Lang, 2014, pp. 137–154

Leistner Matthias, 'The German Federal Supreme Court's Judgment on Google's Image Search: A Topical Example of the "Limitations" of the European

Approach to Exceptions and Limitations' (2011) *IIC-International Review of Intellectual Property and Competition Law*, 42 (4), pp. 417–442

Lepsius Oliver, *Steuerungsdiskussion, Systemtheorie und Parlamentarismuskritik*, Tübingen: Mohr Siebeck, 1999

Lessig Lawrence, *Code and Other Laws of Cyberspace*, New York: Basic Books, 1999

Letsas George, 'The ECHR as a Living Instrument: Its Meaning and Legitimacy', in Andreas Føllesdal, et al. (eds.), *Constituting Europe: The European Court of Human Rights in a National, European and Global Context*, Cambridge: Cambridge University Press, 2013

Levi Ron and Valverde Maria, 'Studying Law by Association: Bruno Latour Goes to the Conseil d'État' (2008) *Law & Social Inquiry*, 33 (3), pp. 805–825

Lievrouw Leah A., 'The Materiality of Mediated Knowledge and Expression', in Tarleton Gillespie, et al. (eds.), *Media Technologies: Essays on Communication, Materiality, and Society*, Cambridge, MA: The MIT Press, 2014, pp. 21–51

Lipton Jacqueline and Wong Mary, 'Trademarks and Freedom of Expression in ICANN's New gTLD Process' (2012) *Monash University Law Review*, 38 (1), pp. 188–227

Lodder Arno R., 'Directive 2000/31/EC on Certain Legal Aspects of Information Society Services, in Particular Electronic Commerce in the Internal Market', in Arno R. Lodder and Andrew D. Murray (eds.), *EU Regulation of E-Commerce: A Commentary*, 2nd edn, Cheltenham: Edward Elgar, 2022, pp. 18–63

Loven Claire, *Fundamental Rights Violations by Private Actors and the Procedure before the European Court of Human Rights: A Study of Verticalised Cases*, Antwerp: Intersentia, 2022

Luhmann Niklas, *Grundrechte als Institution: Ein Beitrag zur politischen Soziologie*, Berlin: Duncker & Humblot, 1965

Luhmann Niklas, 'Normen in soziologischer Perspektive' (1969) *Soziale Welt*, 20 (1), pp. 28–48

Luhmann Niklas, *A Sociological Theory of Law*, translated by Elizabeth King-Utz and Martin Albrow, 2nd edn, Abingdon: Routledge, 2014 (1972)

Luhmann Niklas, 'The World Society as a Social System' (1982) *International Journal of General Systems*, 8 (3), pp. 131–138

Luhmann Niklas, *Social Systems*, translated by John Bednarz with Dirk Baecker, Stanford: Stanford University Press, 1995 (1984)

Luhmann Niklas, 'The Autopoiesis of Social Systems', in R. F. Geyer and Johannes van der Zouwen (eds.), *Sociocybernetic Paradoxes: Observation, Control, and Evolution of Self-Steering Systems*, London and Beverly Hills: Sage Publications, 1986, pp. 172–192

Luhmann Niklas, *Die Wissenschaft der Gesellschaft*, Frankfurt: Suhrkamp, 1990

Luhmann Niklas, 'Verfassung als evolutionäre Errungenschaft' (1990) *Rechtshistorisches Journal*, pp. 176–220

Luhmann Niklas, 'The Form of Writing' (1992) *Stanford Literature Review*, 9 (1), pp. 25–42

Luhmann Niklas, *Law as a Social System*, translated by Klaus Alex Ziegert, Oxford and New York: Oxford University Press, 2004 (1993)

Luhmann Niklas, *Theory of Society*, translated by Rhodes Barret, Stanford: Stanford University Press, 2012 (1997)

Luhmann Niklas, *Die Politik der Gesellschaft*, Herausgegeben von André Kieserling, Frankfurt: Suhrkamp, 2000

Lynch Michael and Cole Simon, 'Science and Technology Studies on Trial' (2005) *Social Studies of Science*, 35 (2), pp. 269–311

Lynch Michael, et al., *Truth Machine: The Contentious History of DNA Fingerprinting*, Chicago: University of Chicago Press, 2010

Lynch Michael (ed.), *Science and Technology Studies: Critical Concepts in the Social Sciences*, London and New York: Routledge, 2012

Mader Luzius, 'Experimentelle Gesetzgebung', in Dieter Grimm and Werner Maihofer (eds.), *Gesetzgebungstheorie und Rechtspolitik*, Wiesbaden: VS Verlag für Sozialwissenschaften, 1988, pp. 211–221

Madhavan Esha Sen, 'Internet and Social Media's Social Movements Leading to New Forms of Governance and Policymaking: Cases from India' (2016) *Glocalism: Journal of Culture, Politics and Innovation*, pp. 1–32

Mahlmann Matthias, *Rechtsphilosophie und Rechtstheorie*, 4th edn, Baden-Baden: Nomos, 2017

Malcomson Scott, *Splinternet: How Geopolitics and Commerce Are Fragmenting the World Wide Web*, New York and London: OR Books, 2016

Markee Numa, 'Emic and Etic in Qualitative Research', in Carol A. Chapelle (ed.), *The Encyclopedia of Applied Linguistics*, Malden: Wiley-Blackwell, 2013, pp. 1–4

Marsden Christopher T., 'Comparative Case Studies in Implementing Net Neutrality: A Critical Analysis of Zero Rating' (2016) *SCRIPTed*, 13 (1), pp. 1–39

Marsden Christopher T., *Network Neutrality: From Policy to Law to Regulation*, Manchester: Manchester University Press, 2016

Marsden Christopher T., 'Zero Rating and Mobile Net Neutrality', in Luca Belli and Primavera De Filippi (eds.), *Net Neutrality Compendium: Human Rights, Free Competition and the Future of the Internet*, Cham: Springer International Publishing, 2016, pp. 241–260

Marsden Christopher T., 'Transnational Internet Law', in Peer Zumbansen (ed.), *The Oxford Handbook of Transnational Law*, New York: Oxford University Press, 2021, pp. 418–436

McGeveran William, 'Friending the Privacy Regulators' (2016) *Arizona Law Review*, 58 (4), pp. 959–1026

McLuhan Marshall, *Understanding Media: The Extensions of Man*, Cambridge, MA: The MIT Press, 1994 (1964)

Merrill Kenneth, 'Domains of Control: Governance of and by the Domain Name System', in Francesca Musiani, et al. (eds.), *The Turn to Infrastructure in Internet Governance*, New York: Palgrave Macmillan, 2016, pp. 89–106

Mertel Kurt C. M., 'Heidegger, Technology and Education' (2020) *Journal of Philosophy of Education*, 54 (2), pp. 467–486

Millett Lynette I., et al., 'Cookies and Web Browser Design: Toward Realizing Informed Consent Online', in Michel Beaudouin-Lafon and Robert J.K. Jacob (eds.), *Proceedings of the ACM CHI 2001 Human Factors in Computing Systems Conference* (Seattle, 31 March to 5 April 2001), pp. 46–52

Möller Hans-Georg, *The Radical Luhmann*, New York: Columbia University Press, 2012

Mostowlansky Till and Rota Andrea, 'Emic and Etic', in Joel Robbins, et al. (eds.), *The Cambridge Encyclopedia of Anthropology*, University of Cambridge, 2020, pp. 1–16

Mueller Milton L., *Ruling the Root: Internet Governance and the Taming of Cyberspace*, Cambridge, MA: The MIT Press, 2002

Mueller Milton L., *Networks and States: The Global Politics of Internet Governance*, Cambridge, MA: The MIT Press, 2010

Mueller Milton L., *Will the Internet Fragment?: Sovereignty, Globalization, and Cyberspace*, Cambridge and Malden: Polity, 2017

Mueller Milton L. and Badiei Farzaneh, 'Inventing Internet Governance: The Historical Trajectory of the Phenomenon and the Field', in Laura DeNardis, et al. (eds.), *Researching Internet Governance: Methods, Frameworks, Futures, Information Policy*, Cambridge, MA: The MIT Press, 2020, pp. 59–83

Mukerjee Subhayan, 'Net Neutrality, Facebook, and India's Battle to #SaveTheInternet' (2016) *Communication and the Public*, 1 (3), pp. 356–361

Murray Andrew D., 'Regulation 2015/2120/EU Laying Down Measure concerning Open Internet Access', in Arno R. Lodder and Andrew D. Murray (eds.), *EU Regulation of E-Commerce: A Commentary*, 2nd edn, Cheltenham: Edward Elgar, 2022, pp. 281–307

Nassehi Armin, *Muster: Theorie der digitalen Gesellschaft*, Munich: C.H. Beck, 2019

Natsoulas Thomas, '"To See Things Is To Perceive What They Afford": James J. Gibson's Concept of Affordance' (2004) *The Journal of Mind and Behavior*, 25 (4), pp. 323–347

Nissenbaum Helen, 'From Preemption to Circumvention: If Technology Regulates, Why Do We Need Regulation (and Vice Versa)?' (2011) *Berkeley Technology Law Journal*, 26 (3), pp. 1367–1386

Norman Donald A., *The Psychology of Everyday Things*, New York: Basic Books, 1988

Nothias Toussaint, 'Access Granted: Facebook's Free Basics in Africa' (2020) *Media, Culture & Society*, 42 (3), pp. 329–348

Oyer Gordon, 'Thomas Merton and the "Pessimism" of Jacques Ellul' (2017) *The Merton Annual*, 30, pp. 131–144

Park Whon-il and Greenleaf Graham, 'Korea Rolls Back "Real Name" and ID Number Surveillance', *University of New South Wales Research Paper*, 2012-57, Sydney: University of New South Wales, https://papers.ssrn.com/sol3/papers.cfm?abstract_id=2187232

Pasquale Frank and Cockfield Arthur J., 'Beyond Instrumentalism: A Substantivist Perspective on Law, Technology, and the Digital Persona' (2018) *Michigan State Law Review*, pp. 821–868

Pasquale Frank, *The Black Box Society: The Secret Algorithms That Control Money and Information*, Cambridge, MA: Harvard University Press, 2015

Patkos Theodore, et al., 'Privacy-by-Norms: Privacy Expectations in Online Interactions', *2015 IEEE International Conference on Self-Adaptive and Self-Organizing Systems Workshops (SASOW 2015)* (Cambridge, MA, 21 to 25 September 2015), pp. 1–6

Perry Stephen R., 'Judicial Obligation, Precedent and the Common Law' (1987) *Oxford Journal of Legal Studies*, 7 (2), pp. 215–257

Pernice Ingolf, 'Multilevel Constitutionalism and the Treaty of Amsterdam: European Constitution-Making Revisited' (1999) *Common Market Law Review*, 36 (4), pp. 703–750

Pernice Ingolf, 'The Treaty of Lisbon: Multilevel Constitutionalism in Action' (2009) *Columbia Journal of European Law*, 15 (3), pp. 349–407

Petersmann Ernst-Ulrich, 'The WTO Constitution and Human Rights' (2000) *Journal of International Economic Law*, 3 (1), pp. 19–25

Pfaffenberger Bryan, 'Technological Dramas' (1992) *Science, Technology & Human Values*, 17 (3), pp. 282–312

Pickering Andrew, 'The Mangle of Practice: Agency and Emergence in the Sociology of Science' (1993) *American Journal of Sociology*, 99 (3), pp. 559–589

Pike Kenneth L., *Language in Relation to a Unified Theory of the Structures of Human Behavior*, 2nd edn, The Hague: Mouton, 1967

Pinch Trevor J. and Bijker Wiebe E., 'The Social Construction of Facts and Artefacts: Or How the Sociology of Science and the Sociology of Technology Might Benefit Each Other' (1984) *Social Studies of Science*, 14 (3), pp. 399–441

Popelier Patricia, et al. (eds.), *Criticism of the European Court of Human Rights*, Cambridge: Intersentia, 2017

Post David G. and Kehl Danielle, 'Controlling Internet Infrastructure: Part 1: The "IANA Transition," and Why It Matters for the Future of the Internet', Washington, DC: Open Technology Institute, April 2015

Post David G. and Kehl Danielle, 'Controlling Internet Infrastructure: The "IANA Transition" and ICANN Accountability, Part II', Washington, DC: Open Technology Institute, September 2015

Pottage Alain, 'Biotechnology as Environmental Regulation', in Andreas Philippopoulos-Mihalopoulos (ed.), *Law and Ecology: New Environmental Foundations*, Oxford: Routledge, 2011, pp. 105–125

Pottage Alain, 'The Materiality of What?' (2012) *Journal of Law and Society*, 39 (1), pp. 167–183

Pound Roscoe, 'Law in Books and Law in Action' (1910) *American Law Review*, 44 (1), pp. 12–36

Pound Roscoe, 'The Scope and Purpose of Sociological Jurisprudence: Part I' (1911) *Harvard Law Review*, 24 (8), pp. 591–619

Preuss Ulrich K., 'The Implications of "Eternity Clauses": The German Experience' (2011) *Israel Law Review*, 44 (3), pp. 429–448

Proferes Nicholas, 'The Development of Privacy Norms', in Bart P. Knijnenburg, et al. (eds.), *Modern Socio-Technical Perspectives on Privacy*, Cham: Springer International Publishing, 2022, pp. 79–90

Qvortrup Lars, *The Hypercomplex Society*, New York: Peter Lang, 2003

Ramcharan B. G., 'The Legal Status of the International Bill of Human Rights' (1986) *Nordic Journal of International Law*, 55 (4), pp. 366–383

Ranchordás Sofia, 'The Whys and Woes of Experimental Legislation' (2013) *The Theory and Practice of Legislation*, 1 (3), pp. 415–440

Ranchordás Sofia, *Constitutional Sunsets and Experimental Legislation: A Comparative Perspective*, Cheltenham: Edward Elgar, 2014

Rao Ashwini and Pfeffer Juergen, 'Types of Privacy Expectations' (2020) *Frontiers in Big Data*, 3, pp. 1–14

Regan Priscilla M., 'Privacy and the Common Good: Revisited', in Beate Roessler and Dorota Mokrosinska (eds.), *Social Dimensions of Privacy: Interdisciplinary Perspectives*, Cambridge: Cambridge University Press, 2015, pp. 50–70

Reidenberg Joel, 'Lex Informatica: The Formulation of Information Policy Rules Through Technology' (1998) *Texas Law Review*, 76 (3), pp. 553–593

Rhinow René A., et al., *Schweizerisches Verfassungsrecht*, 3rd edn, Basel: Helbing & Lichtenhahn, 2016

Rödl Florian, 'Fundamental Rights, Private Law, and Societal Constitution: On the Logic of the So-Called Horizontal Effect' (2013) *Indiana Journal of Global Legal Studies*, 20 (2), pp. 1015–1034

Rogers Karl, *Participatory Democracy, Science and Technology: An Exploration in the Philosophy of Science*, London: Palgrave Macmillan, 2008

Rozakis Christos, 'The European Judge as a Comparatist' (2005) *Tulane Law Review*, 80 (1), pp. 257–279

Ruggie John G., 'Multinationals as Global Institution: Power, Authority and Relative Autonomy' (2018) *Regulation & Governance*, 12 (3), pp. 317–333

Saladin Peter, *Grundrechte im Wandel*, 3rd edn, Bern: Stämpfli, 1982

Sandvig Christian, 'The Internet as Infrastructure', in William H. Dutton (ed.), *The Oxford Handbook of Internet Studies*, Oxford: Oxford University Press, 2014, pp. 86–106

Sayes Edwin, 'Actor–Network Theory and Methodology: Just What Does It Mean to Say That Nonhumans Have Agency?' (2014) *Social Studies of Science*, 44 (1), pp. 134–149

Schefer Markus, 'Kommunikationsgrundrechte', in Oliver Diggelmann, et al. (eds.), *Verfassungsrecht der Schweiz*, vol. 2, 2nd edn, Zurich: Schulthess, 2020, pp. 1413–1451

Schlosberg David, et al., 'Democracy and E-Rulemaking: Web-Based Technologies, Participation, and the Potential for Deliberation' (2007) *Journal of Information Technology & Politics*, 4 (1), pp. 37–55

Schütz Alfred, 'The Well-Informed Citizen: An Essay on the Social Distribution of Knowledge' (1946) *Social Research*, 13 (4), pp. 463–478

Sciulli David, 'Voluntaristic Action as a Distinct Concept: Theoretical Foundations of Societal Constitutionalism' (1986) *American Sociological Review*, 51 (6), pp. 743–743

Sciulli David, 'Foundations of Societal Constitutionalism: Principles from the Concepts of Communicative Action and Procedural Legality' (1988) *British Journal of Sociology*, 39 (3), pp. 377–407

Sciulli David, *Theory of Societal Constitutionalism: Foundations of a Non-Marxist Critical Theory*, Cambridge: Cambridge University Press, 1992

Searle John R., *The Construction of Social Reality*, London: Penguin, 1995

Shaffer Gregory and Halliday Terence, 'With, Within, and Beyond the State: The Promise and Limits of Transnational Legal Ordering', in Peer Zumbansen (ed.), *The Oxford Handbook of Transnational Law*, New York: Oxford University Press, 2021, pp. 986–1006

Simmel Georg, 'Über sociale Differenzierung', in Heinz-Jürgen Dahme (ed.), *Georg Simmel, Gesamtausgabe in 24 Bänden, Band 2: Aufsätze 1887-1890. Über sociale Differenzierung (1890). Die Probleme der Geschichtsphilosophie (1892)*, Frankfurt: Suhrkamp, 1989, pp. 109–295

Sismondo Sergio, *An Introduction to Science and Technology Studies*, 2nd edn, Chichester: Wiley-Blackwell, 2010

Sluijs Jasper P., 'From Competition to Freedom of Expression: Introducing Article 10 ECHR in the European Network Neutrality Debate' (2012) *Human Rights Law Review,* 12 (3), pp. 509–554

Sunstein Cass R., *#Republic: Divided Democracy in the Age of Social Media,* Princeton: Princeton University Press, 2017

Suzor Nicolas P., *Lawless: The Secret Rules That Govern Our Digital Lives,* Cambridge: Cambridge University Press, 2019

Ten Oever Niels, 'Productive Contestation, Civil Society, and Global Governance: Human Rights as a Boundary Object in ICANN' (2019) *Policy & Internet,* 11 (1), pp. 37–60

Ten Oever Niels, '"This Is Not How We Imagined It": Technological Affordances, Economic Drivers, and the Internet Architecture Imaginary' (2021) *New Media & Society,* 23 (2), pp. 344–362

Teubner Gunther, 'Substantive and Reflexive Elements in Modern Law' (1983) *Law and Society Review,* 17 (2), pp. 239–285

Teubner Gunther, '"Global Bukowina": Legal Pluralism in the World Society', in Gunther Teubner (ed.), *Global Law Without a State,* Aldershot: Dartmouth, 1997, pp. 3–28

Teubner Gunther, 'Societal Constitutionalism: Alternatives to State-Centred Constitutional Theory?', in Christian Joerges, et al. (eds.), *Transnational Governance and Constitutionalism,* Oxford and Portland: Hart, 2004, pp. 3–28

Teubner Gunther, 'The Anonymous Matrix: Human Rights Violations by "Private" Transnational Actors' (2006) *Modern Law Review,* 69 (3), pp. 327–346

Teubner Gunther, 'Self-Constitutionalizing TNCs?: On the Linkage of "Private" and "Public" Corporate Codes of Conduct' (2011) *Indiana Journal of Global Legal Studies,* 18 (2), pp. 17–38

Teubner Gunther, *Constitutional Fragments: Societal Constitutionalism and Globalization,* translated by Gareth Norbury, Oxford: Oxford University Press, 2012

Teubner Gunther, 'The Project of Constitutional Sociology: Irritating Nation State Constitutionalism' (2013) *Transnational Legal Theory,* 4 (1), pp. 44–58

Teubner Gunther, 'Transnational Economic Constitutionalism in the Varieties of Capitalism' (2015) *The Italian Law Journal,* 1 (2), pp. 219–248

Teubner Gunther, 'The Constitution of Non-monetary Surplus Values' (2021) *Social & Legal Studies,* 30 (4), pp. 501–521

Teubner Gunther and Golia Angelo Jr, 'Societal Constitutionalism in the Digital World' (2023) *Indiana Journal of Global Legal Studies,* 30 (2), pp. 1–23

Thier Andreas, 'Recht, Rechtswissenschaft und Medialität' (2014) *NCCR Mediality Newsletter,* 1, pp. 7–15

Thompson Clive, *Coders: The Making of a New Tribe and the Remaking of the World*, New York: Penguin Press, 2019

Thornhill Chris, 'Towards a Historical Sociology of Constitutional Legitimacy' (2008) *Theory and Society*, 37 (2), pp. 161–197

Thornhill Chris, *A Sociology of Constitutions: Constitutions and State Legitimacy in Historical-Sociological Perspective*, Cambridge: Cambridge University Press, 2011

Thornhill Chris, *A Sociology of Transnational Constitutions: The Social Foundations of the Post-National Legal Structure*, Cambridge: Cambridge University Press, 2016

Thornhill Chris, 'The Mutation of International Law in Contemporary Constitutions: Thinking Sociologically About Political Constitutionalism' (2016) *The Modern Law Review*, 79 (2), pp. 207–247

Thornhill Chris, 'Transnational Constitutional Law', in Peer Zumbansen (ed.), *The Oxford Handbook of Transnational Law*, New York: Oxford University Press, 2021, pp. 134–156

Trachtman Joel P., 'The Constitutions of the WTO' (2006) *European Journal of International Law*, 17 (3), pp. 623–646

Tribe Laurence H., *American Constitutional Law*, 3rd edn, New York: Foundation Press, 2000

Turow Joseph, 'Media Buying: The New Power of Advertising', in Matthew McAllister and Emily West (eds.), *The Routledge Companion to Advertising and Promotional Culture*, Abingdon: Routledge, 2013, pp. 99–111

Tushnet Mark, 'Internet Exceptionalism: An Overview from General Constitutional Law' (2015) *William & Mary Law Review*, 56 (4), pp. 1637–1672

Vanderstraeten Raf, 'Parsons, Luhmann and the Theorem of Double Contingency' (2002) *Journal of Classical Sociology*, 2 (1), pp. 77–92

Van Schewick Barbara, *Internet Architecture and Innovation*, Cambridge, MA: The MIT Press, 2010

Verbeek Peter-Paul, 'Artifacts and Attachment: A Post-script Philosophy of Mediation', in Hans Harbers (ed.), *Inside the Politics of Technology: Agency and Normativity in the Co-Production of Technology and Society*, Amsterdam: Amsterdam University Press, 2005, pp. 125–146

Vesting Thomas, *Legal Theory and the Media of Law*, translated by James C. Wagner, Cheltenham, UK, and Northampton, MA: Edward Elgar Publishing, 2018

Viellechner Lars, 'The Network of Networks: Karl-Heinz Ladeur's Theory of Law and Globalization' (2009) *German Law Journal*, 10 (4), pp. 515–536

Von Bernstorff Jochen, 'The Structural Limitations of Network Governance: ICANN as a Case in Point', in Christian Joerges, et al. (eds.), *Transnational Governance and Constitutionalism*, Oxford and Portland: Hart, 2004, pp. 257–285

Von Bogdandy Armin, et al., *In Whose Name?: A Public Law Theory of International Adjudication*, Oxford: Oxford University Press, 2014

Von Foerster Heinz, *Wissen und Gewissen. Versuch einer Brücke*, Frankfurt: Suhrkamp, 1993

Waelbers Katinka, *Doing Good with Technologies: Taking Responsibility for the Social Role of Emerging Technologies*, Dordrecht: Springer, 2011

Wahl Rainer, 'In Defence of "Constitution"', in Petra Dobner and Martin Loughlin (eds.), *The Twilight of Constitutionalism?*, Oxford: Oxford University Press, 2010, pp. 220–242

Walter Christian, 'Die EMRK als Konstitutionalisierungsprozess' (1999) *Zeitschrift für ausländisches öffentliches Recht und Völkerrecht*, 59, pp. 961–983

Wang Wallace, *Steal This File Sharing Book: What They Won't Tell You About File-Sharing*, San Francisco: No Starch Press, 2004

Weber Max, *Economy and Society: An Outline of Interpretive Sociology*, translated by Günther Roth, Berkeley: University of California Press, 1978 (1922)

Weber Rolf H., 'A Legal Lens into Internet Governance', in Laura DeNardis, et al. (eds.), *Researching Internet Governance: Methods, Frameworks, Futures*, Cambridge, MA: The MIT Press, 2020, pp. 105–121

Weber Rolf H., *Internet Governance at the Point of No Return*, Zurich: EIZ Publishing, 2021

Weiler Joseph, *The Constitution of Europe: "Do the New Clothes have an Emperor?" and Other Essays on European Integration*, Cambridge: Cambridge University Press, 1999

Weinberg Jonathan, 'Governments, Privatization, and "Privatization": ICANN and the GAC' (2011) *Michigan Telecommunications and Technology Law Review*, 18, pp. 189–218

Wielsch Dan, *Zugangsregeln: Die Rechtsverfassung der Wissensteilung*, Tübingen: Mohr Siebeck, 2008

Wielsch Dan, 'Political Autonomy in the Digital World: From Data Ownership to Digital Constitutionalism' (2023) *Indiana Journal of Global Legal Studies*, 30 (2), pp. 115–130

Willke Helmut, *Stand und Kritik der neueren Grundrechtstheorie: Schritte zu einer normativen Systemtheorie*, Berlin: Duncker & Humblot, 1975

Winner Langdon, 'Upon Opening the Black Box and Finding It Empty: Social Constructivism and the Philosophy of Technology' (1993) *Science, Technology & Human Values*, 18 (3), pp. 362–378

Winthrop-Young Geoffrey, 'Silicon Sociology, or, Two Kings on Hegel's Throne?: Kittler, Luhmann, and the Posthuman Merger of German Media Theory' (2000) *Yale Journal of Criticism*, 13 (2), pp. 391–420

Wittgenstein Ludwig, *Philosophical Investigations, The German text, with an English Translation* by *G. E. M. Anscombe, P. M. S. Hacker and Joachim Schulte*, 4th edn, Oxford: Wiley-Blackwell, 2009 (1953)

Woltag Johann-Christoph, 'Internet', in Rüdiger Wolfrum (ed.), *The Max Planck Encyclopedia of Public International Law*, 2nd edn, Oxford: Oxford University Press, 2013

Woods Lorna, 'Article 11', in Steve Peers, et al. (eds.), *The EU Charter of Fundamental Rights: A Commentary*, Oxford: Hart, 2021, pp. 333–369

Woolgar Steve and Cooper Geoff, 'Do Artefacts Have Ambivalence?: Moses' Bridges, Winner's Bridges and Other Urban Legends in S&TS' (1999) *Social Studies of Science*, 29 (3), pp. 433–449

Wu Tim, 'Network Neutrality, Broadband Discrimination' (2003) *Journal of Telecommunications and High Technology Law*, 2 (1), pp. 141–179

Wu Tim, 'Is Internet Exceptionalism Dead?', in Berin Szoka and Adam Marcus (eds.), *The Next Digital Decade: Essays on the Future of the Internet*, Washington DC: TechFreedom, 2010

Wu Tim, *The Attention Merchants: The Epic Scramble to Get Inside Our Heads*, New York: Alfred A. Knopf, 2016

Wu Tim, 'Blind Spot: The Attention Economy and the Law' (2019) *Antitrust Law Journal*, 82 (3), pp. 771–806

Yu Peter K., 'The Origins of ccTLD Policymaking' (2004) *Cardozo Journal of International and Comparative Law*, 12 (2), pp. 387–408

Zammito John H., *A Nice Derangement of Epistemes: Post-positivism in the Study of Science from Quine to Latour*, Chicago: University of Chicago Press, 2004

Zimmermann Nesa, 'Entre innovations et résistances: La garantie des droits humains dans l'État fédéral suisse' (2023) *Zeitschrift für Schweizerisches Recht*, 142 (2), pp. 151–249

Zittrain Jonathan, *The Future of the Internet and How to Stop It*, New Haven: Yale University Press, 2008, at 67–68

Zuboff Shoshana, *The Age of Surveillance Capitalism: The Fight for a Human Future at the New Frontier of Power*, New York: Public Affairs, 2019

Zumbansen Peer, 'Transnational Law: Theories and Applications', in Peer Zumbansen (ed.), *The Oxford Handbook of Transnational Law*, New York: Oxford University Press, 2021, pp. 2–30

Index

Printed by Integrated Books International,
United States of America